Conversations with the Turtles: On the Ideological Conundrums of Our Times

Polarization often results from deficient forms of social belonging, caused primarily by stark social inequalities. These inequalities then generate psychological responses that both create and worsen polarization. Yet social stability is possible. In this provocative and original book, Nilson Ariel Espino argues that our current ideological polarizations can be best analyzed as springing from the contradictions of modernity and its obsessions. Using culture as a founding and organizing dimension, the author disassembles the typical dichotomies of left versus right, or conservatism versus progressivism, and reveals the opposing sides as mutually interdependent positions that struggle with cultural paradoxes they are ill-suited to address. Written with clarity and verve for the general reader, this book brings classic concepts of cultural anthropology to bear on the key preoccupations of today's world, from poverty and inequality, to political instability and the environmental crisis.

Nilson Ariel Espino is an academic and architect based in Panama City, Panama. His research interests are urban social problems and political ideologies. He is an adjunct professor at McGill University's School of Urban Planning, Co-Chair of the UNESCO Chair for Dialogues on Sustainability, and an associate researcher at Santa María La Antigua Catholic University. He has a Ph.D. in social and cultural anthropology and is the author of *Building the Inclusive City* (2015).

Conversations with the Turtles

On the Ideological Conundrums of Our Times

Nilson Ariel Espino

CAMBRIDGE
UNIVERSITY PRESS

CAMBRIDGE
UNIVERSITY PRESS

Shaftesbury Road, Cambridge CB2 8EA, United Kingdom

One Liberty Plaza, 20th Floor, New York, NY 10006, USA

477 Williamstown Road, Port Melbourne, VIC 3207, Australia

314–321, 3rd Floor, Plot 3, Splendor Forum, Jasola District Centre, New Delhi – 110025, India

103 Penang Road, #05–06/07, Visioncrest Commercial, Singapore 238467

Cambridge University Press is part of Cambridge University Press & Assessment, a department of the University of Cambridge.

We share the University's mission to contribute to society through the pursuit of education, learning and research at the highest international levels of excellence.

www.cambridge.org
Information on this title: www.cambridge.org/9781009441162

DOI: 10.1017/9781009441186

First published 2024

A catalogue record for this publication is available from the British Library

A Cataloging-in-Publication data record for this book is available from the Library of Congress

ISBN 978-1-009-44116-2 Hardback

Cambridge University Press & Assessment has no responsibility for the persistence or accuracy of URLs for external or third-party internet websites referred to in this publication and does not guarantee that any content on such websites is, or will remain, accurate or appropriate.

This one, Susana, is for you

CONTENTS

PREFACE

I'm done with names. Names are nothing but collars men tie round
your neck to drag you where they like.
                    Alasdair Gray, *Lanark: A Life in Four Books*

This is a book about the ideas that move the contemporary
world forward, and also against itself. It's a reflection on the assumptions that underlie many of the debates that crowd the news on politics,
culture, religion, and economics. It is written from the vantage point of
a cultural anthropologist, with support from other social sciences and,
especially, depth psychology. The intended public is the general reader,
however, so I've stayed away from all technical jargon as much as possible, while also moving the more scholarly digressions to the footnotes.

It is a book written in some desperation. I have lived most my
life in Latin America, a highly ideological region of the world if there
is one. I have witnessed first-hand my fair share of ideological waves,
including Marxism and neoliberalism, as well as quite distinct (even
incompatible) versions of Christianity. Many of these swings were
orchestrated by the United States government, an enormously influential presence and force, not only in the world of politics but also education. During my (bilingual) school years in Panama, I had the fortune
of benefitting from the explosion of American cultural production and
promotion that washed up on our shores during the 1976 bicenten-
nial celebrations and the ensuing years. What I read was intellectually
eclectic and displayed a hard-headed pragmatism that impressed and

influenced me from then onwards. In high school, I discovered Emerson and Thoreau, who opened up even deeper perspectives on the American ethos. By the 1980s, however, the mood had changed. By that time, the Reagan administration was more interested in ideological wars than in cultural exchange. Committed to combating the Marxist "structural" interpretation of social ills, the US embassy was now distributing free Spanish translations of Lawrence Harrison's *Underdevelopment Is a State of Mind* (1985),[1] which supposedly offered an alternative "cultural" explanation.

I have lived long enough to see many of these ideological movements dominate the public square and then peter out, and also influence ultimately catastrophic political experiments. I've become wary of their siren calls, their foolproof certainties, and their finalist assertions. I have no conversion story to share in this respect. I was never a "leftist" who turned into a "conservative," or the other way around. My skepticism was always more primordial. It's not that I consider their arguments false; in fact, I'm quite sympathetic to them all. The problem is deeper. The ideological battles that we engage in are a window, I believe, into the modern worldview, into its particular way of framing problems and then dealing with them. The experience feels current because I can see a replay taking place all around me. The ideological polarizations I see today show the same no-holds-barred intransigence and smug confidence that so many times led to disaster. It's a parade of déjà vu.

This book is, then, an attempt at an anthropology of the contemporary moment as it pertains our current ideological battles. It is not an ethnography and is not based on new evidence or hard data either; rather, it is an intellectual, transdisciplinary exercise linking different key authors in order to get a better picture of what we're up against. The authors linked consist, inevitably, of a personal selection. Naturally, other thinkers could have been brought into the picture, and other links could have been developed.

In their best version, anthropologists are cosmologists. We try to explain societies through their view of the world, that is, their culture, which includes their mentality and hidden biases. But the analytical exercise necessarily carries its own assumptions and biases, which nowadays encompass the concept of culture itself, one

---

[1] Harrison 1985.

that has had a rather bumpy ride throughout anthropology's history. From being *the* subject matter of the discipline, the concept of culture came under in-house attack in the late twentieth century for having arguably suggested that it was something self-contained, fixed, and unchanging, and for not taking into account cultural evolution and conflict. As the argument went, to say that a society had a culture that defined it meant implicitly saying that everyone was happy with it, and that revolts and outside influences were ways of changing the "culture," instead of being the dynamics we should be actually focusing on. Recent generations of anthropologists have thus put more import in the ways cultural conventions are contested and manipulated, or are artificial or oppressive, sometimes presenting them as the actual problem, and even questioning the usefulness, or existence, of the concept or reality of culture itself.[2] Thus, the earlier generations focused on what seemed to be stable, while the newer ones on what seemed to be moving. But, of course, something that moves can be still sometimes, and also keep a somewhat recognizable shape while it moves.[3]

The skepticism of anthropologists toward their own master concept came, ironically, at a time when other disciplines started using it more to complement their own theoretical frameworks.[4] Some economists and political scientists understood that not everything was economics or politics, that there is a world of ideas, conventions, and beliefs influencing the course of events, and that sometimes seems to have its own logic. The problem here is that "culture" is frequently brought in at the last minute, when all else has failed; "wheeled in after other explanations are defeated," as Mary Douglas puts it.[5] Culture is seen as the icing on the cake, a topping resting on the more solid realities of

---

[2] See Brightman (1995) for a useful overview and critique.

[3] According to Rosaldo (1993, 209), the classic rule of thumb was that "if it's moving it is isn't cultural." Unfortunately, we then ended up at the other extreme: If it isn't moving, we're not interested. One of the best theorizations of the dynamic relationship between cultural stability and change is provided by Thompson (2017).

[4] The engagement with cultural aspects is more common in the "development literature" written by economists or policy experts (Harrison 1985, mentioned before; Rao and Walton 2004; Bowles, Durlauf and Hoff 2006; Acemoglu and Robinson 2012 & 2019). It is also central, for example, to the groundbreaking work of Elinor Ostrom on collective governance of common resources (Ostrom 1990). On the other hand, such philosophical discussions have always been less significant for anthropologists and ethnographers working precisely on specific development problems.

[5] Douglas 1992, 167.

money and policy.[6] When something cannot be fully explained through those more standard frameworks, it must be a "cultural" thing.

The view from anthropology is that this is precisely backwards. This cake works, in fact, upside down. It is the icing, so to speak, the "softer" parts of the pile, that accounts for how the rest is put together. Culture, or "cosmology," as I will also call it here, is the domain of the ideas that underlie the logic of those other fields. Modern economic or political systems are as much cultural creatures as any supposedly exotic proposition from a recondite tribe, and it is the duty of the anthropologist to treat them like that. In the globalized world we live in, we might not be able to talk about discrete, independent "cultures" anymore, but this doesn't preclude us in any way from analyzing them as all-too-real framing cosmologies. This the case because modernity *is* a culture, however contested. It is akin to what Immanuel Wallerstein called the "geoculture" that legitimizes contemporary global capitalism:

> I believe that we all *today* are living in a singular historical system, a singular society if you will, that I term the capitalist world-economy. Among its basic structures have been an axial division of labor reflected in a core-periphery polarization and a political system of sovereign states bound together within an interstate system. This singular historical system has a geoculture, in my view, which means that there are norms and values which serve to legitimate the world-system as a whole and which receive some important institutional support. Of course, these values may be integrated into individual superegos to varying degrees or not at all. And there may be groups, even institutions, actively opposing these values. But a historical system cannot function unless at least some norms and values of this kind prevail (win out, on the whole, against opposition, disbelief, or apathy).[7]

While it is not my main objective, I hope this book demonstrates that the exploration of social issues through the study of culture is as valid

---

[6] I'm borrowing here Ingold's metaphor (2018, 109). The view corresponds to what Geertz (1973, 44) calls the "stratigraphic" model of human life, where biological, psychological, social, and cultural dimensions are related by stacking and analyzing them independently.

[7] Wallerstein's comments in Wolf (1994, 9. Emphasis in the original). Wallerstein identifies the idea of the nation state and of modern progress as part of this "geoculture." I will cover these aspects, among others, in the following pages.

as ever, and not as an add-on to other efforts, but as an indispensable path in its own right. I will stick here to the traditional notion of culture as "a way of thinking that justifies a way of living," to use Mary Douglas's pithy definition.[8] That this notion incorporates conflict and change I assume as a given, just like Wallerstein does. In the end, no society can function (or exist) without a cosmology; at the same time, no society could evolve if such a cosmology were eternal and unquestionable. That cultures actually change tells us all you need to know about the malleability of the worldviews of humans.

Since the realm of culture is, in consequence, disputed terrain, let me succinctly lay out my main ground premises. First, and as some other anthropologists, I see cultures as *internally* contradictory. While it is common these days to highlight how all cultures are contested, I am equally interested in their internal inconsistencies, regardless of whether we're looking at their hegemonic or rebellious aspects. Cultural conflicts are not necessarily due to clashes of "values," or unresolved disagreements. At base, cultures don't "add up." Some of their principles are in contradiction with others, so that many conflicts are actually self-generated. Societies come apart at the seams because these are all too obvious, and normally consist of those salient fracture lines of incoherence. Second, and in tension with the first point, I present cultures as mechanisms for social integration and, in particular, for establishing modes of social *belonging*. Third, I see cultures as relational phenomena. Especially in a globalized world such as ours, we cannot conceive of societies, or even social groups, as independent universes. We're all interacting and looking over our shoulders – and fashioning ourselves in the process. Finally, I currently see depth psychology as essential for cultural analysis. With Bock and Leavitt, I consider that "all anthropology is psychological" and "all psychology is cultural."[9] I believe many social phenomena cannot be appropriately understood without recourse to psychology, and that any social scientist that does cultural analysis without the psychological toolbox is flying half-blind.

With its wide-ranging overview of the human universe, anthropology has the virtue of defamiliarizing our own culture, in the process helping us imagine a better future. Human cultural diversity highlights

---

[8] Douglas 2004, 107.
[9] Bock and Leavitt 2019.

the arbitrariness of our beliefs and thus sets the stage for adjustment or transformation. Some anthropological work thus present other cultures as alternative models in some dimension or other of social life. The case is also made that, because other cultures work so differently, then change can be clearly envisioned for our own. I will do neither. I tend to find such positions utopian, nostalgic, and escapist. With Ruth Benedict, I believe anthropology mostly illustrates different cultural schemes for dealing with common human problems.[10] In consequence, anthropology's main contribution is to help us *come to terms with the terms of our own culture.*[11] Solutions are not going to be found in a highly exotic elsewhere, and the fact that other peoples do things differently says little about our capacity to follow suit, since we also receive benefits from the system we're critiquing.

An example from my own background can serve as an illustration of this point. For several decades, Latin American countries toyed with the idea of fashioning a unique, regional development model. Normally cloaked with different versions of "socialism," such exercises tried to defend the idea of a singular cultural identity that should generate its own version of modernity. Much political effort was spent defending how different we were, and thus how different our success should look like. The Mexican writer Octavio Paz argued an alternative position: The region is inevitably part of the modern world, and as such, is in the same boat as everybody else.[12] Indeed, the environmental crisis, the problems of social inequality and international migration, or the arms race, are global challenges that speak not only of common tasks but also of common preoccupations. His point was not that the issues had been solved, and so we just needed to follow the path set by others, but rather that we all shared the same questions, along with the same frustrating lack of definitive answers. The riddles we handle are the same. Problems that start in one corner of the world soon spread to another; a solution found in one place is quickly copied everywhere

---

[10] Benedict 1959, 1. This is, admittedly, just one possible approach to the issue of the ultimate purpose of anthropological comparisons (Candea 2019, 47 ff.).

[11] See Marcus and Fischer (1986, 115); the book is a classic exploration of these issues. I thus consider that the most appropriate type of social critique from an anthropological perspective is an *immanent critique* (rather than a "transcendental critique"), that is, a critique that explores the contradictions of the culture and evaluates it in terms of its own principles (see Stahl 2022; and for the argument in anthropology, see Candea 2019, 142 ff.).

[12] Marras 1992, 464.

else. This does not mean that the world is marching (or should march) toward complete cultural homogenization, but it does mean that, at this point, national agendas are not very different from each other. This book will thus focus less on highlighting cultural differences than in exploring the common culture of the world, that is, of the modern world, which I will define, somewhat simplistically, as the one that results from the confluence of industrialization, capitalism, liberalism, and science. While the book is based, to some extent, on my experience of living in my particular side of the world, this is not a book about, or for, Latin America (it is, after all, in English), but tries to cast a wider net. I believe many of the conundrums countries face today relate to how they confront the challenges of a modern capitalist system, such as inequality and environmental degradation, but also of the modern worldview and its putative ideals, such as the equality between men and women, the tolerance for diverse sexual preferences, or the rights of free enterprise. While cultural diversity can pose a resistance to, or can even be a result of this confrontation, my interest here is on what is being confronted.

If the ambition comes across to the reader as a bit hubristic, I must defend it also as a response to my personal history. The region I live in seems to be continuously on the verge of a revolution, always both desired and dreaded. Under such conditions, social theory cannot be of the modest, partial type. The intellectual humbleness of many academics in the global north, their allergy toward integrating theories, and their fears of being "imperialistic" were they to embark in such projects are more appropriate in a world that lacks a sense of urgency. When social upheaval is always on the horizon, you need theories at the scale of the problem. These theories must be both explanatory and propositional, and must avoid an excessive specialization.[13] Otherwise, you end up giving credence, in people's minds, to the humoristic definition of the specialist as "a person who knows more and more about less and less." In this context, I believe knowledge does not come by narrowing your disciplinary gaze on an issue, but by expanding it.

---

[13] Scubla (2002) comments on the intellectual price we have paid for this specialization in anthropology. I should note that my goal here forces me into the formulation of a general, albeit highly abbreviated, theory of culture, even though such efforts have fallen out of fashion at least since the mid-twentieth century due to theoretical atomization within anthropology (Candea 2018, 9). My framework is, in any case, fairly conventional and eclectic.

All of this accounts for the mixed nature of this extended essay: part textbook, part critique, and part manifesto. I will not limit myself to diagnostics, but venture some recommendations as well. The effort also involves the risk of dealing in too many platitudes, for which I plead understanding beforehand. One of the most frequent casualties of ideological polarization is the capacity to see the obvious.

The type of theory also responds to my professional practice. I am only a part-time social scientist. I spend most of my waking hours as an architect and urban planner, frequently engaged in government projects with an explicit public purpose. I have also dedicated a considerable part of my career to public service, working in four different government administrations of (supposedly) divergent political orientations. If, as anthropologist Marc Augé argues, design is "applied anthropology," my design practice necessarily requires an anthropology to back it up.[14] Decisions have to be made, defended, and justified. Being regularly in the design trenches, or in the executive branch, confronts you with both the urgency of a general theory, and the need to keep it close to the ground.

Finally, a note is warranted about the authors used. I have given precedence to relevance over dates or specialties. Although I make ample use of current literature, the reader will note a certain soft spot for "older" works. Some foundational thinkers show up, such as Durkheim, Marx, Freud, and Weber. I draw upon the "classic" anthropological and sociological literature, especially that of Ruth Benedict, Mary Douglas, Victor Turner, Pierre Bourdieu, and Anthony Giddens. In relation to psychology, my choices are also somewhat archaic. In recent decades, dramatic advances in neuroscience and genetics have transformed the mental health disciplines. Genetic and biochemical factors are better understood, and symptoms are better defined and bounded. What the field has gained in diagnostic detail and specificity, it has lost, however, in interdisciplinary openness.[15] The links between the psychological and social realms have not necessarily been invigorated in the process. I'm thus reaching out to an earlier generation of

---

[14] Augé 2001, 110.

[15] The transition is well analyzed by Wilson (1993) for the case of the United States (see also Harrington 2019). The corresponding impacts on anthropology of the important advances in "brain science" are still to be seen (see Ingold 2018, 127 for some perspective), although Bartra (2014) already offers an updated model of an integration of the cultural and the biological based on such research.

authors who were very much concerned about the social and political dimension of people's inner lives, such as Karen Horney, Erich Fromm, and Victor Frankl, and later thinkers who kept those concerns alive, such as, notably, Ethel Person.[16] And then there are the unclassifiable René Girard and Ivan Illich. I believe considerable insight can be attained by keeping our eyes open toward our intellectual forebears. Many problems that seem new are not new at all, and have confronted us since the dawn of the modern era. We suffer frequently not only from ignorance, but also from amnesia. It's as if our hard drive is regularly wiped clean by our momentary obsessions. Lastly, although many of the ideas and ideological positions analyzed have a long and complex history, I will deal with origins sparingly, relying more on what anthropologists call the "ethnographic present," which assumes that whatever is relevant from the past is already included in our current mentalities. This approach is particularly appropriate for the peripheries of the world, which confront modern ideologies as full-fledged ships that regularly show up on the horizon.

The book is divided into thematically oriented chapters, nominally dedicated, following an introductory one, to "religion," "culture," "psychology," "power," "economics," and "politics." The topics continuously overlap, however, since, as I will argue throughout, they are part and parcel of the same thing, namely the "cosmology" of a society, that is, its encompassing culture. Any critique of an ideological system is, necessarily, a critique of its labels.

---

[16] I should note that the study of the interphase between politics and psychology has maintained a valuable vitality in the psychoanalytic tradition (see Stavrakakis 2020), and particularly in the work of Slavoj Žižek.

1 TURTLES ALL THE WAY DOWN

Others said that the earth has nine corners by which the heavens are supported. Another, disagreeing with these, would have the earth supported by seven elephants, and the elephants do not sink because their feet are fixed on a tortoise. When asked who would fix the body of the tortoise, so that it would not collapse, he said that he did not know.

Letter written from India by the Jesuit Emanuel da Veiga (1599)[1]

The idea that the world rests on the back of a turtle has been identified in the mythologies of several North American tribes, as well as in other mythologies from ancient India and China. As a general explanation for the structure of the universe, the proposition has always been found wanting by interlocutors from the West, who logically proceed to ask what, in turn, is supporting the turtle. Historical anecdotes have the natives evading the question. Enthusiastic modern defenders have taken the challenge more seriously, proposing that, obviously, the turtle is supported by another turtle, and dealing with the inevitable riposte with the now classic expression "it's turtles all the way down!"[2]

---

[1] Charpentier 1924, 320.
[2] Ross 1967, v. Geertz (1973, 28–29) offers an alternative story for the expression.

It is unfair, of course, to treat myths as physics theories. The purpose of myths is to explain the moral logic of the world, not its physical scaffolding. The Delaware indigenous cultures had a turtle supporting the world because they saw the turtle as symbolizing, through its attributes, life itself. The turtles they knew showed perseverance, longevity, and steadfastness, lived both in water and land, and, like humans, were omnivores.[3]

The problem posed by an infinite column of turtles has nonetheless been used as an illustration of philosophical positions that cannot account for a clear, solid base. The vulgar question about God is an obvious example. God created the world, but then, who created God? If we sidestep the question of absolute origins, the turtle dilemma can be framed as an issue concerning the underpinnings of our ideas about the world. Is there some solid truth under it all that can explain and justify the way we look at things? Or is the world simply what we make of it? In other words, is the turtle, however much we depend on it for holding up everything, of our own making, too?

It is fashionable these days to posit that our social reality is self-made. Activists of the current sexual identity wars insist, for example, that gender, that apparently most self-evident of all human characteristics, is actually "socially constructed." Indeed, it is. While (most) humans are born with either "male" or "female" genitalia (and their corresponding biology), the historical and anthropological record registers a wide variety of customs regarding sexual practices and roles. But this truth is less of a debate stopper than activists usually hope for, because social constructivism is a double-edged sword. To be consistent, one would have to admit that the belief that there are two genders is as much a social construct as the one that posits that there are actually twenty. "Social constructivism for thee but not for me" just doesn't cut it.

Conservatives, for their part, despair with all this "moral relativism." They hope for a real, independent turtle; a solid base of moral certitude, one perhaps supplied by the sacred texts of traditional religions. The idea that social reality is a human construct is, however, not particularly new, and weaves through several Western and Eastern philosophical traditions. Buddhism, notably, holds that

[3] Miller 1974.

social reality is an illusion (or, rather, a delusion), toward which we need to put some mental and emotional distance.[4] The social nature of our ideas about the world figures prominently in the nineteenth-century work of Nietzsche and Marx.[5] The more recent currents of "postmodern" thought that so unnerve conservatives are just a late chapter in the debate, one that significantly focuses on the role of language in making us believe what we say.[6] In a more pedestrian route, the idea has also been a truism of the field of anthropology since its founding more than 100 years ago. Anthropologists have been, decades in and out, painstakingly documenting quite exotic societies that swear that their view of the universe does not represent one more "culture" to be added to the discipline's catalog, but rather transparent, unadulterated reality. We, of course, believe the same about ourselves.

Admitting to the (mostly) arbitrary nature of our mental world does not necessarily leave us, however, in a moral limbo. Not all anthropologists fell in love with their subjects, even when they tried respectfully and empathetically to record their particular cultural universe. We don't have to approve of other societies in order to respect or tolerate them. We can acknowledge other people's preferences while being at peace with our own. I know the world is full of wonderful women, but that doesn't keep from feeling that I'm married to the most wonderful one of all. When we compare groups or societies we can only, in any case, evaluate them in reference to our own. They can illuminate some of our deficiencies, or point us toward some possible betterment. But these insights are all unavoidably self-serving. We can only be responsible for ourselves, and we have no business telling other people how to live – unless their conduct inevitably affects us.

The best way to handle the pitfalls of a world that seems arbitrary and unstable is to explore its cultural and ideological underpinnings, since that allows us to feel more confident about our own moral choices. The study of our own ideological biases is, however, always a perilous and imperfect business, akin, as the expression goes, to the study of water by fish. But a dynamic society leaves us with no choice,

[4] Wright 2017.
[5] Berger and Lukman 1967.
[6] Lee 1997.

since if we don't have an informed opinion about these matters, others will have them for us, and will act accordingly. The turtles under the ground have to be uncovered and examined, however partially and deficiently.

Let's start with one that's famous as a destroyer of all civil social intercourse: religion.

2 ON BEING RELIGIOUS WITHOUT KNOWING IT

> In reality, then, there are no religions which are false. All are true in their own fashion; all answer, though in different ways, to the given conditions of human existence.
>
> Emile Durkheim, *The Elementary Forms of the Religious Life*

Given how much conflict there seems to be in the world these days around religion, it may come as a surprise to learn that, for anthropologists, defining religion has always been a particularly difficult thing to do. According to Talal Asad, Europeans didn't even start talking about religion as a separate aspect of social life until the seventeenth century, after the Reformation generated different interpretations of how to be a Christian and spawned the religious wars of the continent.[1] The problem with religion is that it normally encompasses ideas and beliefs about topics that are also the purview of supposedly separate areas of social life, such as politics, science, or culture. We tend to deal with these overlaps by assuming that what distinguishes the religious approach is a belief in (a) God and certain "sacred" texts. If only things were so simple.

In the long history of their study of religion, anthropologists have always given a special place to a book by Emile Durkheim, *The*

[1] Asad 1993.

Elementary Forms of the Religious Life, published originally in French in 1912. Durkheim is considered one of the fathers of modern sociology, but like the anthropologists, was interested in cross-cultural comparisons. What makes his contribution important is that he thought hard about what religion was – and wasn't. Since I'm also a fan of the book, I'll use it as a starting point.

The first thing Durkheim does is to present and argue away the definitions of religion that he finds unacceptable. For Durkheim, religion, in its essence, is *not* about (1) a belief in God; (2) the supernatural; or (3) magic and superstition.

The first point he handles summarily, reminding the reader that there are established religions that don't depend on the existence of a God, such as Buddhism and Taoism. They have all the usual trappings that we associate with religions, such as rituals and spiritual doctrines, but they dispense with the idea of a divinity pulling the strings of human affairs. The rules of the universe regarding humans have either an automatic and autonomous nature (as with karma), or are left vague.

On the other hand, the problem with associating religiosity with the "supernatural" or with "magic" is that these terms inhabit a definitional quicksand. To assert that something is "supernatural" you first have to define what "natural" is. We tend to see this distinction as straightforward, since we associate the "natural" with the phenomena that science has been able to account for. But this also means that the distinction is a very modern one. Before the development of the scientific method, it would have made no sense, in any society, to distinguish between the natural and the supernatural. Consequently, to then use this distinction to identify the "religious" part of any culture would make no sense, either.

We also associate the supernatural with some sort of invisibility, but this barely helps, since most societies, including ours, handle some notion of a visible and an invisible world. Humans rarely believe that the world is limited solely what they can perceive directly with their senses. Certainly, there are societies that have very complex invisible worlds, which include all kinds of fascinating entities. Societies with animist beliefs experience an encompassing world of spirits that live in all beings and objects, including animals, plants, and rocks. Other believe in the existence of good and evil spirits that interact with humans. Modern societies tend to limit the invisible realm to dimensions of reality that scientists have told us are there but that we don't experience directly. It can be a busy world. There are atoms, neutrons, and electrons; microorganisms of different types; electromagnetic waves and fields; all kinds of radiations; and different forms of energy. Scientists add elements and dimensions to this realm all the time. They initially based their theories on matter; then they discovered antimatter. Since a very small percentage of the population has actually studied any of this, most people take the existence of all these things on faith. I'm not, to be clear, putting in doubt the reality of the "invisible" worlds of science, but simply making the point that the boundaries of the "natural" are not fixed, but are rather moving all the time. Scientists still don't understand how different types of cells "know" what they have to do, or how they communicate with one another, and might perhaps one day indeed discover that all things are "alive," as the animist societies assert.[2] All of which means that the whole topic can easily be handled as a scientific problem rather than as a "religious" one. This point becomes even clearer when we step into the subject of "magic."

All societies need, in order to survive, a minimal body of cause-and-effect theories about the world. Some problems are clearly more easily decipherable than others. If you throw something into the air, it falls back down. That seems simple enough. But what about predicting rain? Or explaining why someone falls ill? The premodern societies that early anthropologists typically studied offered a combination of folk theories in this respect, some of which we could describe as involving elements of magic or the supernatural. Some were effective anyway; some were clearly wrong. Societies, in any case, usually move with the best explanations they have at the moment.[3] When cholera epidemics ravaged European cities in the nineteenth century, the mainstream explanation for disease was the "miasmatic" theory, formulated initially in ancient Greece, and which argued that illnesses were carried by foul odors. Since cholera was transmitted through contaminated drinking water, all efforts to control smells were useless. The great urban sewer and aqueduct works that eventually brought the epidemics under control benefited from the finally accepted waterborne theory that some more observant physicians were pushing. But it would be

---

[2] See, for example, Lieff 2020.
[3] Shore 1996, 65.

decades before the real cause was located with the discovery of micro-organisms, in this case, the cholera bacillus. By that time, however, the more basic (and incomplete) waterborne theory had done the job.

When an anthropologist observed a rain ritual that combined some practical actions (starting a fire) with an "impractical" one (a dance), the temptation was to classify the latter one under "magic" and send it to the "religion" chapter of the report. But, as mentioned earlier, this only makes sense for societies that distinguish between "natural" and "supernatural" domains. For societies not dominated by the philosophy of modern science, all events are "natural" (or "supernatural"), and every deviation from a natural pattern demands an interpretation. Since the world is not seen as ruled by impersonal, mechanical laws (but, rather, as following a pattern), any unusual event can be taken as an omen, an announcement, or a change in the order of things. This is why the miracles of Jesus are also called "signs" in some of the Gospels, since they announced the arrival of the Kingdom of God. It's also the reason he was treated as a messiah, rather than as a magician.

So, the label "magic" only makes sense as a conceptual imposition from a scientifically minded observer. But since we are the ones making the distinction, it comes as no surprise that our own world can be divided in such a way, and, more importantly, that we live surrounded by plenty of magic ourselves. Durkheim explains that the scientific method had only been applied to a limited number of problems, mainly pertaining the physical world. In the domain of social life, science had much less useful things to say, so people just carried on with their usual, and unexplained, cultural patterns. (Indeed, this situation persists today, where scientific notions in the social sciences are less definitive, more incomplete, and more contested.) The result is that people failed to realize how bizarre (magical) their actual conduct was. Perhaps the best example I can offer is the use of money. The fact that the world can be so dramatically transformed through the exchange of small pieces of colored paper could certainly seem an amazing magic trick to an outside observer. (Although nowadays money is not even that, but rather numerical digits on an electronic screen.) Money works only because we all have implicitly decided that it is what we say it is – a representation of worth and value, rather than just pieces of processed linen and cotton. In this, the mechanism is barely distinguishable from the rituals of many "primitive" peoples that relied on collective suggestion and ceremony to make participants believe in what they were seeing.[4] To understand "scientifically" the nature of money, we would have to throw the whole weight of the scientific method onto the riddle, making use of controlled experiments, and insights from psychology, anthropology, sociology, and economics, among other disciplines. Of course, no banker is going to wait for the results. This is why Durkheim concludes that "It is science and not religion which has taught men that things are complex and difficult to understand."[5]

The view of religion as something immersed in superstition and opposed to science has a long pedigree in the modern era, and shows, unfortunately, no signs of abating, being the basic idea behind the militant atheism of our day. It was also the position, of course, of many of the key architects of the modern worldview. For Freud, religion had three main functions: to provide an explanation for the world, to provide ethical guidance, and to console the suffering.[6] In his opinion, all three functions could be assumed in time by science and rationality. As science advanced, religion would surely retreat. People would come to appreciate the superior explanations of science, would understand social norms as the result of "social necessity" (rather than of divine commandment), and would maturate psychologically enough to be able to dispense of imaginary fathers and paradises. Marx focused more on the consolation component. For Marx, religion provided the poor with an inverted image of their real, dystopian world. It provided a vision that was the exact opposite of what they experienced every day. Religion was "the heart of a heartless world and the soul of soulless conditions,"[7] a compensatory fantasy that nonetheless revealed what the oppressed should have in this world anyhow. Attacking religion meant attacking the social conditions that made religion necessary. In a truly just world, religion would have no place. Enlightenment and psychological maturity were thus the enemies of religion according to Freud; according to Marx, it was social justice. In both thinkers, religion appears as a shoddy substitute, a recourse for people who are missing the real thing. And in both cases, modern science had the critical role to play, by providing

---

[4] Douglas 2002, 86.
[5] Durkheim 1915, 27.
[6] Freud 1961a [1927].
[7] Marx 2002 [1844], 171.

rational explanations and proposals for everything, from the laws of physics, to the laws of the psyche, to the laws of social coexistence. Of course, both Freud and Marx lived in an era of unbound optimism toward science, before it had become a handmaiden of nuclear bombs and environmental destruction.[8]

So, going back to our original inquiry, if religion is not essentially about God, the supernatural, superstition, or magic, what is it about, then? For Durkheim, religions had two main characteristics: (1) they consisted of a set of beliefs and practices that formed a moral community and (2) they concerned the sacred. The first aspect means that religions provide a moral grid for the group, thus defining notions of good and evil, and supporting these notions through established rites (Freud correctly identified this dimension). Religion is thus part of the general practice of mythmaking, through which societies define where they come from, where they're going, and what their ultimate purpose is. It gives moral meaning and direction to the world, unifies the community around a vision of the good life, and establishes what is important and what is not.

It is crucial to note that science cannot play this role. Science can tell us that if we do X, Y will follow. But it cannot tell us if X or Y are good or desirable. Science is mostly concerned about the mechanical logic of the world, not its moral one. Its main mission is explanation, not discernment. As John Gray writes,

> Science cannot replace a religious view of the world, since there is no such thing as 'the scientific worldview'. ... Science cannot close the gap between facts and values. No matter how much it may advance, scientific inquiry cannot tell you which ends to pursue or how to solve conflicts between them.[9]

There are certainly many "secular" views of the good life, and today's modern societies guide themselves by making use of many broadly consented visions, such as the one offered by the Universal Declaration of Human Rights. But, as many authors have pointed out, most of these ideas have their origin (acknowledged or not) in religious doctrines

---

[8] It should be noted that Freud and Marx were reacting to the dominant version of Christianity of their day, a version that was substantially incompatible with modern science – what theologian Torres Queiruga (2000) calls "pre-modern Christianity" (which, in his opinion, needs to be now abandoned).

[9] Gray 2018, 12, 21.

(which then doesn't make them very "universal").[10] One can certainly opt to follow these simpler formulas and dispense with the heavy baggage of traditional faiths. Science also has a lot to offer to the debate. The more recent "science of happiness," the humanist schools of psychotherapy, the contributions of "positive psychology," and many other efforts, have much to contribute to an understanding of human happiness, which is presumably what everyone is after. But however well-armed science can be, we should lay down the idea of a complete scientific takeover of the world of religion. It is difficult to see science, with its ragtag and selective approach to reality, matching the capacity that religions have at integrating and moving people, synthetizing beliefs, and transmitting and enlivening them through symbolism, imagery, ritual, and art. As I will expand in Chapter 3, religions, like cultures generally, try to explain everything when allowed, and science advances precisely by wrestling from them alternative pieces of explanations. "Scientists suspend everyday knowledge and create pockets of disbelief," says Mary Douglas.[11] The "counter-intuitive" results of science are, in consequence, always also countercultural, because they upend our assumptions of how the world works. The clashes between science and religion are thus not fundamentally different from the clashes between science and culture in general.

On the other hand, it is a mistake to see science as occupying a space completely "outside" of religion. At least since Thomas Kuhn's book *The Structure of Scientific Revolutions* (1962), we have understood that science does not necessarily advance through a simple accumulation of objective knowledge, but that it can change course when new "paradigms" burst the scene. New scientific paradigms establish a sort of new master metaphors of the world, which then change the way science elaborates hypotheses and prioritizes research. Very different types of science practice result from, say, James Lovelock's "Gaia hypothesis" than from the paradigms of Newtonian or Einsteinian physics. In a way, by working through paradigms, science also engages in a form of mythmaking, or an imaginative reflection on the nature of the world.

Much of the opposition that religion generates relates to its purported, rigid dependence on preestablished beliefs. But religion (or

[10] Taylor 2007.
[11] Douglas and Isherwood 1996, 50.

spirituality) is actually more than belief, and also less. Many people ascribe to a religion because it confers a certain cultural identity, not because they believe every single one of its postulates.[12] Being Catholic, Muslim, or Jewish may mean many things, some of which may entail a certain way of looking at things, a certain way of living (a "culture"), or an identification with a certain social group or community. Regularly attending religious rituals or accepting all the faith's tenets may be secondary, or beside the point. So, religion can be, in a sense, "all over the place." Religions can also supply virtuous role models through their founders or some exceptional followers (e.g., saints). Whatever the official faith says about these personalities may be less important than their example as exceptional human beings. In this sense, the attractiveness of a religion may come mainly from the power of its message, rather than from the plausibility of its beliefs.

Some people also pursue deeper waters. Deep religious experiences (such as, but not limited to, religious extasy, bliss, or trance) have been associated with a sense of unity with the universe and of surrendering to something bigger than ourselves, with a transcendence of the self and of the barriers that separate us from others or the cosmos. This is how the famed environmentalist and scientist Jane Goodall describes it:

> I believe that there's an intelligence, a spiritual power that I don't understand. I call it God because I don't know what else to call this great spiritual power. It gives me strength. I've also had amazing times alone in nature when for a moment you forget you're human. Your humanness goes away, and you're part of that natural world. It's the most amazing and wonderful and beautiful feeling.[13]

These kinds of experiences are part of almost all religious traditions, which means they can be pursued through different spiritual paths. Once you get there, though, you're basically *beyond belief*, since the specific ideological content of the path taken is secondary to the experience.

* * *

[12] Douglas 1996a, 37 ff.
[13] Marchese 2021.

In sum, religion is all about values, philosophical outlooks on life, and about transcendence. What about Durkheim's other point of religion being about the "sacred"? If you think this point is self-explanatory, and that it simply implies that religious societies or groups naturally deal with sacred things, think again. Durkheim saw the stark division of the world into separate spheres of sacred and profane things as an absolutely essential element of the religious phenomenon. Most religious practices in fact dealt with the relationships between these two spheres – how to demarcate sacred spaces, objects, and times; how to protect the sacred from profanation; how to invoke the sacred and actualize it. Durkheim saw the formalization and regulation of the sacred by an established Church as one of the foundations of religion. But a more abstract use of the notion of the sacred can allow us to do much more with it, and to also go beyond Durkheim's narrower framework.

The sacred has two attributes. It is, on the one hand, something supremely important; one could say cardinal and foundational. On the other hand, it is also set apart and insulated from manipulation. A believer cannot just add paragraphs to the Bible or the Koran, or insert an eleventh Commandment. By relating the sacred to God, we put it beyond our reach, since God is, of course, "above" or "beyond" us. In more general terms, and moving away from conventional religious contexts, sacred things are important things that no one should be messing around with. This is the sense conveyed by the expression "there's nothing sacred anymore!" One can argue that, in general, a society's most important values are always sacred, and, conversely, that the sacred always encompasses a society's most important values. This is the case even if a society doesn't consider itself "religious" at all.[14] By the way sacred things are established and treated, the existence of an explicitly "religious" dimension is immaterial.

In the societies that anthropologists normally studied, the sacred usually encompassed the whole set of myths and social norms that defined the culture of the group. The relations between the sacred and the profane were handled through a set of taboos and rules regarding purity and pollution that controlled the interactions between the

---

[14] As Durkheim argued in an earlier work (1984 [1893], 119), "it is invariably the fact that when a somewhat strong conviction is shared by a single community of people it inevitably assumes a religious character." See also Douglas 1992, 271.

group's members and upheld the social order.[15] The community itself, and its social makeup, was sacred, since the ultimate objective was the survival of the group. In modern societies, these types of small, integrated communities have mostly disappeared. Our societies are seen as composed by individuals, families, and nations. Since we see these components as essential to our wellbeing, they in turn have been sacralized.

Benedict Anderson has analyzed culturally the phenomenon of modern nations, calling them "imagined communities," since they are so radically different from the face-to-face societies of the past.[16] Nations are now seen as the main group of communal allegiance, even though they may consist of millions of people, a great majority of whom we will never meet. But once the nation replaces the local community, it becomes also, and inevitably, a sacred thing. People are willing to die for their country. When protesters attack the symbols of the nation by, for example, burning the flag, a commotion ensues, since these symbols are, of course, sacred too. In the context of a capitalist economy, where everything seems to have a price, the goods and representations of the nation, such as national monuments, lands, and historical collections, are declared inalienable, that is, priceless, which is another attribute of sacred things.[17]

On the other end of the scale spectrum, the individual is then also sacralized. The rights of the individual are paramount, and so is the body and the interior world of the individual person. As Arthur Brittan explains,

> In a society in which the individual is made the focus of political and ideological commitment, it seems impossible to envisage other cultural frames in which privacy and the self are not taken for granted. The belief in the interiorisation of a world of meaning and uniqueness of experience is embedded in the language and literature of western society ... Privacy is not only taken for granted, it is elevated to a moral category. The violation of an individual's privacy is viewed in the same way as the desecration of the sacred by the unfaithful.[18]

[15] Douglas 2002.
[16] Anderson 1991.
[17] Kopytoff 1988.
[18] Brittan 1977, 49.

Since the individual body is sacred, its parts and reproductive processes are sacred too. Human blood and organs cannot be bought and sold; babies can only be adopted free of charge.[19] The current abortion battles are fought precisely in this terrain. It is not difficult to see how they are framed by the emergence of individualism and the sacralization of the rights of the individual person, in addition to a better understanding of prenatal development. In the abortion debate, two individualistic perspectives on the sacred clash. For the opponents of abortion, the embryo or fetus is a unique and irreplaceable individual in the making, and thus a sacred being. For the defenders of abortion, what is sacred is the rights of the pregnant woman and her inalienable freedom to choose. It's individualism fighting itself.

I'm not suggesting that the controversy is a wash, or that the arguments shouldn't be taken too seriously. If we believe in the dignity of individual life, abortion *is morally repugnant*. But so is the imposition of a full-term pregnancy on a woman no matter what. In Chapter 3, we will see how paradoxical situations like these are quite common in all cultures.

Once we understand the relationship between social values and sacralization, the theoretical division between religion and other dimensions of social life starts falling apart. Modern political systems can be seen simply as just another cosmology that has its own demarcations of the sacred and the profane. The reader might object that the constitution is not the same thing as the Bible, that religious systems are authoritarian and ruled by self-serving, dogmatic despots. But religions, as well as political ideologies, evolve and change in response to new realities, social pressures, knowledge, and ideas. As we will also see in Chapter 3, all rules made by humans, religious or otherwise, are ambivalent and subject to interpretation. The Bible was used to justify slavery, then to abolish it. If religious precepts were really set in stone, theologians would be out of work. A political constitution is, of course, always being interpreted, too. In light of the fancy costumes, formal rituals, and elevated surroundings, the proverbial Martian would find it difficult to differentiate a supreme court from a council of theologians. The same accusations of arbitrariness and political unaccountability are hurled at appointed judges all the time.

---

[19] Kopytoff, op. cit.

The religious echoes of many political ideologies have been, of course, amply noted, especially in the case of radical movements. The same terms are commonly used: There are political bibles, creeds, and dogmas. The reason might be a poverty of vocabulary, but I think the sharing belies a deeper identification. The nominally atheist Friedrich Engels, intellectual partner of Marx, wrote a "Communist Confession of Faith" for the First Congress of the Communist League, organized in London in 1847. Given his opinions about religion, he might have been somewhat sarcastic with the title, but he was definitively being more literal than he thought.

The view of religion as something fundamentally "separate" from the domains of politics and culture is responsible for the confused nature of many of the debates involving religion in the world today, such as those pertaining the "separation of Church and State" in the United States, or *laïcité* in France. Rather than seeing them as a conflict between "secular" and "religious" positions, we are better served by framing them directly as a clash of different sets of sacred principles, that is, as an outright clash of religions in the sense I have described them. In the case of those debates that are always on the front pages of the news, and that never seem to go away, we can be sure to be dealing with the cardinal values of a society, which, by definition, are unnegotiable. These values and principles cannot be negotiated away because they form the bedrock of a society's identity and cosmology. You either believe men and women are equal, or you don't. The same with free elections, a free press, or an independent judiciary. The fact that any views about these kinds of matters are supported or not by allusions to God or an established Church doctrine should be, in the end, irrelevant. People that advocate for the legal protection of just any kind of religious practice or belief in the name of social tolerance and the right to the free exercise of religion demonstrate a grave misunderstanding of how societies are put together. The issue is not about tolerance, but compatibility. If a religious group's basic principles are incompatible with those of the host society, you have a real problem in your hands. Religious tolerance can only really be applied to secondary matters – lifestyle freedoms that we afford everyone else who demands them, such as the young, the eccentric, or the foreign. But we cannot blame any society for drawing the line on the essential items.

The degree of religious tolerance of any society is thus going to relate closely to its degree of tolerance for any type of unconventional behavior. The more "open" a society is, the more it will tolerate all kinds of "religions," but only as long as they don't threaten the overall openness of the system that supports the freedoms of everyone else, including those who have no interest in "religion."

Before the modern era, "religious tolerance" was mainly practiced through physical segregation and distance. Ancient empires allowed foreign rural or urban communities to live their cultures independently as long as they paid their tributes on time.[20] When such arrangement became problematic, they were simply intervened in militarily. Modern societies are not organized in this fragmented manner. They are rather assembled as large nation states that function under unitary legal systems. This makes culture and ideology, as socially integrating mechanisms, and into which religions are basically rolled, key variables in the quest for social stability and viability. Let's now examine these topics directly.

[20] Southall 1998.

3 THE FANTASIES WE LIVE BY

The king dreams he is a king,
And in this delusive way
Lives and rules with sovereign sway;
All the cheers that round him ring,
Born of air, on air take wing.
And in ashes (mournful fate!)
Death dissolves his pride and state:
Who would wish a crown to take,
Seeing that he must awake
In the dream beyond death's gate?
                    Pedro Calderón de la Barca, *Life Is a Dream*

When analyzing the phenomenon of culture in a general sense, it is convenient to start with biology. Humans are animals, after all, and are subject to the same basic evolutionary imperatives as the rest: to survive and reproduce. What makes humans unique is mostly the form these imperatives take – and the enormous consequences that derive from that.

The main difference between us and all other animals is the disproportionate role played by learning in humans. Most animals depend on instinct for their survival, with some added margin for learning, which varies depending on the species. With humans, it's the opposite. Most of our behavior is learned, with biological drives playing a more limited role. As other animals, humans need to eat, hydrate, sleep, and engage in sexual activity (most, at least), but any scholar who pretends to explain the form of any human society out of this meager list is going to fail miserably. Humans don't just "satisfy" these needs, but they do that in the context of particular cultures, fashioned by humans themselves. We don't just eat; we eat specific things, prepared and presented in specific ways, at specific times, in specific places, and accompanied by specific types of fellow diners. Many people will forgo eating if the context, companions, or food is the "wrong" one. The important thing is that all these variables are cultural, and vary from one society to the next. There is no universal "human" way of eating, or sleeping, or having sex. Two different colonies of ants of the same species will look very similar, even if they are kilometers apart and have never interacted. With human colonies, this would be practically impossible.

The fact that there are many ways of fashioning social life means that all cultures are selective. Their ways consist of a limited repertoire of behaviors and beliefs that, by their very nature, are particular and somewhat arbitrary. Humans are, in consequence, cultural creatures. There is no human nature outside of a specific society. There is no universal human language, for example, like the specific sounds of a bird species, but cultural languages, such as English or Mandarin. As Clifford Geertz summarizes it,

> One of the most significant facts about us may finally be that we all begin with the natural equipment to live a thousand kinds of life but end up in the end having lived only one.[1]

The fact that most human behaviors are learned means that the teaching process is necessarily extended. This is then made possible by the incredibly long human childhood. Human infants are not only born completely helpless; they also take a lot of time to become an adult. Horses (foals) can walk and run within ninety minutes of birth; chimpanzees within six months – human babies take a year. Mastering language, a hugely powerful learning tool, also takes years; attaining sexual maturity, more than a decade. During all this time, the child does not become "human," as much as a full member of her specific society or group. In the classic words of Ruth Benedict,

---

[1] Geertz 1973, 45.

> The life-history of the individual is first and foremost an accommodation to the patterns and standards traditionally handed down in his community. From the moment of his birth the customs into which he is born shape his experience and behaviour. By the time he can talk, he is the little creature of his culture, and by the time he is grown and able to take part in its activities, its habits are his habits, its beliefs his beliefs, its impossibilities his impossibilities.[2]

As an evolutionary strategy, the bet on learning over instinct has been an unalloyed success for humans. By being able to accumulate knowledge and experience, and transmit it to succeeding generations, first through spoken language, and later through its written form, human societies have become the undisputed masters of the living world (and its main threat). But all of this depends on the social nature of human life – another key biological premise. Humans only survive and thrive as part of a group. It is the group that first guarantees the survival of the child and then teaches her how the world works. Of course, as noted, this group has a particular culture to transmit. In this sense, cultural diversity is the price we pay for both the open-ended nature of learning, and of the social nature of human life.

It should be noted that, for any of this to work, the integration of the individual to the group is key, which is supported by another crucial biological disposition: the capacity to form emotional attachments or bonds, which also take a particular character (we just don't equally "love" anyone). Anthropologists have long documented the fact that many tribal societies' name for themselves was simply the word for "humans" or "people." Any other group was not another "culture," but simply considered not that human at all. The necessary and unavoidable group cohesion tends to make us ethnocentric. The key premise of group belonging also means there are no humans that do not belong to an established culture, or that do not live in the context of cultural parameters, however complex or disputed. I will come back to this basic point in further chapters.

Because survival depends on being part of the group, and because the group does not behave instinctively, a mechanism is needed to keep everyone in line with whatever the group's culture

---

[2] Benedict 1959, 2–3.

has established as the "correct" way to behave. This is where human morality comes in. Humans are exceptional in that everything they do, feel, and think is framed in moral terms, that is, within parameters of "good" or "bad."[3] We function in our daily life according to the moral grid that our particular society establishes for all kinds of activities and interactions. (We don't necessarily do this consciously; as we will see later in this chapter, culture is lived mostly subconsciously.) There are "appropriate" and "inappropriate" ways of eating, walking, speaking, greeting, and generally behaving in a whole set of different contexts, places, and situations. As Herbert Gans has summarized it,

> Everyday life is, among other things, a never-ending flow of moral surveillance. We all survey each other to see if actions live up to the norms and expectations we carry in our heads.[4]

The surveillance is not only between people but also within ourselves. We continuously police our own conduct in order to comply with whatever social norms are expected in every particular situation. Am I dressed properly for the occasion? Should I greet with a handshake or a kiss? Should I use the little fork or the large one? If all this sounds a bit stressful, it's because it is. This is why jokes and humor have an element of catharsis. Humor consists of a release of stress at the expense of the social order.[5] We laugh when things don't go quite as expected, or according to the rules. Slapstick humor, which consists of a string of faux pas, capitalizes on the funniness of the unexpected breakdown of social norms, mostly naively or accidentally. (If the breakdown were intentional, we would see it as antisocial behavior, and would not necessarily be funny.) Our enjoyment has an element of identification and complicity: We feel that the "mistakes" are the kinds of things we are always on the verge of committing, given the impossibility of

[3] There are, arguably, dimensions of social life that have a more "instrumental" character, that is, that do not necessarily follow a moral logic, and work within parameters of "right or wrong," rather than "good or bad" (see Faubion 2011). I'm taking here a more general perspective, in the classic sense of Durkheim: "Society is not a simple aggregate of individuals who, when they enter it, bring their own intrinsic morality with them; rather, man is a moral being only because he lives in society, since morality consists in being solidary with a group and varies with this solidarity. Let all social life disappear, and moral life would disappear with it, since it would no longer have any objective" (Durkheim 1972 [1893], 101).

[4] Gans 1995, 11.

[5] Douglas 1975.

navigating the social world completely victorious. Humor has also a subversive element, since it indirectly reveals the arbitrariness and frivolity of all those social conventions. (Nothing really terrible happens, after all, to the comic hero.) When we say that the truth is really only being spoken by comedians, this is what we mean. Comedians dispense of all the euphemisms and doublespeak we are all continuously practicing, and just tell it as it is. When we laugh, we admit to the charade.

One of the main psychological weapons human societies have for keeping everyone in check is the emotion of shame. Societies regularly dispense shame and ridicule, in different doses, to those who are not up to standard in one way or another. Since human societies work with a template of "good" and "bad" behavior, which then translates into "better" and "worse," all members may be judged in their performance in a myriad of ways, the number of which depends on how many roles and occupations a society offers, as well as its level of social stratification. In very unequal societies (like our own), where social esteem (i.e., status) is consequently badly distributed as well, shame, in the form of feelings of social inferiority, is the most common cause of social unrest and violence. Feelings of pride, dignity, and respect, in other words, of social acceptance (the opposite of shame) are enormously important for humans, highlighting once again the evolutionary centrality of group belonging. Psychiatrist James Gilligan has argued that intolerable feelings of shame, humiliation, and hurt pride are at the base of all violent antisocial behavior.[6] I will come back to this issue.

We should not see shame, however, exclusively as a mechanism of social control, because it also assists the individual. Shame (frequently internalized as guilt) signals to the person that she is in danger of being disconnected and marginalized from the group and can thus stimulate corrective behavior.[7]

It is important now to reexamine the source and consequences of social standards. Human societies work with notions of "better" and "worse" behavior because they have no recourse to biological instincts. Appropriate behavior can only be defined culturally (but never definitively, since we can always discover or develop an even

---

[6] Gilligan 2001.
[7] From this point on, I will be dealing with the unfortunate partialness of conventional gendered pronouns in the following way: I will be mostly using the female pronoun in the first half of the book, up to Chapter 4, and the male pronoun in Chapters 5–7.

"better" way). This state of affairs confers human societies their moral character, but it also demands from them moral direction. Human cultures have the critical task of providing their members with a sense of purpose and meaning. Since our agenda is mostly open, it is incumbent on our society to help us fill it up. The feeling of moral disorientation is another one of those intolerable emotional states for humans. We need direction, *some* direction, for our lives, even if we later on find it wanting or defective.[8]

Now, the fact that we understand that "better" is definitively better than "worse" doesn't necessarily make us pursue "better." Why go through all the trouble? Why do human societies strenuously engage in all kinds of activities that have no clear relation to biological survival? One reason is the promise of enhanced social esteem or status, which is related to increased social power. If, from an evolutionary perspective, being part of the group is good, then being a more esteemed or powerful member is definitively even better. To climb further up the social ladder, according to one standard or another, theoretically improves your survival chances and makes evolutionary sense. If, for example, "better" means having more money, and having more money means better life chances and better control of your life, then pursuing "better" is a no brainer. We will dedicate Chapter 5 to this topic of social power and inequality. But another is the fact that humans just seem fond of challenging themselves. In a world with few instinctual imperatives, it seems not only logical that humans be free to set their aims, but also motivated to pursue them. When all other animals encounter obstacles, they respond through their instinctual repertoire. Most of these obstacles are going to be standardized, since most animals live in the particular ecosystems for which they are adapted. For humans, obstacles are less predictable, and many of them are self-generated, all of which demands not only creativity, but also tenacity. While we can speculate if tenacity is a trait of all living creatures, it is mainly in humans that we see the surmounting of obstacles as a potentially pleasurable thing that is actually practiced and pursued *intentionally*. Humans, indeed, commonly make their lives far more complicated than is "needed." Sports, contests, artistic endeavors, scientific research, explorations, and the rest, all committed to the pursuit of excellence (however defined), speak of

---

[8] Fromm 1976, Ch. 7.

a restless spirit that takes pleasure in challenging its perceived limits, which is after all, what learning unbound leads to. It is perhaps no coincidence that the most popular sport in the world prohibits the use of arms and hands, the most physically versatile parts of the human body. It is as if we were telling ourselves, "What nice arms and hands you have there! Now take this ball, and let's see what you can do without them!"

* * *

In sum, humans live in groups that share a somewhat arbitrarily established culture and that includes a set of moral standards that define the good life and the standards of social success. This culture then conforms what we understand and assume as "reality."[9] It is important to note that reality is, in this sense, *a property of the group*. We all assume that, as individuals, we have a good grasp of the world out there, since we are definitively a part of it. But the last word of what classifies as real belongs to society. A simple thought exercise demonstrates this point. If you leave your residence and the first person you encounter praises your "beautiful red hat," even though you have nothing on your head, you will think that person has gone insane. But if every single person you meet afterwards does the same thing, you will quicky start questioning your own sanity, and making an appointment with a psychiatrist in no time.

But how are these cultures, this reality, actually put together? We can mention several key components. One of them is social roles. All societies establish a set of standardized positions or roles that are then occupied by its members. Some of these roles are related to kinship relationships (such as father, mother, wife, brother, aunt, or cousin), while others relate to occupations or positions of social command (such as architect, governor, bus driver, or legislator). Of course, many people fill both types simultaneously.

All of these roles come with different degrees of social power. Being an engineer usually entails more social power (i.e., status and means) than being a carpenter. Some roles are, however, relatively equal among their type (e.g., different types of engineers). All social roles also come with expectations of behavior. If you call yourself a

---

[9] Van Der Elst 2003.

banker (hopefully because you are one), people are going to expect a certain demeanor and style. These expectations follow a rich catalogue of stereotypes, which are an unavoidable part of social life. In Erving Goffman's words,

> To *be* a given kind of person ... is not merely to possess the required attributes, but also to sustain the standards of conduct and appearance that one's social groupings attaches thereto.... A status, a position, a social place is not a material thing, to be possessed and then displayed; it is a pattern of appropriate conduct, coherent, embellished, and well articulated.[10]

The number of roles and positions that a culture offers is generally dependent on its degree of "complexity." What anthropologists call "small-scale societies" (such as bands or tribes) usually have a very short list of social roles and positions. By contrast, "complex societies," like our own, have a seemingly infinite list. This is closely related to the society's economic system. The bigger, more complex an economy is, the more occupations it encompasses, leading to a multiplicity of roles and positions.

Attaining any social role or position is usually well regulated. Not just anyone can become a judge, an electrician, or a witch doctor. Depending on the culture, requirements may entail years of training and tests, "supernatural" signs, or exceptional performance. By contrast, some other positions, such as "adult" or "elder," only require living long enough. Regardless, the transitions to most social positions are usually marked with some sort of ceremony (which formalizes the attainment and makes it "real"). Anthropologists call these ceremonies "rites of passage."[11] Graduation ceremonies are the rites of passage for professional occupations, while weddings signal a change in family status and romantic availability (in theory, at least).

Rites of passage are just one type of social *ritual*, which is another common component of cultures. In general terms, rituals are scripted events that organize social life. They also make the culture "real" and confirm its norms and parameters. As Edmund Leach puts it, "We engage in rituals in order to transmit collective messages

---

[10] Goffman 1959, 75. Emphasis in original.
[11] Van Gennep 1960.

to ourselves."[12] Christmas dinners, birthday parties, carnivals, and coffee breaks are all rituals.

Finally, cultures also organize themselves through particular divisions of space and time, following the expression "a time and place for everything." Our world is divided into different types of physical settings that are appropriate for certain activities and not for others, and into time slots that follow the same logic. We don't expect to see a wrestling match in a bank lobby, or a Happy Hour on midday Monday. Every setting, as well as every occasion, is not, however, simply an empty container waiting to be filled with an activity. Every event tends rather to be predefined culturally in space and time and brings a whole set of expected behaviors, as well as attendants. (As Goffman says, "only individuals of a particular kind are likely to be found in a given social setting."[13]) Weddings tend to occur in certain types of places, at certain days and hours, with people dressed in a certain manner. We normally expect a certain coherence between setting, the people in it, and their behavior and appearance. The particular sequence of repetitive events strewn in a calendar and distributed in different physical settings is what gives every culture much of its character (and its rush hour traffic jams). As Anthony Giddens says, "all social life can be represented as a series of episodes."[14]

All these social dynamics and properties – roles, rituals, events – depend critically on the use of symbols. Humans live in a "forest of symbols," to borrow an expression from anthropologist Victor Turner.[15] If we accidentally step into a party, we can probably figure out fairly quickly what the occasion is about by observing the way the place is decorated, how people are dressed and are behaving, and the accompanying paraphernalia (props, food, music, etc.). All of these variables work as symbols – they "stand for" or "represent," say, a "Bar Mitzvah." When deploying symbols, we tend to pile them up and use redundancy in order to reinforce the message of the particular role, ritual, or event, and also to enhance its emotional impact. Christmas arrives with decorated pine trees, a profusion of lights, nativity scenes, nutcrackers, snowmen (even in tropical countries), special music, food and dress, scripted rituals, and so on. There's no escape from it.

[12] Leach 1976, 45.
[13] Goffman, op. cit., 1.
[14] Giddens 1984, xxix.
[15] Turner 1970.

Symbols are always relational, and they always work in sets.[16] We tend to believe things have an essence, but they rather derive their meaning through contrast. There is no "beautiful" without "ugly," "masculine" without "feminine," "luxurious" without "ordinary," "rich" without "poor," or "clean" without "dirty." In general, you can't have something without its opposite. In addition, the best way to enhance and emphasize something is to play on the contrast. A Catholic nun's appearance, envisioned to block any reference to female sexuality, uses a repertoire that contrasts in every aspect with the Western image of a sensual woman: covered head instead of flowing hair; lack of make-up; long, closed dresses instead of skin-revealing attire, etc. (In some other culture, however, it would be possible for a nun's outfit to be considered sexy.) In the West, the formal/informal divide in dress follows closely a covered/revealing opposition. Normal business attire is relatively covered-up for both men and women (although always less for the latter), and turns more revealing for both as we move toward the informal end. When we move toward the high-end pole of formality, however, as in "red carpet" events, men's attire gets even more closed (as with tuxedos), while the women's then opens up (as with dresses with plunging necklines). All cultural forms can be analyzed through this method of identifying opposing attributes.

* * *

In sum, cultures function through the distribution of roles, the enactment of rituals, and the division of space and time, all mediated through the use of symbols. This might give the reader the impression of a mental cage, a system that engulfs the individual and offers her very little wiggle room. But, in fact, cultures are fragile and rickety constructions, and are usually self-contradictory.[17] They can also be, as we all know, full of conflicts between different groups. Finally, they are frequently confronted with (or formally incorporate) episodes or rituals of deviance or breakdown of social norms. Let's address these topics in that order.

While we tend to imagine cultures as based on explicit rules, these, in fact, play a rather small role in social life. Most cultural

---

[16] Leach, op. cit.
[17] Nuckolls 1997; 1998.

behavior is routinized, that is, subconscious, and is practiced as habit.[18] A very large proportion of our daily conduct is completely scripted, and the cultural parameters that frame it are incorporated into these routines as a matter of course. The regular sequence of waking up, dressing, having breakfast, getting to work, and so on, consists of tasks that we put minimal thought into, since they have been already mentally incorporated as behavioral "programs." Likewise, in social situations, we function rather automatically with what sociologist Pierre Bourdieu calls "a sense of compatibilities and incompatibilities."[19] We tend to know "in our gut" when something is "off" or "wrong" in any kind of social interaction or event. Explicit rules are usually brought into play only when the danger of misunderstanding is large. You usually would not hang a sign in a fancy restaurant telling patrons that you need a shirt on in order to enter; but if you do require a dinner jacket, that might need an explicit notice. Likewise, in the political system, what gets legislated consists in what is not going to happen anyway (and that we *really* need people to do). We don't have laws mandating people to sleep, but we do regulate parties that disrupt people's sleep.

Rules or norms, explicit or implicit, are, moreover, always ambiguous. We can interpret rules in different ways, or just bend them to our benefit. Interpreting apparently transparent written rules is, of course, what lawyers get paid for, but we all live like lawyers of a sort. One could argue that social norms exist not just to be followed, but also *to be used strategically*. Depending on our interests and agenda, certain rules can be emphasized, reinterpreted, flaunted, or ignored. Some rules are drafted in an intentionally ambiguous manner, precisely to be able to play with them. In societies with marked social divisions and conflicts, rules are going to be challenged all the time, since by definition they support a certain way of living, which inevitably favors some groups over others. Any movement of social reform will take aim at the society's norms, roles, and rituals, since they form the building blocks of the culture. This highlights the fact that cultures are not just purveyors of meaning, but ways of organizing society, that is, *of organizing relationships between people*. I will emphasize this point throughout the following chapters.

---

[18] Giddens 1984.
[19] Bourdieu 1990, 13.

In a more abstract sense, social norms relate to expectations in the context of communication, or, in sociologist Niklas Luhmann's formulation, "expectations about expectations."[20] We carry expectations in our heads of how things should work, and other people should react, to our presence and conduct. When things don't pan out as expected, we are forced to change our assumptions, learn and adapt, or fight for adjustment in the external world. Given the fact that we're dealing with interactions between any number of separate brains, Luhmann believes that, in principle, "communication is highly improbable," in other words, that it is striking that we can understand each other at all. The answer is, of course, that all these independent brains are integrated through *culture*, which functions as a sort of external, interpersonal neurological circuit.[21]

The fact, however, that cultures provide values and ideals does not mean that they do so coherently. Frequently, one highly valued ideal is in conflict with another highly valued ideal, and there is no clear mechanism to conciliate them. This is just a logical result of cultures being concoctions wrought out of a very large field of possibilities. (In other words, there is no reason why cultures *should* be completely coherent.) Turner's classic study of the Ndembu culture (in present-day Zambia) is a case in point.[22] The Ndembu lived in small villages of grass huts, with a subsistence economy based on hunting and cassava cultivation. Their culture stipulated what anthropologists call "virilocality" and "matrilineality," which in plain English means, in the first case, that when the woman married, she moved with the husband's family; and in the second, that only descendants through the mother's side were actual relatives. (In other words, an uncle and cousin from the mother's side were relatives, but an uncle and cousin from the father's side were not.) In consequence, men imported wives from other villages and exported sisters. The system split power between men and women (since men ruled over place of residence, and women over family composition) but was also a source of constant tension and conflict. Women had to abandon their village and family when they married; at the same time, in the case of a divorce, women could return to her original village with all the children, leaving the former husband alone

[20] Luhmann 1990, 45.
[21] Bartra 2014.
[22] Turner 2020 [1957].

and threatening his capacity to consolidate his village, and his power in it. The dynamic accounted for many broken marriages and village fissions. Ndembu social rituals thus incorporated considerable taunting and aggressive joking between the sexes, which had the effect of diffusing the tensions that caused all the troubles. The Ndembu also favored marriage between cross-cousins (marrying the child of one's mother's brother or father's sister), which had the advantage of cementing allegiances on both sides of the divide. It is important to highlight that the conflict here was, as Turner emphasized, "between opposed goods, not between good and bad."[23]

In "small-scale" societies like these, the main production unit is the household or residential group, which together cultivates the land, hunts, takes care of the children and the elderly, and shares the rewards. Kinship relations are, therefore, everything, since they define who is related to whom (and thus who is responsible for whom) and also who inherits what from whom. In modern societies, kinship rules are less relevant, because we get relatively less from our families, and relatively more from large-scale institutions such as the capitalist market or the government. The key conflicts thus move to this plane.

An obvious contradiction in our societies is the one between individual initiative and social responsibility. (As we will see later in this chapter, this is a practically universal contradiction.) We wax unendingly about the rights of the individual and the possibilities that the system offers for self-realization and "finding oneself." At the same time, we preach incessantly about the need for social cohesion and solidarity. The fact is, of course, that these are opposing goods, and the ways they can clash are legion. Our societies, furthermore, don't really have any established ways of conciliating these opposing pulls. Anthropologist Bradd Shore has argued that, in US society, baseball is one of the social rituals where the interaction between communitarian and individualistic impulses are "modeled" and can thus be psychologically processed by the fans, much like Ndembu rituals do with relations between the sexes.[24] In general, modern team sports are indeed a privileged form of enactment of the various ways in which individual and group efforts can work together. But, to judge on the evidence, our ritualistic repertoire is clearly insufficient. This is best illustrated

[23] Ibid., 330.
[24] Shore, op. cit.

by the political fights around these values, which frequently take a pen-
dular character. A "left-leaning," "socially responsible" government
comes to power to reign in inequality, which is then replaced in the
next period with a "right-leaning" administration intent on curbing
the excesses of that "big government" and its "suffocating" effects on
individual initiative. And then, of course, the cycle just repeats itself,
leaving in its wake a string of resentful voters, zigzagging public policies, canceled government initiatives, and waste. The whole process
feeds on the cultural fantasy that these contradictions can be solved;
that there is, somewhere in the future, a system (of whatever political
sign) that can get it right. But paradoxes cannot be solved; they can
only be managed. As I will argue later in this chapter, the obsessive
quest for a definitive solution to these kinds of issues is what actually
gets us into trouble.

Finally, many societies incorporate rituals that allow for the
temporary suspension of social norms. In general, rites of passage
involve a transitional stage between the two states (the old social position and the new one), when the individual is in a social limbo, and
her status is undefined. In societies where roles are rigidly enforced,
these "liminal" states, as they are called, can be considered dangerous
or polluting, a fact that can be observed, for example, in puberty or
initiation rites in many cultures.[25] In some societies, the novice can be
segregated or expelled from the community during this period. During
this transitional phase, the person can also be allowed to engage in
antisocial behavior, which reflects the condition of being temporarily
outside the moral grid normally enforced through established roles.
In modern Western societies, this pattern can be noticed in the rowdy
behavior tolerated in bachelor parties and in the activities of high-
school students in their last year, both involving people in obvious
social transitions.

Turner has related these kinds of stages, when conventional
social roles are suspended, with the concept of "communitas," the
social modality that occurs when individuals renounce to all social
hierarchies and predetermined roles, and relate to each other sponta-
neously and in conditions of radical equality.[26] Communitas is typical
of some millennial or utopian movements and groups, or of religious

[25] Douglas 2002.
[26] Turner 2008.

or secular communes, that break with the larger society and establish alternative forms of social living where everyone is treated equally as "brothers" and "sisters." Social protest movements frequently invoke a vision of communitas in their ultimate vision for society. Some cultures offer the experience of communitas as part of established, common rituals. In the Western world, carnivals originally had this connotation, and included an important component of social satire. During carnival, mocking rulers and authorities was allowed and tolerated, and the celebrations included all kinds of games involving role reversals – women dressed as men, commoners as nobles, and so on. This served to upend temporarily the social hierarchy, releasing social tensions in the process. In part for this subversive character, however, they were eliminated in most of Europe and other regions.[27]

* * *

In the previous pages, I have presented cultures as the framework of human life, as the scaffolding of reality, as a system that provides people with meaning, purpose, and organization. On the other hand, I have made clear that cultures can be unstable and full of contradictions, either because their values are in conflict or because their different subgroups are. I will close the chapter with a brief discussion on some of the key cultural components of the modern worldview, to which I will be referring back in the following chapters. But first, I want to comment on the issue of activism and cultural change, which has a special salience in this dynamic world we live in. A key point is how modern activism is related to utopian thinking, which is both an intrinsic component of modern societies and a constant challenge to their stability and viability.[28]

One of the most peculiar aspects of many contemporary social movements, especially in richer countries, is their negation not only of the reigning social order (which is to be expected) but also of *any* social order.[29] What is presented as oppressive is not just this or that

---

[27] Ehrenreich 2006.
[28] "To be modern is to find ourselves in an environment that promises us adventure, power, joy, growth, transformation of ourselves and of the world – and, at the same time, that threatens to destroy everything we have, everything we know, everything we are" (Berman 1988, 15).
[29] Morgenthau and Person 1978.

limitation, custom, or rule, but the idea itself of any social (or even biological) restriction at all. Freedom is presented as that which results from the elimination of any obstacle to the realization of the unique identity of the person, which is then seen as originating in the depths of the individual, a realm where society apparently has no role to play. This is evident in the activism around the ever-expanding list of discovered sexual identities in wealthy countries. In poorer nations, the prevalence is rather on utopian social visions, where the negation of the social order consists of ignoring it completely, and imagining a radically different state of affairs, whose realization does not demand a change in, or evolution of, the present order, but an integral replacement with a new model that simply sweeps the old one away. The perennial alure of a definitive socialist revolution in these parts of the world is an obvious example.

These social utopias work with what I will call "limit scenarios," an imagined future where the particular social problem that concerns the movement has been completely eliminated, and forever.[30] Utopianism is, in essence, a staple of the modern worldview, and makes itself present throughout the current ideological spectrum, influencing different versions of Marxism and libertarianism, as well as more recent radical movements.[31] Utopian visions usually end up generating dogmatic, intolerant, and sectarian movements and regimes, since they shun complexity and incoherence, two basic features of contemporary cultural systems. They usually assume that there is only one evil, or rather a "master evil" (such as economic exploitation, racism, patriarchy, or government overreach), whose eradication is a simple moral redress that needs no postponement. Utopian ideological movements are usually reductive (complex problems are reduced to one issue), Manichean (the social scene is neatly divided into allies and enemies), and apocalyptic (there is a clear and definitive solution at hand). Modern history is, of course, full of appalling utopian experiments, in the form of totalitarian communist revolutions, repressive

---

[30] I'm here fashioning my own version of Hinkelammert's (1984) utopian "limit concept" (*concepto límite*). Samuels (2016) characterizes this as the pursuit of a "shadow-free politics."

[31] According to Mannheim (2000 [1936]), utopianism is only possible in a society that allows for social mobility (such as modern ones). Many societies handle visions that are incongruent with their reality, but that are also situated beyond this world. In Mannheim's formulation, only transcendental visions that entail the transformation of the status quo merit the label "utopian."

theocracies, and brutal neoliberal dictatorships. This makes a discussion about social change such a key topic, especially from an anthropological perspective.

I have argued earlier that all cultures are selective, that is, whatever their cosmology establishes, it does so at the expense of other possibilities. Inevitably, this condition is shared by many protest movements. In the words of Mary Douglas:

> Public outrage is a mysterious thing. To foreground certain crimes means ignoring others. Each generation finds something to condemn in the moral record of its immediate ancestors.[32]

Douglas proceeds to highlight how in the world of the ancient Greeks, slavery was so central to the system that its abolition was simply unthinkable. For Aristotle, the exemplary person was the free citizen who participated fully in the political and judicial affairs of the city-state. For this (male) citizen to do this, someone else had to take care of the mere necessities of life, a task which then fell on women and slaves. (The use of slaves for the generation of profit, rather than discretionary time, belongs to more recent centuries.) In our times, the corresponding moral scandal is the unprecedented levels of poverty and social inequality that we are willing to tolerate. We simply derive too many benefits from our unequal system, such as enormous wealth and private initiative, to do anything serious about it. Or perhaps we are too traumatized with the alternative experiments we have already tried, such as communism. Be that as it may, Douglas speculates how forgiving historians in the future will be with us, as compared perhaps to how forgiving we are willing to be with the ancient Greeks. In the meantime, we are forced to engage in justificatory mental gymnastics not very different than those of Aristotle, who deemed slaves incapable of deliberation and independent judgment, and thus unsuited for citizenship.[33] We, of course, want to believe that the modern poor are just too uneducated, lazy, or fond of the wrong values, to deserve any better.

These kinds of "big" underlying issues are the true "rigid" or "sticky" parts of a cultural system, the taboo corners of social debate that we try to avoid whenever possible. As I will argue in the following

---

[32] Douglas 2004, 85.
[33] Arendt 1998 [1958], 84.

chapters, social inequality accounts for many of today's social ills and sufferings, but this does not make it any easier to recognize or handle. Poverty and inequality are also part of a longer list of issues covered in what sometimes is called "emancipatory politics," which focuses on combating sources of discrimination and oppression, as suffered by certain social classes, racial and ethnic groups, women, or sexual minorities.[34] It is important to examine the objective, general limits of these types of movements.

As argued before, all cultures restrict human life by establishing specific norms and types of social relations. Any culture is only one culture among many theoretically possible. At the same time, human life can only develop in the context of a specific culture. Human beings cannot mature and grow in a culturally undefined social universe. To be human is to be historic and particular. That is why Giddens describes social institutions as both "constraining" and "enabling."[35] You can only build a new society by using the existing one as your starting point. As the saying goes, in order to change the rules, you first have to know them. A rebel needs something to rebel against.

In addition, you can only replace one cultural system with another, which will be, of course, constraining in its own way. You cannot replace a system with a non-system. This means you can never have a society without marginalized individuals or groups. All societies have outsiders. The idea that you can build a society without any type of social exclusion is, objectively speaking, an impossibility. Such an effort would end not with a completely just society, but, rather, with nothing. Culture is selection, and selection is exclusion.

Historically and culturally, societies have had different ways of dealing with nonconformists. In the most extreme cases, they were simply eliminated or expelled. In more humane cases, outsiders might be given a legitimate role, or at least one tolerated halfheartedly. Seers, prophets, artists, and intellectuals are examples of social outsiders that presumably play an important role, even if sometimes reluctantly acknowledged. (Of course, such tolerance can transform such rebellion into an actual form of social belonging.) The modern democratic, liberal world is noteworthy in the degree of legal protection it affords to many forms of social deviancy. In this sense, the true test of a free

---

[34] Giddens 1991.
[35] Giddens 1984.

society is not if it can prevent the generation of marginalized citizens, but rather on how it treats them.

Nonconformism is, in any case, rarer than we think. Truly independent thinkers are few and far between. Most contrarians, however eccentric in their minds, simply join a breakaway group and fall in line with its viewpoints. Most individualisms devolve into tribalism. People's opinions tend to depend on what their reference group thinks of the matter, or on the social status of the person making the argument. Humans are, in general, and as argued before, terrified of being socially isolated. The Roman philosopher Seneca perhaps said it best: "We live by the principle, not of reason, but of imitation."[36]

As a general rule, the existing society provides its individuals with the available menu of life choices, which then those same individuals, through social action, can try to expand. There is no "deep" identity inside the individual that needs to be discovered, if by this we mean a personal essence that is not already a social role. Exactly zero individuals grew up in the seventeenth century frustrated because they couldn't be an airline pilot, for the obvious reason that air travel was not then a real possibility. What lurks in the deeper recesses of every person is not a unique project that society needs to accommodate, but a variation of society itself.

Social activism is frequently presented as an activity that prioritizes moral dimensions over the purely technical, economic, or political ones that other social actors concern themselves with. But this is mostly an illusion. Since most social life is organized around moral values, every social endeavor is steeped in moral action, whether it is acknowledged or not. As I will analyze later in Chapter 7, technical languages of all sorts are a convenient and particularly modern way of concealing the moral choices implicit in many institutions and processes. Moreover, *every* actor believes in the morality of her actions. The moral nature of social life leaves no other option. We all justify our actions in moral terms. Activists defend the rights of the weak and oppressed, businesspeople create jobs, the military protect the nation, scientists invent technological solutions to the world's problems, and so on. Antisocial behavior can be justified as a righteous reaction to a rotten society. Even history's most noteworthy mass murderers

[36] Seneca et al. 2007, 85.

believed they were acting morally. The real choice in cultural conflict is not really between morality and immorality, but rather between different understandings of morality.

As noted before, many social conflicts involve paradoxes that have no real solution, at least in the terms of the current system. The struggle gives the impression of moving toward a resolution that ultimately proves elusive, and that generates even more conflict. Anthropologist Charles Nuckolls has described some ways in which societies deal with these paradoxes, especially in relation to the conflict between individualism and communality mentioned before.[37] One answer is to deal with the conflicting values in a temporal sequence, that is, in different moments in time. So, for example, people are usually more concerned with social solidarity ("progressive") when they are young, but become more individualistic ("conservative") as they get older. But this mechanism only guarantees a perennial intergenerational conflict. Another one is to assign the different values to different kinds of people and then assume that the different groups embody such values. Nuckolls argues that this is what US society has done with gender, by assigning the traits of independence and individual initiative to men, and dependence and commitment to women. This was indeed a key cultural model of modern society in its initial phases and still endures in many social realms, and even whole countries. In psychoanalyst Karen Horney's words, it consists of the "cultural belief in man's superiority in all but love."[38] As a result, women have been limited historically to domestic roles that have constrained their ability to exert power in society.

But we should not see this conflict as based exclusively in gender relations and thus approachable only at this level. Part of the problem (as I will expand in Chapter 6) is that capitalist societies assign a higher value to business initiatives that generate money and less value to those activities that concern the care of people. But these more domestic labors are absolutely essential for social life. *Someone* has to take care of the children, the house chores, or the elderly relatives. The fact that women are disproportionately in charge of these tasks, and devalued for it, does not entail that it is exclusively a misogynistic issue. The problems generated by the disparate valuation of social roles would endure even if we

[37] Nuckolls 1998, 30.
[38] Horney 1937, 204.

made all the men homemakers and all the women left for the office. We would be shuffling the actors, but not changing the play.

* * *

Let's now then conclude with the identification of some of those key components of the modern worldview – of its cosmology or "religion," so to speak. These are some of its deeper cultural notions, akin to what Shore calls "foundational schemas,"[39] that is, the bottom-most turtles.

The first one is the preponderance given to the individual at the expense of the group, something we have already touched upon. The individual is seen as the basic unit of society. Both capitalism and classical liberal politics privilege individual rights (of the consumer or the citizen) over the claims of communities of any sort, save the nuclear family or the "imagined community" of the nation. That this serves neatly the logic of a capitalist system will become clear enough, but we can see its presence in other areas as well. Medicine, for example, tends to see illness as a mostly individual affair. The social relations or social environment of the patient are seen frequently as irrelevant. The cures concern changes in the lifestyle of the individual, not in her social milieu or relationships. Culturally, there is a constant exhortation to "find oneself" by looking inward for a unique identity, instead of simply searching for a particular place or role in society.

A second salient component is a mechanistic view of the world. The world is like a big machine. This is clear in the physical sciences, where impersonal, fixed laws rule the universe. But the economy is also like a machine. Economic actors supposedly make free and independent decisions, but the "market" is a coordinating mechanism that renders the whole process intelligible and somewhat predictable. Policy makers can then influence the machine by lowering an interest rate here or increasing a tax over there, as if playing with the knobs on a dashboard. The human body is also a machine. Illnesses can be eliminated by introducing particular substances or modifying certain parts, as when one fixes an engine. Sexual problems are mechanical failures, rather than relationship challenges. Professionals with a less reductionist outlook have to struggle against this mind/body or body/

---

[39] Shore, op. cit., 53.

environment ideological split within their fields. Since the body is like a machine, its "needs" can also be clearly identified and addressed (if realistically possible). Governments and aid agencies can thus design programs based on the "basic needs" of the poor. Tied to all this is a special privilege afforded to quantification. Things that can be measured and quantified are deemed somewhat more "real" than those that are not amenable to this approach. Performance and success are best measured in numbers.

Lastly, modern societies have a linear view of time. In contrast to other civilizations that experienced time as cyclical, modern societies see time as open-ended, nonrepetitive, and extending infinitely into the future.[40] Key institutions and processes depend critically on this linear property: scientific progress, compound interest, and mortgage loans. With an open-ended future comes the idea of a final destination at the end of the road, since such an indeterminate framework is perhaps too anxiety-provoking. We have thus adopted a secular version of the Christian heaven that awaits us all.[41] The evolution of society is a trip toward perfection. All our historical visions contain an element of advancement and overcoming: We moved from the Dark Ages to the Enlightenment, from barbarity to civilization, from backwardness to progress, and from underdevelopment to development. Tied to this is a split and external view of evil. Evil, or lack, is not something that is intrinsic to this world, but a defect that can be, and must be, excised. Douglas finds a similar view in the Lele (from Central Africa), who believed that most of life's misfortunes could be traced to sorcery, a late arrival to creation according to their cosmology. The Lele could clearly imagine a world without sorcery, so they strived to eliminate all sorcerers. Says Douglas:

> A strong millennial tendency is implicit in the way of thinking of any people whose metaphysics push evil out of the world of reality.[42]

Our exorcists and healers are, of course, our scientists, whom we've given the task to eliminate all suffering from the earth. To accomplish

[40] Koselleck 2004.
[41] According to Blumenberg (1983), the modern idea of progress is the result of moving into this world the otherworldly Christian heaven, which solved a problem for a religion whose promises were always postponed.
[42] Douglas 2002, 211.

this task, what they mostly need is time, which we can offer plentifully, since it is infinite. But if our politicians and scientists bet on the future, our contrarians do so too. The utopianism of our rulers is matched by the utopianism of our revolutionaries, who also place their faith on a perfect future, when all injustices will find their ultimate demise. It is an end state without any form of inequality, domination, poverty, or sexual conflicts. Ours is a society permanently hungry of communitas, since we understand it as a fallen world in need of redemption, and whose original sin is injustice. When the desire for emancipation cannot find an outlet in one topic (e.g., poverty), it finds it in another, perhaps more accessible one (e.g., language politics).

To be clear, I'm not suggesting that social change is unnecessary, or that utopian visions are pure folly. In a globalized world careening toward catastrophe, change, and its orienting ideals, are essential and urgent. Utopian thinking is an intrinsic part of the modern culture, both a necessity and a potential liability. In this sense, the best approach is perhaps suggested by political scientist Norbert Lechner, who warns of two dangers regarding utopias: to try to live without them and to try to implement them.[43]

The immobile alternative is clearly unacceptable given our current challenges, but it does have its defenders. Alberto O. Hirschman has famously described three frequent arguments against social change deployed historically by conservatives: the perversity thesis, the futility thesis, and the jeopardy thesis.[44] The first one argues that any action aimed at improving the social order will ultimately only make it worse; the second, that the effort will be useless, since it will not make much of a difference; and the third one, that it will worsen some other accomplishment that we're not looking into. These "reactionary" positions are also part of our social landscape, and given what we've commented on the contradictory and paradoxical nature of cultural systems, they are not completely unmoored from reality. The road to hell is, indeed, frequently paved with good intentions.

In the end, progressives and conservatives are both, in their own way, right. Conservatives are prescient in distrusting social change, since as they correctly sense, all change is relative, and there

[43] Lechner 1986, 6.
[44] Hirschman 1991.

is no gain without loss. For their part, progressives are right to push for change on situations that are clearly unacceptable, and on their insistence that society not put up with conditions that generate unnecessary suffering. The stalemate can be broken if progressives renounce to "limit scenarios" and conservatives admit that some things do need to change. Both camps would then meet on the bland proposition that all societies have things to change and others to conserve, and that the real issue is what these lists consist of.[45] At that point, however, the distinction between conservatism and progressivism falls apart.

---

[45] Of course, at a more abstract level, "conservatism" can be identified with cultural stability, and "progressivism" with cultural change, two basic modes of cultural dynamics of modern societies (or of any society, for that matter).

4 THE COSMOS WITHIN

It is a matter of indifference who actually committed the crime; psychology is only concerned to know who desired it emotionally and who welcomed it when it was done.
Sigmund Freud, *Dostoevsky and Parricide*

In Chapter 3, I have described rules and norms as an indispensable component of societies and cultures. I also clarified that these rules and norms can be unspoken, ambivalent, and contested. For humans, rules or norms can never be fixed, because that would make them work as mock instincts. We would behave as ants, but with rules provided by ourselves, instead of by biology. The learning capacities that make us human entail that every person, group, or generation has the possibility of transforming the received social order and of proposing something new, that is, of changing the rules.

The view that derives from this formulation is that of social actors who use rules strategically. We comply with rules if and when it is convenient for us as individuals or as members of a social group or class. When it is not, we contest the rules and fight for changes, transforming the culture in the process, and advancing our interests.

This scenario presupposes that people behave somewhat "rationally" – they purportedly asses the social order and decide to comply or contest. It is an approach used by many social scientists in fields such as sociology, anthropology, and political science. What's missing here is depth psychology. What if people not always consciously know why they behave in a certain way? We have seen that culture, in general, is a subconscious affair. It consists of routinized, preprogrammed behavior. In addition, the whole cultural edifice is supported by implicit assumptions about how the world works, that is, by a cosmology, or a whole column of underground ideological turtles. Both behavioral programs and ideological assumptions can be brought to partial or full consciousness, which tends to happen in the face of unexpected events, misunderstandings, cultural shocks, or social conflict. When something out of the ordinary happens, we are forced to make explicit, and ponder on, what used to be simply the habitual ways of responding to, and thinking about things. Giddens calls these modes of knowing "practical consciousness" and "discursive consciousness," respectively.[1] Practical consciousness is what we engage in mindlessly and regularly as we go about living our routinized lives. Discursive consciousness is what we engage in when we formalize, regulate, write down, or give reasons for that behavior; in other words, when the rules become explicit. Both are then contrasted by Giddens with the *unconscious*, the domain opened up by Freud that deals with the things we rather not know, but that are nonetheless steering our behavior.

The human unconscious is a terrain of conflict, just as the social and cultural worlds. In this case, the conflicts do not concern disagreements between different individuals or groups, but rather between what we desire as individuals and what the world out there is willing or able to give us. The origin of this conflict is the same as that which explains cultural diversity, human learning, and human freedom in general. As individuals, we all want certain things, which, although chosen from the repertoire that our society offers, it is not necessarily ready to give us. If there were an exact match between the environment and our behavior, in other words, if our desires and behaviors adapted automatically to changes in the social or natural worlds, we would be back in the realm of animal instinct. Even though we are all part of the society we belong to, we are not necessarily satisfied with it, and this mismatch is what generates social and cultural change. Since societies are, in the end, composed of individuals, cultural and social conflict have, unavoidably, an individual dimension.

[1] Giddens 1984.

The "world out there" that frustrates our desires has different components.[2] It includes the norms and rules of our culture, which define the parameters of good and bad. We internalize these norms as "conscience" (what Freud called the "super-ego"), and we are all familiar with the corresponding psychic conflict: We desire something that our society (and ourselves as part of it!) does not approve. The world out there also includes other people; first of all, the people we share our lives with and depend on (such as partners, families, friends, bosses, and colleagues), but then everyone else that has power over our destiny. Finally, there's "reality" – the events that are out of our control and that have the power to wreak havoc in our lives: accidents, earthquakes, economic crises, or pandemics.

The conflicts with our own culture, other people, and external events are a source of stress and danger to us. We can end up isolated. We can lose our most meaningful relationships, or our social standing. We can also lose ourselves, by having to renounce to our most cherished desires. We handle these stresses and threats in several ways.[3] We can lean on the support of other people, especially the ones closest to us. Our society can also offer coping mechanisms in the form of established rituals that diffuse tensions. Our hostility can be vicariously lived as passionate fans of a sports team, for example, instead of letting it loose in the workplace where it actually originates, but where it would get us fired. Normally repressed behaviors can perhaps be practiced during carnival, an established period in which society tolerates them. We can also cope by internally planning for conflict. We rehearse in our minds what might happen, and prepare ourselves psychologically for it. We can also take a more philosophical attitude toward problems that lessens their potential psychological impact. When none of this works, the unconscious takes over. Unconscious mechanisms of dealing with stress and danger function, as the word implies, outside of awareness, but have the same purpose of relieving tensions for the individual. They also work, moreover, at the group level, since, due to our social nature, unmanageable stresses are frequently shared.

In the proverbial example, a little boy is angry because his baby brother has taken possession of his favorite toy. Because he knows he should not get angry with his small brother (a social norm transmitted

---

[2] Vaillant 1993, 29 ff.
[3] Ibid., 10.

to him by his parents), he takes it out on the dog and hits it. In psychology, this is a "defense mechanism" known as "displacement." It works as a "defense" because it protects the child from the anxiety resulting from the internal psychological conflict (he wants to hurt his brother but understands that it would be wrong, and would have consequences). The anger is thus "displaced" to a third party that poses no threat. The reaction is wholly unconscious, and the child would not be able to make the connection. In addition, from a "rational" point of view, the behavior makes no sense (the dog didn't do anything). Unconscious mechanisms are an essential component of social life, and if we don't take them into account, many social processes don't make much sense, either.

Psychologist Albert Bandura has conceptualized social dynamics as a triangle with the vertices occupied by "person," "behavior," and "environment."[4] The environment consists of external events, the actions of other people, the culture, the natural world, and so on. The person encompasses the inner reality of the individual, while behavior is simply what people end up doing. The fact that behavior and person are placed in separate vertices implies that our behavior does not always match our thinking or feeling, or at least the totality of it. We saw an example with the "rational" model earlier. I know that the environment (the social rules) demands a certain behavior from me, but I choose to do otherwise because of strategic motives. Unconscious mechanisms are another example of a split between behavior and person, but one in which our response to the environment occurs outside of our own awareness.

It is important to understand the relevance of the three interacting poles for analyzing social life. If our behavior was to respond uncomplicatedly to environmental events, we would be functioning as instinctual animals. If, on the other hand, our behavior was to respond solely to our internal world, without any attention to the environment, we would be living in a psychotic state. This is the realm of the self-declared Napoleons and Jesuses. People do behave oftentimes as automatons and, of course, psychosis does exist, but we would normally not consider these to be the proper or ideal conditions of human life. The conscious and unconscious dynamic tug between social conformity and individual assertion is what we find at the base of human psychology.

* * *

4 Bandura 1986.

As explained in Chapter 3, culture provides a meaningful order and a template for social relations. This framework then provides the context for individual and group psychology. At the most basic level, culture provides a "ground" that allows the individual to make sense of the world and be able to act – what Giddens calls "ontological security," or a sense of "confidence or trust that the natural and social worlds are as they appear to be."[5] The disruption of this order always generates disorientation and anxiety, regardless of whether we consider it just or unjust, legitimate or illegitimate, since our sense of agency and self depends on the existence of a predictable world out there to which we can respond. Culturally determined daily rituals and routines thus function as coping mechanisms that provide a sense of certainty and reduce anxiety.[6]

The dramatic effects on the individual of the total collapse of any predictable social order have been documented in the case of the Nazi concentration camps, where prisoners where subject to random insults and beatings, and arbitrary changes in routines involving vital matters, such as food and sleep.[7] The corresponding loss of a sense of personal autonomy, and the inability to predict and plan ahead, generated in many prisoners an attitude of extreme fatalism, apathy, and passivity, a sort of renouncement of will, which was accompanied by depression and followed by prompt death. Those able to survive the trials of the camps were generally prisoners who retained some sense of inner freedom and faith in the future, inspired sometimes mentally by personal plans that they expected to fulfill after the war.[8] As described by Victor Frankl, a camp prisoner himself, these survivors tended to be those with a rich inner life (with strong intellectual, artistic, or spiritual orientations), who paradoxically were usually the least physically robust.[9] Still others turned into accomplices of the guards, collaborating with them on repressive tasks and assuming their outlooks, what psychologically is called "identification with the aggressor." Since the aggressor is the only party that retains power, such identification has the advantage of reinstating some sense of purpose, even when you remain a prisoner. In these cases, the prisoner recovers some form of agency by switching sides.

[5] Giddens 1984, 375.
[6] Giddens 1991, 46.
[7] Giddens 1984, 61–64.
[8] Frankl 1985 [1959].
[9] Ibid., 55–56.

Having a predictable social order involves, as is obvious in this example, controlling the future. This is one of the purposes of norms. Norms aim not only to regulate what you should do today, but, equally importantly, what you should do tomorrow as well. The future is forced to be an extension of today (and of yesterday). Some things, however, are allowed to change. Luhmann calls norms "expectations not disposed towards learning."[10] We regulate those aspects of life where we don't want any surprises, while leaving open those where we "are willing to learn," that is, to accept or evaluate whatever comes our way. Societies and individuals differ in the set of dimensions that they are willing to leave open to the unexpected. The activity of planning is, in addition to the enforcement of norms, a typical mechanism for reducing the possibilities of undesired future events or outcomes. Both reduce anxieties generated by the intrinsic uncertainty of the world. We meticulously plan weddings, for example, to avoid any surprises, and we're usually successful.

Modern societies tend to tolerate uncertainty in the realms of art, sports, science (where learning is supposedly the whole purpose), and, to a certain extent, in the capitalist economy, where innovation and change are seen as key to progress and social welfare. Economic disruptions usually entail social disruptions, however, which means they're rarely conflict-free. The capacity to deal with uncertainty increases, in fact, with social power.[11] The wealthy are always better prepared to confront drastic economic transformations, especially if the industries they command are already placed to potentially benefit from the new economic tendencies. For this reason, they are usually supportive of following the next best thing, and of deregulation in general (i.e., the abandonment of norms in the economic field). The costs of transformation are usually transferred to society's weakest members, who can end up losing their jobs, their status, and their sense of identity. As we will see in Chapter 5, the control of uncertainty, that is, the ability to control the future, is one of the most important prerogatives of power.

* * *

The earlier section dealt with the psychological dimensions of culture's role as a provider of meaningful order. Let's now address the

---

[10] Luhmann 1995, 321.
[11] Marris 1996.

other key role: that of organizing relationships between people. Here we are concerned with people's psychological responses, especially unconscious responses, to the expectations of society. This is a tricky topic, because it entails the definition of what "normal" behavior consists of. As argued earlier, when we analyze people's behavior at the social level, we might be content enough to do so based on different groups' purported interests. But if we want to pursue psychological avenues, which may better account for the "odd" behaviors typical of defense mechanisms, we are forced to define a baseline of normality. Given what we've said already, the obvious answer would be that "normal behavior" is, in principle, what the society says it is. Under this assumption, abnormal or unhealthy behavior would simply be that which deviates from the norm and impedes the integration of the individual to society.

The dangers of this position are clear. In a "sick" society, the abnormal person may be the only healthy one around. We are familiar enough with indictments of whole social systems and cultures as inhuman, or contrary to healthy human development. To hold such society's eccentrics and contrarians as psychologically unhealthy would be the height of injustice. This reminds us of the medical practices of totalitarian regimes, which use mental health pretexts to persecute and lock up political opponents. To get around this dilemma, we also need a definition of normality that transcends particular social standards. This is how psychoanalyst Eric Fromm saw the problem:

> The term *normal* or *healthy* can be defined in two ways. Firstly, from the standpoint of a functioning society, one can call a person normal or healthy if he is able to fulfill the social role he is to take in that given society ... Secondly, from the standpoint of the individual, we look upon health or normalcy as the optimum of growth and happiness of the individual. If the structure of a given society were such that it offered the optimum possibility for individual happiness, both viewpoints would coincide. However, this is not the case in most societies we know, including our own. Although they differ in the degree to which they promote the aims of individual growth, there is a discrepancy between the aims of the smooth functioning of society and of the full development of the individual. This fact makes it imperative to differentiate sharply between the two concepts of

health. The one is governed by social necessities, the other by values and norms concerning the aim of individual existence.[12]

It could be objected that the "aims of individual existence" are, in themselves, culturally defined, which would make the distinction irrelevant. Normalcy is what's socially adaptive but also "healthy," but since the definition of healthy is also social, the two concepts collapse onto one another. The way out of this loop is to realize that a society's standards of human maturity and happiness do not always coincide with its adaptive needs, that is, societies usually fall short of their own ethical standards. This discrepancy is what actually accounts for moral conflicts. Debates about right and wrong confront what we are doing with what we believe we should be doing, that is, our behavior with our standards. In order to work with Fromm's distinction, we thus need to take every civilization at its word.[13]

The view of the emotionally healthy individual, from the standpoint of the modern therapeutic disciplines, is that of a person that knows herself, and is able to consciously recognize and reasonably handle her inner emotional conflicts, thus rendering her a more responsible person. I highlighted earlier that intrapsychic conflicts are unavoidable, since every person has to confront discrepancies between inner desires and external world. When such conflict is unmanageable, that is, when the level of anxiety it generates cannot be handled by the person, psychological defense mechanisms kick in, effectively moving the problem elsewhere. Many defense mechanisms are forms of "externalization," that is, of getting rid of an internal problem by moving it outside.[14] As noted, they work unconsciously, and inevitably distort what's going on, since it is precisely because we can't handle the truth of the matter that they activate to begin with. They are, in other words, "lies we tell ourselves to evade pain."[15] In theory, and, again, according to the Western paradigm, the emotionally "healthy" or "mature" individual is more able to recognize and manage her internal conflicts and make less use of defense mechanisms, or at least the more socially destructive ones.

[12] Fromm 1969 [1941], 137–138. Emphasis in original.
[13] Faubion 2011.
[14] Horney 1945, 115 ff.
[15] Burgo 2012, 10.

As theoretical concepts, defense mechanisms are just useful metaphors for describing general psychological processes, so there is no definitive list of them, or even an agreement on precise definitions. Some of them, however, have already become part of colloquial language: We talk of people being "in denial," or "projecting." Denial, as we all correctly understand it, entails ignoring the existence of the conflictive fact. "Projection" means assigning other people what we are actually feeling ourselves. I am angry with my spouse, but since I don't allow myself that feeling, I accuse her of being angry with me. "Passive aggression" consists of being hostile in a backhanded way. I don't approve of my company's policies, but instead of discussing it with the owner, I start being irresponsible at work. "Acting out" involves misbehaving in contexts that have nothing to do with the actual conflict. I'm frustrated with my parents, but pick up a fight with a classmate. "Reaction formation" involves turning our emotions into their very opposite. I'm in love with an indifferent woman, so I state that I'm really repulsed by her type. I'm economically ambitious but unsuccessful, so I start praising the virtues of voluntary poverty. "Splitting" consists of dividing people or issues into clear black-and-white, or good-and-evil, categories. It helps in handling intolerable feelings of ambiguity, especially if that means recognizing faults in ourselves that are too painful to see because they shatter a cherished self-image. By splitting, all evil is assigned to specific individuals or groups, and all goodness to other, the latter of which we identify with. The result of splitting is always a feeling of self-righteousness, because we always end up on the right team. So, all businesspeople are greedy sociopaths, and all environmental activists are virtuous defenders of society (perhaps because I'm an activist, but I'd rather be a businessperson). All immigrants are slackers, while all nationals are hard-working people (perhaps because, as a national, I'm sort of a slacker too). I have already commented on "displacement," where the conflict is retargeted to an innocent bystander that takes the role of a scapegoat.

This quick (and incomplete) overview makes clear that defense mechanisms can wreak havoc in society. People that have nothing to do with the actual problem can end up being insulted, unfairly labeled, or attacked. Defense mechanisms not only deceive their own practitioners, but also misrepresent the reality of other people, who are not judged according to their actual attributes, but rather according to the particular psychological needs of the offender. But not all defense mechanisms are socially destructive. George Vaillant also classifies some as "mature" defenses, precisely because the end result is beneficial to both the person and the people around her.[16] The mechanism of "altruism" allows us to channel the intolerable emotions into a socially valuable cause. Through altruism, the person does for others what she would like for herself. For example, a parent who has lost a child in a car accident dedicates her life to an organization that promotes car safety. "Sublimation" transmutes a problematic desire into a less conflictive form that is nonetheless equal in intensity and satisfaction. A violent and belligerent person becomes a highly successful boxer, thus sublimating the aggressiveness in the process. Religious extasy can be the sublimation of sexual energies in highly spiritual people committed to celibacy.

Mature defenses tend to be more conscious than immature ones, that is, we are more aware of what we're doing. This relates to the aforementioned idea that a psychologically mature person is, in general, more aware and in control of her emotions. The psychologically healthy person has thus more internal autonomy, and a greater capacity to choose, which translates into more responsible behavior. Instead of being a marionette of her unconscious, she is able to more objectively asses her feelings and those of others, and act according to her more authentic desires.

"Immature" defenses can have, nonetheless, legitimate uses in social and personal life. Denial is almost an integral part of daily living, since we could barely get through the day if we were constantly thinking about all of life's dangers, or all the world's disasters. We all also tend to ignore the indisputable fact that we are going to die someday. In general, denial helps us to be selective in our attention and to focus on the moment or task at hand. Splitting is highly valuable in the world of sports, since team rivalries would not be so exciting if we weren't convinced of the perfidy of our opponents and the superiority of our own team. During wartime, splitting is almost a requirement for the troops, since we could with difficulty kill our enemies if we weren't truly convinced of their evil nature.

Regardless of their degree of virtuousness, psychological defense mechanisms all replicate the functions of the other forms of consciousness: They allow us to reduce anxiety and engage daily life

[16] Vaillant 1993.

flowingly. Gidden's "practical consciousness," assisted by his "discursive consciousness," helps us function in a culturally efficient manner and in a sort of auto-pilot, without the stress of having to constantly think everything through. Unconscious defense mechanisms likewise "solve" problems on the spot by moving the uncomfortable issue elsewhere, allowing us to cope more effectively with the situation (even if other people pay the price). The whole set of modes allows humans to live *as if* they were instinctual animals, and assists the individual in reducing stress and protecting her (perceived) social standing, that is, in surviving more effectively as part of the group. In this picture, a greater degree of individuation and freedom can only mean a greater degree of awareness of these processes. In Frankl's version, "being human is nothing other than being conscious and being responsible."[17]

* * *

The distinction between "mature" and "immature" defenses begs the question of where psychological immaturity or pathology comes from. It is not surprising that the origin has a lot to do with problems of social belonging. As highlighted, social belonging is not negotiable for humans – we have to belong to a group, and any sign of social exclusion or rejection is a source of acute anxiety. On the other hand, we are all unique individuals, and the assertion of our individuality in the context of a particular society is equally fundamental to our well-being. Psychological pathology originates in an imbalanced or inadequate resolution of this tension, and the long and treacherous human childhood is normally the battleground where the corresponding psychological wounds are generated.

The individual can handle the relationship with the group in different ways. In Karen Horney's typology, you have the option of moving *toward* people, *against* people, or *away* from people.[18] Moving *toward* people means being empathic, loving, and considerate toward them. It entails tuning mostly to the needs of others, and then trying to be responsive toward those needs. In this mode of relation, the needs of the individual take second place, or are ignored. We sacrifice our needs for others. We thus guarantee our belonging to the group or our

---

[17] Frankl 2020 [1946], 41.
[18] Horney 1945.

commitment to the other person, but at the expense of our individuality, at least for the time being. This is the mode of selfless love. Moving *against* people is almost the opposing mode. We assert our individuality and put our needs first. Others have to sacrifice their desires and comply with our wishes, or negotiate. We move against people when we assert our social power. Bosses and leaders are frequently moving against people, even when they have consulted others in making their decisions, since it's impossible to please everyone. Moving against people detaches us temporarily from the group and asserts our individuality, but may not imply isolation if others need us anyhow, and if they acknowledge our right to independent thought and action. This is the mode of healthy individualism. Finally, moving *away* from people means avoiding the social challenge *tout court*. The individual isolates herself from the group, renouncing both attending to others and asserting her place in it. We retreat within ourselves and claim alone time. We engage in introspection, we tune out the noise of the world, and search for ourselves instead. In this case, our individuality is protected, but at the price of a very weak social presence. This is the mode of healthy detachment.

The psychologically healthy individual uses all three modes flexibly, and depending on the circumstances. It is oftentimes necessary to be empathic and sacrifice ourselves for others. In other contexts, however, individual assertion is essential if we are to survive as a unique personality in the midst of others, and to advance our personal life projects. And sometimes we do need to temporarily sever our ties with the group and retreat, especially if our continued involvement threatens our well-being. Compliance, assertion, and detachment are necessary components of a healthy relationship to the world, and we ideally engage in them flexibly as we navigate life in pursuit of our place in it. But only the self-confident person that has used these modes flexibly since childhood can use them thus as an adult. And only psychologically mature parents that have this capacity themselves can foster it in their children.

In theory, a child's unique personality should be recognized by her caregivers, and cultivated in tandem with the complementary respect for others. The child needs to learn to live as a responsible member of society and to honor the rules of social exchange. At the same time, the child's autonomy needs to be valued, cultivated, and respected as well. If the child's autonomous desires are ignored or rejected, say, by tyrannical, abusive, or neglectful parents, she will invariably repress them, since the child will learn, subconsciously and early enough, that the expression of her true desires will only bring trouble and conflict with the people she critically depends on.[19] Obliged to choose between individual assertion and social compliance, the defenseless child can only choose compliance, at least until open rebellion is discerned and deemed possible.

This kind of forced and shrouded submission produces in the child an alienation from the self.[20] She develops limited capacities to explore her feelings and desires, since such an endeavor brings very few benefits in the context of her household life. Critically, she will also develop a very low self-esteem, since the message she is receiving from her immediate surroundings is that she is unimportant as a unique individual. The lesson internalized is that she is not worthy of attention and respect. Since, for reasons already discussed, a feeling of worthlessness is intolerable for any person, it will be psychologically concealed from awareness, and handled through defensive and compensatory mechanisms that will lead to a more problematic engagement with the world first as a child, and later as an adult.

The main problem will be the barred access to an autonomous self. The self is unconsciously perceived as worthless and damaged, which means it will be kept inaccessible as much as possible. But since the person still needs social recognition and praise, a counterfeit solution will be found in the form of a stereotypical, ideal self. Intensely oriented toward social approval (given that it springs from deep feelings of social rejection), the ideal self will invest itself in one of the three

---

[19] The conflict can originate in a severe *mismatch* between the child and the caregivers, not only as a result of "bad" parenting (see Solomon 2012). Since the parents inevitably participate of the encompassing culture, the mismatch can echo or reproduce a conflict between the child's individuality and the society at large (Solomon 2012, 26–27). It is clear that the theoretical framework presented here belongs mostly to the world created by the massive and historically recent demographic transition to an urban society, which replaced the "group-based" childrearing of many premodern cultures with one more closely dependent on a "nuclear" family. It also corresponds to what Lancy (2022) calls a "neontocracy," that is, a world where the child is a privileged focus of society, and treated as a unique individual with rights. As Lancy makes clear, many premodern societies were rather "gerontocracies," where children occupied the lower rungs of the social order, and treated accordingly.

[20] It should be noted that the concept is the individual "self" (more than, I would argue, the reality of it) has also been amply documented as a modern creation (Douglas 1992, 211 ff.; Sahlins 2013, 24–25; Strathern 2018), since in many premodern societies, the self was conceived as constituted mostly by social categories and relations.

classic modes of social engagement, and fashion a grandiose representative of it. For Horney, the pathological version of moving "towards" people is the "self-effacing" personality, which makes love toward others the supreme value and orientation in life. The "expansive" personality, which values domination and aggressiveness, is the corresponding version of moving "against" people, while the "resigned" type would correlate with moving "away" from people. All three represent neurotic "solutions" to the unperceived problem of a dodged self, deemed defective.[21]

The self-effacing person is radically oriented toward the welfare of others, is highly sensitive and perceptive to injustice suffered by other individuals and groups, and impresses with her capacity for abnegation and selfless action. At the same time, her own personal agenda (beyond empathy and generosity) is blurred to herself and others. She avoids conflict and always bets on understanding. At the same time, she has trouble defending herself from abuse or the self-interested conduct of others, and even difficulty identifying such abuse or conduct. The self-effacing person is quick to forgive and forget, and slow to identify aggression, and her heroic generosity presents a jarring contrast with her doormat psychology in many aspects of life. She is frequently self-critical and apologetic, and prone to feelings of guilt. This can be interpreted as evidence of a superior moral sense, or even saintliness, which is her supreme prize. Her capacity to withstand suffering and abuse can be described as masochistic.

By contrast, the expansive type is all about the domination of others. If the self-effacing person can excel in social activism and aid industries, the expansive type is more common in the higher echelons of business and politics. The heroic aspect here refers to her purported talents for leadership and getting things done, which tends to hide and justify the abuse she heaps on everyone around her. The expansive person tends to be tyrannical and manipulative, and has trouble being empathic. She comes across as narcissistic, selfish, and self-centered, but like the self-effacing type, has difficulty locating an ultimate personal purpose beyond, in this case, being on top of the social pyramid. The social recognition for her success and executive capacities is here the ultimate reward, which hides the haziness about true tastes and enjoyments. Her proclivity for aggression can be described as sadistic.

---

[21] Horney 1991 [1950].

Finally, the resigned type chooses to cut her ties with a society that is deemed deficient or untrustworthy. Society is observed as an external, alien, or menacing body, suitable for analysis and criticism, but not for engagement. The challenge of social belonging is here "solved" by losing interest in the whole affair, and by restricting one's ambitions. This can be virtuously interpreted as independence or rebellion. The resigned type can be an excellent social critic, but the criticism tends to be always destructive, if not outright cynical. Her rebelliousness is always about attaining freedom *from* social restrictions, never freedom *for* enhanced social possibilities. Her emotional and intellectual detachment can be interpreted as tolerance and broadmindedness but are traits rather based, as in the other two cases, on fear. Like the self-effacing types, they can be idealistic, but they will likewise pursue not a better society, but a *perfect* one. Resigned types can end up being recluses or underperforming people in unremarkable jobs or, in contrast, admired intellectuals and social critics. Their proclivity for detachment can be described as misanthropic.

This characterization is somewhat simplistic and reductive, since neurotic personalities tend to combine traits from all three types; but in virtue of individual temperament, one tends to be always dominant. As important as distinguishing the three approaches, however, is keeping in mind what they have in common. All three are escapes from a more authentic self, deemed worthless. They are a refuge, a fortress, built to conceal and replace. But since this ideal self is largely stereotypical and unrealistic, it is a house of cards, a castle built on sand. The castle is there to protect a feeling of deficiency, and does so by erecting an image of perfection: a person that is, respectively, all love, mastery, or freedom. This perfection is threatened by any and all criticism. In consequence, the neurotic person is always thin-skinned. An enormous amount of energy is spent responding to perceived offences, slights, or attacks, and on preparations against anticipated ones. Expansive types respond with vindictive aggression. Resigned ones might retreat even more. Retaliatory attacks are infeasible for self-effacing types, since they would contradict the wholesale image of goodness, so the response takes the form of passive aggressiveness. This all highlights the crucial role of hostility in neurotic behavior.

For Horney, aggression and hostility are a basic component of neurosis in whatever form it takes. At bottom, all three neurotic personalities feel disrespected and unvalued by others. In addition, since my self-image is inflated, available social praise will always be scarce for my needs. Others are always at fault by not acknowledging my true worth; in consequence, I'm always a victim. Feelings of victimhood are thus a constant presence, as well as generalized envy, a chronic dissatisfaction with life, and insensibility toward other people's real interior reality. Other people's attacks are actually a form of projection: I have a very low opinion of myself, but since this is invisible territory, I assume that it is other people who have this feeling toward me. Regardless, perceived aggression demands a response. Humans, like other animals, defend themselves and respond aggressively to attacks, real or imagined. As is commonly framed, one can fight or flee. I can repress my vindictive aggression, which can then show up through somatization as anxiety, chronic tiredness, and other conditions or illnesses. It can also be directed inward as self-loathing, which is, at base, the feeling that I'm actually trying to run away from, which could then trigger depressive states. Fear, anxiety, and panic are also logical responses to the situations of danger that a catastrophic loss of face represents.[22]

Expansive types are those more prone to answer aggression directly with aggression, although one should never underestimate the hostile impulses of the other two. There's a sadist behind every masochist (and vice versa), as Freud eloquently expressed in his harsh assessment of Dostoyevsky:

> ... in little things he was a sadist towards others, and in bigger things a sadist towards himself, in fact a masochist – that is to say the mildest, kindliest, most helpful person possible.[23]

If this type of aggression is a nuisance in most cases, it can become lethal in the hands of more extreme carriers. Gilligan has argued that the "basic psychological motive" behind the behavior of most of the jailed violent criminals he worked with in the United States was "the wish to ward off or eliminate the feeling of shame and humiliation ... and replace it with its opposite, the feeling of pride."[24] Murders and assaults had the purpose of avenging perceived aggressions, and to

---

[22] See Maté (2011; 2022) for a stimulating discussion of the connection between disease and psychosocial dynamics.
[23] Freud 1961b [1927], 179.
[24] Gilligan 2001, 29.

"force respect from other people."[25] These men were highly insecure, thin-skinned, and violently reactive to any perceived offense, and could not imagine responding to humiliation in any other way than through physical attacks and the retaliatory humiliation of the offenders. They had grown in the lower rungs of society, suffering, throughout their lives, the social stigma that came with poverty and discrimination. They felt left out and disrespected by society, and their violence was just their way of getting even. In terms of Horney's classification, they clearly fell under the expansive type. Not surprisingly, as Gilligan explains, their childhoods had prepared the terrain for their conduct:

> ... they had been subjected to a degree of childhood abuse that was off the scale of anything I had previously thought of describing with that term. Many had been beaten nearly to death, raped repeatedly or prostituted, or neglected to a life-threatening degree by parents too disabled themselves to care for their child. And those who had not experienced those extremes of physical abuse or neglect, my colleagues and I found that they had experienced a degree of emotional abuse that had been just as damaging: being focused on as the parents' emotional "whipping boy," in which they served as the scapegoat for whatever feelings of shame and humiliation their parents had suffered and then attempted to rid themselves by transferring them onto their child, by subjecting him to systematic and chronic shaming and humiliation, taunting and ridicule.[26]

For Gilligan, most criminal behavior is a response to humiliation, a revenge against social exclusion and rejection. It is vindictive, but at the same time tries to obtain, through a restitution of pride, a sense of belonging and respect that has been denied, albeit through a "solution" that is completely counterproductive. One can argue that political violence shares some of the same framework. Armed insurgencies or terrorist groups likewise seek to correct a situation of social exclusion, offense, or unequal treatment, real or perceived. At the same time, they tend to generate a sense of belonging *within* the group, one that is precisely denied outside it. It is commonly pointed out that one of the main benefits that violent organizations provide to their members is a

---

[25] Ibid., 35.
[26] Ibid., 36.

sense of purpose, meaning, and belonging, that is, the usual scaffolding of culture.[27] In order to understand these processes, we thus need to see both political and economic rights as forms of social integration. As I will further discuss in Chapter 6, this demands that we analyze economies not as systems that distribute only goods, but also social status.

* * *

It is clear that most of the victims of violence are innocent bystanders. Most violence is misdirected. Pathological rage can be diffuse, and the logic of vindictive aggression can be simply to deny others what has been denied to us. If it avenges a real crime, it is commonly one long lost in time. Furthermore, most violence is justified as legitimate defense. We attack others because we have been attacked first, or so we tell ourselves. Our need for moral legitimacy inevitably provides cover for our violence, however arbitrary.

Physical violence is, of course, just one form of a more generalized pattern of mistreating others. We have already commented that immature or pathological defense mechanisms deny other people's individuality, and treat them as stereotypes or "representatives" of this or that "identity" or interest group. Neurotic personalities are particularly adept at this, of course, since they treat *themselves* as stereotypes, rather than as unique individuals. Splitting, projection, and displacement rule the days, and are put at the service of the person's grandiosity, entitlement, or self-loathing. This is how Horney describes the alchemy that neurotic personalities perform on other people:

> His need for admiration turns them into an admiring audience. His need for magic help endows them with mysterious magic faculties. His need to be right makes them faulty and fallible. His need for triumph divides them into followers and scheming adversaries. His need to hurt them with impunity makes them "neurotic." His need to minimize himself turns them into giants.[28]

That common immature defense mechanisms are the same used by neurotic personalities already tells us that this is a far more generalized problem. Psychological immaturity comes in many forms and degrees,

[27] Borum 2004.
[28] Horney 1991 [1950], 292.

and the neurotic personalities that we have discussed are just the ends of a spectrum. In fact, we can argue that psychological immaturity is the default condition of most societies. A self-confident and genuinely compassionate self is a lifelong project for most of us, and the goal of many religious and spiritual traditions that also see it as the final result of a prolonged inner struggle. We are all insecure and alienated from ourselves to some degree, and we all have difficulties handling the tricky balance between social compliance and individual assertion. Difficulties in childhood are, of course, also quite common.[29]

If violence is understood as a negation of the other person as a person, then it is quite extensive and regular. (Murder would then be the most absolute form of negation.) "He who is reluctant to recognize me opposes me," says Frantz Fanon.[30] All societies engage in violence and deception to some degree. As we will see later in this chapter, capitalism would be unthinkable without its particular forms of depersonalization. We are all treated these days as "labor," as a category, as a number. But at many different levels, we can do much better. The only true way to be nonviolent toward others would be to acknowledge their radical individuality, and also their radical equality to us. We must be able to see in others another struggling human being, a fellow traveler in life, a person like me in every way except circumstance. Only under such a perspective can hurting or disrespecting others seem senseless.

As political movements go, nonviolent struggles are, in this sense, the most radical of all. Nonviolent action, as practiced by Gandhi and Martin Luther King through peaceful protests and civil disobedience, bets on engaging the opponents as real people, and on winning their hearts and minds, all the while renouncing to exert violence on them. It treats opponents not as faceless oppressors, but as people capable of understanding, empathy, and change. It is a bold approach, because by restraining violence, it undermines all impulse or pretext on the opposing party to exact revenge and "defend" themselves. It is unsettling for the opponents, for it closes off the easy path of retaliation, and forces them into the more difficult journey of introspection and reform. Many of us would rather suffer a violent attack.

* * *

[29] What nowadays are referred to as "adverse childhood experiences" or ACEs.
[30] Fanon 1967, 218.

I have highlighted earlier the role of childhood and upbringing in the generation of psychological pathology, and have also pointed out forms in which society itself mistreats its members and contributes to psychological ill health. But, of course, these are related domains. Modern notions of privacy make possible the isolation of families, so that you can actually have sick families in the midst of a more or less healthy society. But, as a general rule, what happens inside the home is a reflection of what's happening outside in one way or another. Childrearing is as much a social and cultural activity as anything else. In order to appropriately understand psychological pathology, even stemming from childhood, we thus need to adopt a forthright cultural outlook.

How does culture affect personality? At the most basic level, the interrelation goes back to the selective nature of culture. Just as a culture is inevitably selective in the behaviors it approves and promotes, it cannot be but selective in the psychologies it prescribes as well.[31] Although societies can incorporate all kinds of people, some personality profiles tend to dominate, since they support that society's sanctioned modes of social advancement or success. In the small-scale societies that anthropologists used to study, the whole group typically shared a restricted set of motives, emotions, and values that conferred a certain common psychology to the group. Each case represented a particular way of balancing social compliance with individuality. In Benedict's well-known overview, the Zuñi (one of the Pueblo cultures of New Mexico) could be squarely identified with Horney's "self-effacing" personality continuum (Benedict calls their culture "Apollonian"). The Zuñi avoided all conflicts and violence and valued inoffensiveness above all virtues. In these peaceful societies of farmers and herders, moderation and cooperation were applied to interactions and institutions across the board. That this attitude guaranteed social harmony goes without saying. It also worked, of course, against any significant individual initiative. By contrast, the Dobuan of New Guinea valued treachery and cut-throat competition (which would locate them in the "expansive" range in Horney's scheme). One's success, say, in terms of one's more productive garden, was deemed always the result of theft or cheating. It was a paranoid society that valued the capacity to take advantage of others in order to get ahead. Like manic and greedy modern businesspeople, value was placed on ruthlessness. Magic was used

[31] Benedict 1959.

covertly and as a weapon, just as modern trade secrets. Social stability was guaranteed in this case by the cultural regulation of hostilities between people, households, and villages: when and with whom one could be hostile was preestablished.[32]

By playing up certain emotions, these two societies also neglected other options. All societies accentuate certain values and play down others – we are always showing our back to something. A violent man would be shunned among the Zuñi, just as a peaceful one would be among the Dobuan. They wouldn't be very successful either. In these contexts, personalities outside of the norm usually end up as outsiders and marginals. This does not mean, however, that rejected emotions cannot be considered virtuous. In more dynamic societies, revolution comes by the hand of shunned values. As Benedict writes, "no social order can separate its virtues from the defects of its virtues."[33]

Due to their social complexity and multiple stratifications, modern societies do tolerate a wider variety of personalities, but they also inevitably reward some more than others. That capitalist systems reward aggressive types is clear enough. They end up usually with more money (i.e., power), while mild-mannered, empathic people end up frequently with the low-paying jobs. As Benedict also points out, societies have difficulties recognizing extreme behaviors within their preferred psychological ranges.[34] In a society that glorifies individual prowess, greed can be mistaken for virtuous entrepreneurship. This might be the reason so many obvious sociopaths end up being promoted to leadership positions, voted into office, or lionized in the media these days.

Culturally appropriate childrearing is the primary mechanism through which society reproduces itself and passes on these psychological traits. In general, society tries to produce the members it needs. In unequal societies such as ours, the process differs by class, since society demands different things from different social classes, including psychology.[35] For all the talk about individual freedoms in modern

---

[32] Benedict analyzes three societies: the Zuñi, the Dobuan, and the Kwakiutl (of Vancouver Island), which she characterizes, respectively, as "Apollonian," "Paranoid," and "Dionysian." For purposes of this particular illustration, I will limit my references to the first two.

[33] Op. cit., 249.

[34] Op. cit., 277.

[35] See Douglas 1996a, 26 ff. for an example of how language within the family, and toward the child, can change according to social class and its particular relation to society.

societies, individual initiative is not frequently expected from the poor, who usually end up taking care of the simple and repetitive jobs no one else wants. Freedom of choice in the labor market varies by wealth (or by things wealth can buy, such as education) so that creativity and independent thinking is more valued in those classes that can actually take advantage of these traits. Working-class parents (as all parents) have a sense of their children's prospects for success, and will try to rear their children with the attitudes they think will best serve them in life. In a more subconscious way, they will simply model their children in the terms of their own adaptive traits, that is, on their own mode of social belonging. If success or survival for their class depends on submissiveness and obedience, this is what the child will be subject to at home.[36] By contrast, wealthier parents will emphasize more independence in the child if navigating their own economic spheres requires more individual decision-making and initiative, as is more common, for example, in the business-owning class. In every case, different weights will be afforded to individualization and social conformity.

So far, I have presented childhood as a prominent terrain of psychosocial adaptation and potential trauma, but societies can be plenty traumatizing to adults too. Horney coined the term "situation neurosis" to account for people's neurotic responses that do not respond necessarily to the person's particular psychological issues (which she calls "character neurosis"), but rather social situations and stressors that would be psychologically challenging even to fairly healthy and mature people.[37] We have seen before the case of the Nazi concentration camps, where all prisoners suffered dramatic psychological changes, many of which later surprised, by their swiftness and extent, therapists who struggled to help people change in more normal circumstances.[38] (Since then, similar processes have been documented in victims of torture, war, and natural disasters). In less radical contexts, societies can regularly create situations, such as loss of employment,

---

[36] Of course, subaltern classes can just as well cultivate rebellion instead of submission.

[37] Horney 1937. Seen from the perspective of traumatic events that generate neurotic responses, Horney's framework recalls Maté's (2022, 21 ff.) distinction between "big-T trauma" and "small-t trauma," where the former originates in a difficult childhood or specific life events, and the latter includes the alienation that the larger culture generates in the individual. The relationship between trauma and alienation from the self is analyzed also by Van Der Kolk (2014), who also emphasizes the individual's alienation from her own body.

[38] Giddens 1984, 61.

income, or general prospects, that are psychologically unmanageable for certain individuals, groups, or classes, and that can trigger neurotic responses. As always, the impact of these stressors will be due to their upending of established modes of social belonging. In highly unequal capitalist societies, for example, poor people can enjoy relatively healthy and sheltered childhoods among family and neighbors, only to discover later on that they belong to the lower rungs of a highly stratified and stigmatizing social pyramid. As a young politician once told me, "I never realized I was poor until I turned fifteen."

* * *

In order to show how these processes play out at the social scale, we thus need to first understand the characteristics of our current societies and the psychological challenges they impose on their members. Anticipating further discussions, we can characterize modern capitalist societies as extremely weak in their commitments to social integration, as well as highly unstable in their modes of such integration. While Marxists tend to highlight the abusive nature of capitalist labor markets, the main iniquity of capitalist societies is not exploitation but indifference. In countries with flimsy Welfare State infrastructure, the message the common citizen receives is that no one really cares about her. At the end of the day, the critical topic in capitalist societies is economic growth, not social welfare or integration. Quality public education, adequate healthcare, or decent housing are always seen as onerous expenses, dependent on the dynamism of the private economy that funds the whole effort. Citizens are mostly on their own – "free" to offer their talents in a labor market that might or might not need them, but that, in any case, has made no commitment to find a role for them. On the other hand, "success" in capitalist societies is always being redefined, since one can always have materially more than at present, and the whole social discourse is indeed about always having materially more, with no end in sight.

This is all, of course, highly anxiety provoking. Everyone is concerned about their social status, which is always both insufficient and unstable. What in economic discourse is called a free market is frequently translated socially into an environment of free conflicts, where everyone's social standing is besieged on multiple fronts. One is anxious to "improve" one's social standing; at the same time, one is also compelled to defend one's current position, which is always threatened by subaltern groups that are trying to move up. Since the whole issue is about relative standing, social inequality, that is, differentials of power, becomes the key variable and the source of most social problems and conflicts. In consequence, the most unequal modern societies tend also to be the most violent, the most unhealthy, and the most distrustful.[39]

The frustrations that all this generates in adults find their way into the home, generating all kinds of perverse feedback loops between "situation neurosis" and neuroticizing childrearing. The threats to self-esteem that marked inequalities inevitably entail can generate insecure, bitter, and resentful parents. Economic poverty translates into time poverty, since parents have to work long hours or several jobs, reducing the time they have available to spend with their children, who then end up alone during the day or in makeshift childcare arrangements.[40] Lack of money also means scarce possibilities for after-school activities and early childhood stimulation that can support exploration of talents and preferences. All this limits the child's growth, who then ends up more disadvantaged for competing in the labor market later on, but also, crucially, more alienated from herself. But the problems are not limited, by any means, to poor parents. In a society riddled with envy and dissatisfaction, parents from all social classes are subject to similar anxieties. Neuroticized parents end up raising neurotic children, who then dully repeat the cycle when they become parents themselves. It is very difficult to raise self-confident children when your own confidence is being constantly eroded.

According to the common individualist ideology mentioned before, these problems are the fault of the individual actor, whose economic trajectory is deemed to be wholly her responsibility. In a free and competitive society, one's economic security is the direct result of one's own effort, or so the story goes. Psychologically, this discourse makes things even worse, since failure is placed exclusively on the individual's shoulders, thus emotionally isolating the person and opening a royal road to all forms of self-recrimination. But, as we know, inequality is critically related to how the productive sector splits its (after-expenses)

---

[39] Wilkinson and Pickett 2009. The psychological consequences of unbridled capitalism, which I describe next, are well explored by Maté (2022, 276 ff.).
[40] Dodson and Albelda 2012.

income between salaries, taxes, and profits, which is more of a political question than an "economic" one. What workers receive is the result of their bargaining power and what the laws demand, not only their productivity. Likewise, inequality is affected by how much the public sector receives through taxation, and how it uses it to create conditions of enhanced opportunities for the general population, such as those offered by better education. In this respect, things have been getting *worse*. As demonstrated by the work of economist Thomas Piketty, in the last fifty years, inequality has worsened globally as the tax rates of the wealthy have been reduced, the salary gap between high and low earners within corporations has widened, and the opportunities for making money off capital have increased.[41] It is now commonplace to see present inequalities as a real threat to the stability of liberal democracies around the world.[42]

The situation has nothing to do with people working more or less, or being more industrious or lazy. The shift responds rather to the success of moneyed interests in changing in their favor the regulatory landscape and the terms of the ideological debate. In fact, the people making the most money these days are the ones who don't work at all, and just watch as the stock market increases their fortunes. Inequality, the real crux of the modern economic problem, is thus not something that can be tackled exclusively at the individual level, but requires rather a systemic look, which makes any narrow discourse about individual responsibility suspect. While morality at the level of the individual is obviously important in any society, in the policy realm, morality is best tackled at the social scale. It is just not reasonable to expect people to behave cooperatively and compassionately if the system in which they live conspires against those emotions. In order to have a good society, you need to make it easy for people to be good. We've been living in an increasingly unequal world; not surprisingly, we also live in a very angry one.

How is this situation reflected psychologically in the culture of today's societies? I'm interested here in the patterned psychological responses of individuals and groups to these particular threats to social belonging. (A likely response is a surge in drug use and alcoholism, deployed as an escape and a coping mechanism, but I will leave this

[41] Piketty 2014.
[42] Fawcett 2018, 461–462.

option only noted.)[43] There seem to be at least three main responses that then tend to contribute in different ways to social conflict and instability. The first one I will call the "classic utopian," since it accompanied the modern capitalist project from its beginning. The other two are "masochistic nationalism" and "positive nationalism," which I am borrowing from sociologist Göran Adamson's provocative and suggestive work, although I'm renaming the latter as "aggressive nationalism" for reasons that will be obvious.[44]

In the "classic utopian" mindset, inescapable conflicts about inequality are handled by solving them in the future. Societies embrace the modern ideology of infinite progress and assume that, as long as economic growth is visible and continuous, everyone will benefit eventually, allaying current concerns about inequality. You might be poor today, but do not worry, we tell everyone, because your condition is likely to improve. Classic utopianism depends critically on a forward dynamism of the system, or what Hirschman calls the "tunnel effect," based on an analogy with a car traffic jam in a two-lane highway tunnel.[45] I'm stuck in a lane of gridlocked traffic, but then the adjacent lane starts moving, and I my hopes are raised that mine will start moving soon too. As long as both lanes are moving, I'll be relatively indifferent that mine is moving slower, or that it stops every now and then. But if my lane stops for good and the other one continues to move, my tolerance will run out and I will react angrily to the injustice of the situation. In other words, I don't mind that other groups progress, as long as I'm advancing too. For some authors, the liberal democracies of our days have *always* depended on continuous and vigorous economic growth for guaranteeing stability and dealing with capitalism's inevitable inequalities.[46] In this classical utopian mode, stability depends on movement. Classic utopianism explains why modern revolutions are less about living conditions than about expectations about living conditions.

Classic utopianism is more common in fast-growing economies, typical of "developing" countries. When growth stumbles, social unrest

---

[43] Although one should never forget that addictions are also culturally mediated. Stein, for example, considers that alcoholism functions as "an acceptable means of social revolt" in the United States, albeit in contradiction to the official discourse of sickness and deviancy (Stein 1994, 203).

[44] Adamson 2021.

[45] Hirschman and Rothschild 1973.

[46] Fawcett 2018, 399 ff.

follows, even if inequality has not changed substantially. Attitudes toward inequality can vary by country in accordance with history and national ideology, affecting these responses. Some countries (such as the United States or Argentina) see themselves as "middle-class" countries, commonly underestimating their level of inequality, and being more tolerant of it. There is an imagined "middle-class" status, usually associated with certain key possessions and resources, that creates a certain sense of equality among a significant portion of the population, and that serves as a goal for the rest. By contrast, other countries see themselves as mostly poor, and correspondingly might have a lower tolerance and a heightened sensibility.[47] Regardless, trouble is never far away when the humming stops. Discontent can then transform the utopianism about the future into utopianism about regime change. Absolute faith is placed on a charismatic leader or a revolutionary movement that can restore the lost vitality or exact revenge on the now clear foes. Psychological splitting is, of course, an essential component at this point.[48]

Developed economies typically have lower economic growth rates, which means classic utopian arguments are less effective. As we have seen historically, once the basic infrastructure of consumer goods and services of a modern nation is in place, growth slows down as the economy is forced to rely on new technologies that, however innovative, are less transformational than the ones that completely reshaped peasant societies.[49] The overall economic impact of digitalization is just more modest than that of the wholesale electrification of a society and of the accompanying flood of home appliances. In the last half-century, this slow growth in wealthy countries has then been accompanied, as noted, with increasing inequality, an explosive combination that has opened the field for two dueling, alternative psychological paths: masochistic and aggressive nationalisms. According to Adamson, they enact the main ideological conflict of our times in the developed West.

Masochistic and aggressive nationalisms correspond neatly with Horney's self-effacing and expansive neurotic personalities,

---

[47] For an overview of different attitudes toward inequality in a sample of Latin American countries, and some preliminary explanations, see Assusa and Kessler 2021.

[48] Fromm (1969 [1941]) famously explained the popularity of Nazism among large sectors of the German population as the result of a prolonged economic crisis that led to the embrace of a vengeful, messianic leader.

[49] Gordon 2017. See also DeLong 2022.

respectively, but at the level not of individuals, but of whole sectors of society. The term "nationalism" is somewhat misleading here, because, although these outlooks do characterize the way national societies relate to foreigners and other countries, they also critically affect social relations within countries, giving shape to their key internal conflicts.[50] They can be seen simply as cultural features of groups, but also as common mentalities that individuals adhere to. As with Horney' self-effacing and expansive types, masochistic and aggressive nationalisms are the polar opposites of one another, which then accounts for much of the antagonism.

In Adamson's telling, masochist nationalists are all about solidarity and empathy, which translates into an overriding concern with discrimination, exclusion, and injustice. These emotions, however, are always aimed *outward* – they are not applied to their own group or society, which is, in contrast, sternly judged. Minorities, immigrants, and foreign countries tend to be deemed faultless and in need of attention, while their own nominally "white" fellow citizens are assigned historic abuses, which merit an attitude of permanent condemnation and a demand for contrition. Purportedly oppressed populations are seen as authentic and in possession of a deep and wholesome cultural identity that needs to be defended against the usurpations (i.e., "cultural appropriations") from Western societies or certain elite classes. "Multiculturalism," "diversity," and "inclusion" are the key words in this universe, which is dedicated to the celebration of the particularities of certain groups at the expense of those of others deemed the heirs of past oppressors.

The arbitrary hostility toward their own country or group (which explains the "masochistic" label), combined with their idealized view of oppressed others, generates all kinds of inconsistencies. Women's rights are defended tooth and nail in their own country, but waived in the case of foreign women subject to patriarchal religious institutions. Mindless consumerism is condemned when practiced by Westerners (such as in the derided *Sex and the City* films), but celebrated in the hands of foreigners (as in the lauded *Crazy Rich Asians* film). Conventional gender stereotypes are considered beyond the pale,

---

[50] Adamson uses as a point of departure the piece *Notes on Nationalism* (1945) by George Orwell, who also considers the term "nationalism" less than ideal for his purposes. Orwell identifies, in the Leftist intellectual elites of his time, the masochist type that Adamson develops. Today, it seems to have become mainstream.

unless they're practiced by foreign cultures or the poor. Terrorist violence is condemned when practiced by nominally "white" extremists, but justified in the hands of "oppressed" groups.

Since the focus is on defending victims, these tend to multiply. The identification of excluded and oppressed groups becomes a highly contentious affair, and also a source of new antagonisms. Since the whole exercise is based on psychological splitting, it inevitably entails its own forms of persecution. As is the case with masochism generally, sadism is never far away. People purportedly committed to empathy and understanding turn vicious toward not only their direct opponents, but also any fellow traveler who dares question the orthodox discourse, as in the case of the "cancel culture" of the United States and other parts. In general, masochistic nationalism tends to be exoticizing, fatalistic, and pessimistic. Things are always getting worse, regardless of what the actual facts say.

Aggressive nationalism is, of course, its mirror image. If masochist nationalists see their nation as a source of sin, aggressive nationalists see it as the source of all virtue. "Diversity" is not something to be pursued, but rather avoided, since there's nothing to improve on the domestic cultural front. If masochist nationalists see other cultures as having a wholesome essence that must not be disturbed, aggressive nationalists see that same type of essence in their mainstream culture, which then has to be defended from foreign intrusions. Aggressive nationalists generally oppose humanitarian aid and immigration, and see cultural differences as a threat to internal social cohesion. Their foreign policy tends to be belligerent, since it is fueled by the decisiveness that comes with arrogance. Rather than abstract principles, they just follow the formula of might makes right. They have no patience with the obsessive quest for difference of the masochist nationalists, since they see cultural differences as destructive of the national soul. "Equal representation" of minority groups in public and private organizations, another key cause of masochist nationalists, is also rejected as an attack to a culture based on merit and strength. Their customary sadism is, of course, closely followed by their respective masochism, since they can as easily resort to their own version of victimhood. Aggressive nationalists feel under siege by the nefarious forces that masochist nationalists summon in their quest to destroy the national culture with multiculturalism and minority power. In general, they are imperialistic, cruel, arrogant, and triumphalist, but can be as querulous as the masochist national-ists when convenient.

What both of these cultures provide is a sense of belonging and power by integrating the individual to something bigger (the social jus-tice movement, the true national culture), but at the price of social divi-sion, since they are based on psychological splitting and scapegoating, where friends and foes are clearly delineated and deemed irreconcil-able. They present, of course, different forms through which individu-als are incorporated into the community. But it is difficult to avoid the conclusion that something is amiss in societies where significant portions of the citizenry behave as either victims or bullies, or alternate between the two.

It should be emphasized, that, as forms of splitting, both mentalities are self-serving, and use the "other" (the foreigner, the oppressed group) as a detour for self-assertion. For aggressive nation-alists, the other is evil and we are virtuous. For masochist nationalists, we are evil and the other is virtuous; but by defending the other, I become virtuous myself. The one rehashes the colonialist logic, while the other inverts it, though ending in the same place. In the process, the other is barely addressed as a real and complex being.

As an overarching ideology, aggressive nationalism is mostly an option for wealthy countries, since developing countries do not have the resources and armies to be regional or global bullies. What developing countries do require is an adequate dose of healthy national pride. As Hirschman pointed out half a century ago, development not only involves an increase in per capita incomes but also an "ability to strike on one's own, economically, politically, and intellectually." For Hirschman, development was also "a quest for self-discovery and self-affirmation" and was thus inseparable from nationalist struggles and feelings.[51] When such self-confidence is impossible, developing countries sometimes adopt their own version of the victim narrative, effectively complementing the arguments of the masochist nationalists of wealthier countries. The perennial anti-imperialism of some Latin American politi-cal forces is a good example. Imperialism is real enough, of course (in the Latin American case, mostly from the United States), but it is one thing to confront foreign aggression, and another to use it as a constant pretext for internal political persecution, as has been frequently the case.

---

[51] Hirschman 1971, 304.

The need for a healthy national pride applies, of course, to developed countries as well. A society full of self-doubt is hardly equipped to tackle challenges of any real significance, such as the construction of a completely new "green" economy. The required self-confidence comes inevitably with a certain egotism that feeds on a sense of uniqueness. As anthropologist Claude Lévi-Strauss has argued, "In order for a culture to be really itself and produce something, the culture and its members must be convinced of their originality and even, to some extent, of their superiority over the others."[52] The challenge seems to be how to handle a good degree of self-regard that does not degenerate into a destructive sense of supremacy, an issue I will come back to in Chapter 7. But it is clear that the inequalities and social exclusions that characterize many societies today hardly provide the right environment for such "healthy" balances. Rather, the current crises of social belonging are perfect breeding grounds for all kinds of radicalizations.

The reader might object that in a world so devoid of empathy, my characterization of "masochist nationalism" ends up condemning important values that we desperately need to build a better world, and this is no doubt true – but not only regarding that side of the conflict. Following Horney, we should never forget that neurosis is always a radicalization of legitimate emotions. *Both* profiled "nationalisms" encompass important values. Empathy and solidarity are obviously essential if we are to address the inequities that are the root of these problematic cultural tendencies. We need a clear-eyed analysis of the factors that contribute to social marginalization and exclusion, and of the policy alternatives available to us. At the same time, once these options have been identified, we need a forceful process of implementation. Aggressive nationalists have something important to transmit in their advocacy of a common vision and decisive action. Masochist nationalists correctly identify many sources of exclusion, but then subvert the potential paths of solution by splintering the social scene into an interminable parade of grieving minorities. Governing is impossible if society is nothing more than a sum of particular demands, however legitimate. Without a compelling vision of a common good, democratic debate leads to paralysis and impotence, since it is impossible to satisfy all demands, many of which will be in conflict with one another. For the process to work, a minimum level of social cohesion is a must,

---

[52] Lévi-Strauss 1995 [1978], 20.

which depends, among other things, on a sense of national unity and the adequate assimilation of newcomers (in also reasonable numbers). Under the abusive style of aggressive nationalists, there's a legitimate desire for accomplishment. The constant apologizing, self-flagellation, and endless consultations of the masochist nationalists are irritating for many aggressive nationalists (and less radical people) because it reflects a passive and reactive attitude that frequently can't get anything done.

Following Benedict, we should also remember that the virtues of all cultural psychologies already encompass their defects. As always, societies need to juggle the contradictory pulls of their different motivations. People that promote cultures of permanent love or aggression are promoting a neurotic society, one that is acting compulsively, not context-appropriately. There is a time for listening and a time for doing. Modern societies also distribute their rituals and cultural creations as varied distillations of distinct emotional states and attitudes and offer them to their members as vicarious enjoyments and fantasies. It makes no sense, as is increasingly common these days, to try to "balance" certain cultural products to make them more "inclusive," since their popularity depends precisely on their specialization. James Bond or mobster movies are celebrations of an excess or an imbalance, in their case of virile traits, just as romantic movies celebrate a purified version of love. Through its creations and institutions, cultures channel a society's varied impulses, and allows it to flex all the emotional muscles it needs in order to survive.

5 THE CORRIDORS OF POWER

It is the main duty of government, if it is not the sole duty, to provide the means of protection for all its citizens in the pursuit of happiness against the obstacles, otherwise unsurmountable, which the selfishness of individuals or combinations of individuals is liable to interpose to that pursuit.

> Frederic Law Olmsted and Laura Wood Roper, *The Yosemite Valley and the Mariposa Big Trees: A Preliminary Report*

Those who overcome others have strength. Those who overcome themselves are powerful.

> *Tao Te Ching*

In Chapters 1–4, I have covered the topics of power and inequality in passing, as part of larger reflections on religion, culture, and psychology. The purpose of this chapter is to tackle the topic head on.

It is important to clarify that I see power and inequality as intimately linked. While we tend to understand inequality as an economic issue related to the distribution of wealth, in a more abstract sense, inequality is nothing else than an uneven distribution of power. Although money is currently seen as the main source of power in society, it is not the only one, and historically it has seldom been the most important. I will expand on this point later.

We also tend to see power as synonymous with domination. Whoever has power rules at the expense of the subalterns and weaker players in a lopsided, zero-sum game. One party decides the course of action and gives orders, while the other obeys and perhaps resists. It is an image not very different from the one afforded by the alpha males of the animal kingdom. It is a *negative* view of power, which then generates alternative visions of more democratic forms of social organization, where power would be more evenly distributed within nations, corporations, institutions, or households.

Indeed, the modern world is obsessed with power and its allocation, perhaps because it has produced the most socially unequal societies history has ever seen, but also due to the way its cosmology frames the topic and makes it so central to its identity. We tend to see power as an imposed hindrance to autonomous action, that supreme value of modern ideologies. We see power as a constraint, and constraints are what we most abhor. In order to see this critically, we need to take a step back and start with a definition of power less encumbered by its modern ideological bent.

We can begin with the still fertile characterization by Max Weber, another one of sociology's key pioneers. For Weber, power was simply "the probability that an actor within a social relationship will be in a position to carry out his own will."[1] In other words, power is the capacity to influence others in the direction of our desires. If we can easily make other people do what we want, we are powerful; if such thing is generally difficult, we are less so. Note that power refers here to influences in a social context. Humans are also powerful in regards to nature and other living beings – a power that, at this point in time, we have thoroughly abused – but the issue here is power within society. Most people today are not afraid of what lions and snakes can do to them. The main obstacles in our lives are other people.[2]

The desires that are thwarted for lack of power are also, as we have emphasized before, culturally defined. We usually desire what our culture or group values. As social animals, it makes no sense to desire something that absolutely no one else values in any way or form, since we would have trouble considering it valuable to begin with. This

---

[1] Weber 2019, 37.

[2] Of course, global warming and environmental devastation have definitively become natural threats to humans, but ones that are self-inflicted, and whose solution runs through changes in social organization, the subject of this book.

means that desirable things have a tendency to become scarce; on the one hand, because everyone wants them, but on the other, because desirable things tend to be so because they afford social distinction, which is always, by definition, scarce. If everyone is famous or successful, then no one is. Because all human accomplishments are graded on a scale of worse to better, desire crowds at the more prestigious pole, and those with more power use it to get there more effectively, displacing other contenders. As we will see later in this chapter, one of the key tasks of any culture is to devise effective ways to manage these kinds of conflicts generated by its own system of values and desirable things.

Power can also be equated quite easily with freedom. The capacity to fashion the world according to idiosyncratic desires is the very definition of human exceptionalism. Humans have more power than other animals because they are free to follow their experience and desires, rather than just their instincts. Their freedom entails power, and their power is a demonstration of their freedom. In a social context, those that have more power are also freer, since they have an increased capacity to influence the world and follow their unique wishes. As many wealthy people are fond of admitting, the main benefit of having money is the possibility of doing what one truly wants. It follows that most humans are free, but due to the unequal distribution of power, some are more free than others.

The question of power, or freedom, is central to both capitalist and socialist ideologies, but with different emphases. While capitalists focus on its production, their critics are all about its distribution. For Marxists, the struggle for power between different social groups is the key to all of human history. As Marx and Engels famously argued in the first passages of the *Communist Manifesto* (1848), "The history of all hitherto existing society is the history of class struggles."[3] For Marx and Engels, capitalism had finally unleashed the productive forces that had "rescued a considerable part of the population from the idiocy of rural life."[4] Capitalism had liberated humanity from the purported drudgery, uncertainty, and enchainment of subsistence agriculture and other forms of nonmechanized, primitive economies, and had created the promise of that leisure time that only kings, nobles, and slave-owning elites had enjoyed in the past. Of course, that potential

[3] Marx 2018, 8.
[4] Ibid., 14.

had been squandered by the capitalists, who had created instead a new form of servitude in the form of exploited workers, and kept the liberating benefits of industrial production to themselves. The promise of communism was to socialize the modern productive apparatus, so that not only its goods could be distributed more evenly, but also the free time that such an extraordinarily efficient system allowed. By making it possible that the necessities of life could not only be more massively produced but also more massively distributed, communism promised a life of kings for everyone, not just for the greedy few. The selling point of capitalism has always been more freedom; that of communism, its sharing.

It is important to understand the cultural universe that preceded the capitalist industrial revolution. During most of their history, humans had organized themselves in the form of relatively egalitarian societies, where material inequality was kept in check or, in contrast, as explicitly hierarchical social formations.[5] By "explicitly hierarchical," I mean societies whose ideology organized the social universe into distinct ranked positions that were fixed and unchanging, and that could even have a hereditary character.[6] This was common in most complex societies in all continents, the Indian caste system being a paradigmatic case. In the West, during the Middle Ages, the nobility, the clergy, the peasants, and the urban artisans all constituted highly regulated orders of belonging in which people were born into and tended to stay in. There was always, of course, a certain degree of mobility and social change, but these types of societies nonetheless *imagined* themselves as unchanging. In addition, the social order was divinely sanctioned; the order of society was just a reproduction of the correct order of the universe. The official religions sanctified and legitimized the social pyramid. Societies with hierarchical ideologies can be profoundly unequal, but they typically try to integrate all its members, even if most end up in a subordinate position. All positions, however, come with certain rights and responsibilities, since the survival of society is seen as depending on the appropriate participation of all its members, including the weaker ones. Society is

---

[5] This is a broad, although useful, simplification. A recent overview of the variety of social organizations in regards to the issue of equality from the anthropological literature is provided by Graeber and Wengrow (2021). I follow here Douglas's (1992, 137 ff.) much simpler, tripartite classification: hierarchical, egalitarian, and market.
[6] This is the concept of "homo hierarchicus" posited by Dumont (1980).

imagined as an organism, whose parts, although of differing stature, are all nonetheless necessary for its overall health.[7]

Capitalism did away with such worlds, and promised freedom from all such constraints. People were now free to climb the social ladder and even to change the design of the ladder itself. This meant that the final social structure was unpredictable; where anybody ended up depended on their individual effort. All the system could offer was more opportunities and less restrictions. Capitalism also developed in tandem with liberal ideologies of equal rights. Our whole political spectrum rejects hierarchical ideologies and commits to the idea that "all men are created equal." We reject any notion that a person's value is predetermined by any circumstance for which the individual is not responsible, such as her place of birth, sex, race, or social condition.

For Marxists, this was all well and good, but ignored the fact that people's degree of freedom depended on their degree of power, that is, on the resources they had on hand, rather than on any formal rights they had on paper. The argument is perhaps best expressed by Anatole France's famous aphorism: "The law, in its majestic equality, forbids the rich as well as the poor to sleep under bridges, to beg in the streets, and to steal bread."[8] In other words, being equal under the law means little if I live like a pauper, and if my chances of escaping that condition are limited. Today, defenders of capitalism frame the equality that the system offers as *equality of opportunities*, while its critics emphasize, in contrast, the importance of *equality of outcomes*. Libertarians like to talk about freedom, while Marxists like to talk about power. They are both talking about the same thing, but emphasizing different dimensions. Rights and resources are both necessary to exert freedom, and having one without the other will not take you very far. Wealth is of little use if you are discriminated against; rights are rather inconsequential if you don't have a penny. I will come back to such challenges of an open economic system in the following pages.

* * *

As noted before, we tend to see power in negative terms, as related to the domination of some people over others, and as something that

---

[7] Taylor 2004, Ch. 1.
[8] France 1924, 91.

can be perhaps eliminated, or at least ameliorated. But as discussed, power is intrinsic to the human condition. We are different from other animals because we have power to willfully change the world, and in our case, this implies changing the human world itself. Without power there is no self-determination, no freedom. The fact that this power is exerted at someone else's expense is not necessarily a bad thing, since the social order is contested terrain anyway. We saw in Chapter 3 that all social roles incorporate specific degrees of power. At the personal level, we assert our individuality by exerting power. We could never accomplish anything otherwise. In general, power is not only destructive, but also constructive, or rather, both things at the same time. In Ethel Person's words, "Power relationships are the ground of human experience."[9] The negative view of power is problematic for several reasons. It is superficial, in the sense that it focuses only on those power relations that involve formal positions of command. It is also usually limited to the political or economic realms, ignoring all the other domains of social life where power is exerted. Finally, it consists of an external view of power in that it doesn't take into account its psychological dimension.

A superficial view of power asks simply who has nominally the power and then asks what can be done about it. But power is not about having the rights to command, but about *getting your way*. The real question is not who theoretically has the power, but rather who's actually influencing the course of events. Informal networks can be as important as formal positions; we talk, for example, about "the power behind the throne." Some very powerful actors actually prefer *not to assume* the formal power positions and rather operate behind the scenes, so that they cannot be blamed when things go wrong. Subaltern actors can also make use of what are called "the weapons of the weak."[10] Submission, deference, flattery, manipulation, and self-victimization can all be used to influence more powerful people by stroking their ego or provoking feelings of guilt. The reader might object that these are desperate measures that don't compensate for the lack of real power, but societies can be as critically run and stabilized by its informal mechanisms as by its formal ones. If you identify a series of social rules that are not only acknowledged but also ignored, something noteworthy is going

[9] Person 2002, 162.
[10] Person 1988, 35.

on. Some societies are highly invested in a formal façade of values that are nonetheless subverted regularly in daily life. This means that their ostensible values and their transgression are both important.

A limited view of power likewise fails to see the pervasiveness of power dynamics. If power is the means for self-assertion, then it is ubiquitous and diffuse. Power dynamics are going to be present in relationships not usually associated with "domination," such as those between lovers, spouses, friends, and colleagues, and, of course, between parents and their children. Power dynamics can also vary, and even flip, according to context, spatial, or temporal. A business CEO can be all powerful at work but submissive with his wife at home. Conversely, a low-pay employee can compensate for his powerlessness at work by becoming a tyrant with his family. Parents can rule over their children when they're small, only to see them rule over them when they're old. Modern romantic relationships involve key dimensions of "possession" and "surrendering," which involve complex power dynamics in couples.[11] As commented above, some power differentials are institutionalized, that is, formalized in rules and procedures, while others exist as informal mechanisms. One can also voluntarily cede power in some fields of activity in which one feels not particularly competent, or interested in. All divisions of labor, both voluntary and institutionalized, are divisions of power or control. In many traditional societies, women ruled over the house, while men ruled outside it. From a modern feminist perspective, the problem here was the rigidity of the system; in other words, the impossibility of shifting or reversing roles. But regardless of how porous the social structure is, different fields of activity will always be bounded in terms of the power they assign. No one can be, or would necessarily want to be, all powerful in everything. This overall complexity of the power phenomenon is perhaps why anthropologists have given up in their quest for truly "egalitarian" societies, normally associated with certain cultures of hunters and gatherers. If the egalitarian label is justified on the basis of material culture (everyone lives basically under the same material conditions), power inequities are then identified between the sexes, or between age groups. As anthropologist James Flanagan concludes, "There are no egalitarian cultures ... there are egalitarian contexts, or scenes, or situations."[12]

[11] Ibid., Ch. 7.
[12] Flanagan 1989, 261.

If power is about my ability to impose my will, then I must be psychologically capable to do that. Ethel Person argues that there are actually two types of power: personal power and interpersonal power.[13] Personal power is related to self-knowledge, self-confidence, and self-control (in other words, power over *ourselves*). Interpersonal power is the freedom of action that other people, or society, allows us (Weber's definition). They are interdependent, but "they also retain a necessary degree of separation."[14] It is much more difficult to be self-confident if you are demeaned socially because of your gender, race, or social class. If society systematically blocks your possibilities of action, you are bound to internalize feelings of powerlessness and weakness. As we know, poverty and social exclusion can easily threaten your general morale. At the same time, you can also retain an internal sense of strength, and fight back. As a general rule, the more restrictive the social environment is, the more personal power is necessary in order to prevail. Those who change the terms of the world around them by deploying their personal power are usually described as having determination and courage. Conversely, socially powerful people can be internally weak; plagued by insecurity, doubts, or psychological conditions that diminish their capacity to act in the world, such as depression, inhibitions, or crippling anxieties or phobias. Moreover, having ample possibilities to transform the world does not entail that you know what to do with that. It doesn't much matter to be able to do anything you want if you don't know what you want.

For Person, personal power is the more important of the two, because it's the one the individual can really control, and is the actual basis of human fulfillment:

> We often assume that worldly power confers inner strength. Yet the feeling of authentic power, of inner strength, is not necessarily, and perhaps only rarely, associated with power in the external world. To establish a *raison d'être* whether in work or love or religious devotion, to commit to activities that one chooses, to be able to live in the moment without abandoning either the past or the future; to have a life relatively free of fear, anger, or envy and filled with love and concern for at least a few others – these are all facets of authentic power.

[13] Person 2002.
[14] Ibid., 185.

> Authentic power is the ability to live fully, with few regrets and fewer recriminations. When we are internally free to pursue our goals, we experience neither excessive apathy nor doubt, and we remain untroubled by fear of failure or of success.[15]

Likewise, for Frankl, the highest possible achievement of a human life is not to be found in external accomplishments, but in the manner the person reacts to her "fate," that is, to the limitations imposed on her by the world. According to Frankl, meaning in life can be found through acts of creation, through experiences, and by internal endurance and adaptability; but it is the last one that holds the highest form of heroism.[16]

Personal power clearly depends on the self-knowledge and authentic self-direction that Horney saw as the hallmark of the psychologically mature person. Only the person who knows herself, including weaknesses and strengths, and who knows what she wants, can consciously navigate the social world in pursuit of her aims, changing the external environment or adapting to it, depending on the possibilities of the hour. Personal power explains why different people occupying the same social roles can have dramatically different internal responses, since personal power involves the individual's intentions, as well as her sense of purpose and meaning. A normally considered "dead-end job" can be a source of frustration for one person but a blessing for another, depending on how it fits into the larger picture of the person's personal project, her expectations, and her sense of what's realistically possible. In other words, depending on the level of internal choice involved, one same act can consist of pure submission, pure conformity, or pure will.

This also means that personal power expands in tandem with interpersonal power, as befits their interdependency. When the external environment opens up more for us, we get a sense of enhanced personal power and can expand our ambitions. As the narrator of V. S. Naipaul's *A Bend in the River* puts it, "After all, we make ourselves according to the ideas we have of our possibilities."[17] The modern sensibility, focused as it is on always moving forward, critically favors seizing such opportunities. For Simone de Beauvoir, to *not* take advantage of enhanced

---

[15] Ibid., 19. For Person, personal power, or inner strength, is inevitably, something "we must struggle to reach on our own," is only partially dependent on circumstance or personal history, and is "seldom the gift of youth" (Ibid., 25).

[16] Frankl 2020 [1946], 59.

[17] Naipaul 1989 [1979], 152.

possibilities is actually a "positive fault," a dereliction of the duties one has with oneself.[18] Like the other authors, de Beauvoir sees human realization as the result of a self-directed process based on self-knowledge and experience, rather than on social demands or imperatives:

> ... any man who has known real loves, real revolts, real desires, and real will knows quite well that he has no need of any outside guarantee to be sure of his goal; their certitude comes from his own drive.[19]

Personal power is, in consequence, as threatened by any experience that precludes self-knowledge as it is by external restrictions. The traumatic childhood experiences that generate Horney's neurotic personalities are an obvious example. The alienation from the self that results from childhood abuse or neglect can be seen as a form of internal weakness, a condition that precludes the person from being an effective social actor regardless of external constraints or possibilities. Paradoxically, such weakened self can also be the result of an *excess* of gratification during childhood. Spoiled children, whose every desire is promptly satisfied by parents and caregivers, grow up with the expectation that the social world will behave the same way during adulthood, and have a very low tolerance for its inevitable constraints and their concomitant frustrations. They are not internally strong because they have little experience in dealing with adversity, that is, with external limitations, and because they have had very little need to "reach inside" for clarity and will.[20] External obstacles should thus not be seen always as a negative variable, but rather as an inevitable presence that sets the terms of our personal battles. A world where everything is possible is as disempowering as one where nothing is. Our capacity to confront our "fate," and work around it, depends on having experienced enough of ourselves, and enough of a resistant world, so that we are not crippled by either excessive entitlement or despair.

* * *

---

[18] de Beauvoir 2018 [1947], 41.

[19] Ibid., 173.

[20] Person, op. cit., 190. Lukianoff and Haidt (2019) have argued that, in the United States, the more recent generations of students have been brought up with less autonomy during childhood, leading to psychological fragility and a sense of entitlement that is having a considerable impact on the ideological debate on university campuses.

Let's now go back to the interpersonal level, that is, to the plane of social power, so that we can transition better into the forthcoming discussions on economics and politics. The best guide at this level is, in my opinion, the work of Pierre Bourdieu, who draws on both Weber and Marx to explore the different forms social power takes.[21] For Bourdieu, there are, in modern societies, three forms of "capital," the term he uses for power. "Economic capital" consists of material resources; that is, money and wealth, as we understand and deploy them today. "Social capital" consists of social prestige, reputation, or honor. Finally, "cultural capital" is education, knowledge, expertise, or "culture," in the sense of erudition. The social class of a person, or her location in the power structure of a society, is determined by the relative amounts of each form of capital that the person has. Different social classes are precisely defined by their different "compositions" of capital. Of the three, economic capital is the "dominant" one in capitalist societies, because it can frequently "purchase" the other two.[22]

Thus, for example, a business magnate may have plenty of economic capital but little cultural capital (e.g., educational credentials), while an academic might have the opposite composition. A political leader may have plenty of social capital (in the form of reputation among her constituents), but be short on money or education. All forms of capital are forms of social influence, of course, and social classes are always trying to access those they lack, even in the face of economic capital's overwhelming supremacy. Millionaires donate to universities, cultural institutions, and "noble" causes in order to acquire honor (i.e., social capital). University professors and liberal professionals fight for higher salaries or fees while defending their position as the main holders of knowledge and expertise. Power in precapitalist societies consisted mostly of different forms of social and cultural capital (what Bourdieu conflates as "symbolic capital"), mostly because their economies were largely nonmonetized, that is, there was not much you could do with money. Positions of influence and command were acquired rather through reputation, exceptional performance, or inheritance.

In the modern world, social power is critically expressed and deployed through consumption patterns and taste. Social distinction is the key issue and is guaranteed by having tastes that contrast with

---

[21] Bourdieu 1984; 1990.
[22] Part of this summary is loosely reproduced from my previous book (Espino 2015), specifically Chapters 2 and 6.

those of your adversaries, and that undermine their social pretensions. For Bourdieu, who based his analysis mostly on late twentieth-century French society, the lifestyle of the working class is characterized by its "naturalism," so that the goods and activities it consumes or engages in are understood as simple pleasures that meet immediate needs, rather than sophisticated entertainments that, of course, require previous education. Food is food (which is either good or bad) rather than "high" or "low" cuisine; sex in the theater is sex, rather than "art." The classes that tend to engage in these distinctions (e.g., those high in cultural capital, such as artists) are then seen by the working class as effeminate snobs, while these, in turn, may see working class tastes as reflecting ignorance and lack of education. Those high in economic capital may actually share their antipathy toward the cultural elites ("why do they think they're so smart?") and, at the same time dismiss the working classes as helplessly tasteless and vulgar (they don't know how to behave or dress, or use cheap or unknown brands). When money is accompanied by culture (such as in older, wealthy families), antipathy will be directed also toward those with money but no "taste" (i.e., the "new rich"), who flaunt their wealth in an inappropriately flamboyant manner. Bourdieu's work is replete with examples of these opposing styles, which exist both to reinforce the identity of their bearers and to distinguish them from their social adversaries, covering the production and consumption of food, clothing, music, sports, and art, as well as other aspects of class "style," such as body language and accents.

In general, social mobility is achieved, by any family or individual, by accessing the social group immediately above in the social ladder, which can be done, for example, through more luxurious consumption, higher educational credentials, or through marriage. These advances will always tend to be resisted by the superior group, especially in the case of a large-scale movement, since the end result would be a drop in the value of the threatened social position, which, by definition, *depends on its relative scarcity*. Like the real estate advertisements that promote "exclusive" projects, status groups protect themselves with entry restrictions that preserve the privilege and the exceptional nature of the social position. Any upward movement from lower classes will tend to produce an equivalent movement from the superior group, which will immediately increase the membership prerequisites, say, through higher consumption levels or more sophisticated tastes. All this means, as Louis Dumont points out, that the social hierarchy is always imposed from above, that is, the reason lower groups cannot "move up" is to be found in the restrictions and movements of the higher groups.[23] This is logical, since as Peter Marcuse argues, "No group desires low status; it is imposed on them."[24]

Bourdieu's scheme is useful because it goes beyond the merely economic in explaining social inequality and conflict. By identifying noneconomic modes of social influence, grouping them as forms of "symbolic capital," and finding a way to relate both as assets that groups have and defend, he is able to paint a less reductionist picture of "class struggle" than the one we usually receive from Marxist analyses. The model can be used to understand social conflicts that have multiple dimensions, but which relate ultimately to struggles for social power. An example is contemporary racism.[25] In countries where slavery was practiced in recent centuries, or where colonialism entailed the domination of European elites over indigenous populations, the upward mobility of the subaltern groups represents a threat to those classes who have historically benefited from full citizenship, such as the nominally "white" middle or upper classes. The status of these benefited classes is also, of course, precarious, given the dynamism of the whole capitalist system. Those with more possibilities move up, while those left behind cling more desperately to what little they have, which means opposing more fiercely the upward surge of those on the bottom rungs, that is, the formerly subjugated classes. These dynamics are bound to worsen in times of economic crises or during periods of rising inequality, which is what we are witnessing in many parts of the world today. It makes little sense to analyze racism independently of social power dynamics, as a kind of evil psychological disposition or an aversion to "diversity." We should see race, like gender, as just one more potential dimension of social capital, that is, a social characteristic that can be drawn into power struggles as a convenient form of social distinction. Racism, as well as xenophobia, is highly dependent on the overall power dynamics of a society, including its levels of social inequality and the perceived prospects of its economy. They are bound to worsen when jobs are scarce, when an excess of laborers push salaries down, or when social advancement of different groups is generally

[23] Dumont 1980.
[24] Marcuse 2005, 23.
[25] Dumont, op. cit., 262.

perceived as a zero-sum game, so that the progress of one group is seen as occurring at the expense of another. There is no effective solution to these ills at the level of education or sensibilization, because they have more to do with inequality than with difference. In such contexts, the more tolerant people are usually those who have less to lose by the increased mobility of those below.

***

Let's now close the chapter highlighting some additional aspects of social power, as well as the analytical boundaries of the earlier discussion. First, as indicated in Chapter 4, power is also about controlling uncertainty, not only about displaying status.[26] Having a more predictable future is an important part of being powerful. A person who has an adequate income, but who lives under conditions of extreme uncertainty, is actually weak even economically, because she has slim possibilities to plan ahead and forge personal projects. In this sense, it is often preferable for many people to have a modest but steady and predictable income, rather than a higher income that can disappear anytime. Much of the socially destructive nature of today's "gig economy" is related to its unstable character, not only its income levels. A person who cannot control the future can end up with a passive and fatalistic attitude that logically responds to the feeling that everything is temporary.[27]

It is also important to examine the relationship between power and morality, and power and difference. Because cultures are, as a whole, morally organized, it should come as no surprise that power is too. As a general rule, societies tend to associate more power with higher virtue, and less power with immorality.[28] It cannot be otherwise. It would make little sense to be socially powerful but considered thoroughly depraved by everyone, since that would undermine the person's capacity to influence and lead others. In fact, one of the prerogatives

---

[26] Marris 1996.

[27] "Casualization [job insecurity] profoundly affects the person who suffers it: by making the whole future uncertain, it prevents all rational anticipation and, in particular, the basic belief and hope in the future that one needs in order to rebel, especially collectively, against present conditions, even the most intolerable" (Bourdieu 1998, 82). Around the world, according to Banerjee and Duflo (2011, 227), "... stability of employment appears to be the one thing that distinguishes the middle classes from the poor."

[28] For Kelly (1994), inequality consists of social differences that include differential moral evaluations.

of power is to be able to define what is moral and what is not, and to establish a society's value system.[29] You cannot have a stable society where its value system and power structure are at odds. Of course, one of the most frequent forms of attacking those in power is precisely by questioning their morality. Any effort to change the power structure of a society involves delegitimating the moral pretensions of the ruling groups or individuals, and locating the moral center in their opposing social forces. All power struggles are moral struggles, since those seeking power must inevitably legitimize their effort morally.

These dynamics are not limited to political battles but are present throughout the social structure. This is clearly observable in modern societies' relationship to the poor.[30] Throughout the history of modern capitalism, the poor, a product of the system itself as we will see, have been consistently characterized as morally deficient; otherwise, why else would they be poor? Nineteenth-century labels, such as "the dangerous classes," or the more recent ones of "undeserving poor" or "welfare cheats," frame the poor as depraved, lazy, or dishonest, which are all forms of moral condemnation. In highly stratified and dynamic societies such as ours, the poor play a key role of maintaining and reinforcing the social and moral status of the nonpoor. They can be used as scapegoats and blamed for all kinds of problems; they can provide services, such as prostitution and drug distribution, which would morally taint its upper-class consumers if practiced by themselves; and they generally provide the moral foil for everyone above them. Whatever moral shortcomings the middle and upper classes have, they are at least not poor, and are generally more hardworking, disciplined, and driven, which is precisely why they're not poor. Their social position proves their moral worth, and their moral worth explains their social position. Disadvantaged racial groups frequently play the same role. Naturally, when the poor are also racially distinct, which means that some physical, cultural, or historical variable has been used to define a distinct "race," both characteristics can work in tandem to justify their subordinate status. Being black, indigenous or from the wrong country entails having the wrong values, which then explains and justifies their social condition. By implication, the more successful classes are, of course, the ones with the *right* values.

[29] Thompson 2017; Graeber 2001, 88.
[30] Gans 1995.

Let us now conclude with some reflections on the relationship between power and difference, which will help us prevent the issue of power from gobbling everything up. It is clear that any social difference, be it related to gender, race, lifestyle, or social class, can be interpreted as representing or embodying different degrees of social power. For an author like Bourdieu, and for Marxism-inspired thinkers generally, all social differences enact power differentials. Differences in lifestyle and taste are embodiments of different positions in the social ladder. The cultural landscape is nothing more than an integrated display of different forms and degrees of power. Given what we've said about the power-laden nature of human life, this thesis is both true and banal. Unless one believes that all forms of social power can be eliminated, which would make one a devotee of "limit scenarios," to argue that all social relations and institutions include power differentials is to state the obvious and the inevitable. In any particular society, the main issue is not eliminating all the existing power differentials, which would be impossible, but assessing their particular noxiousness.[31] Let's try to throw some additional light on this matter.

All societies police the potential reach of their dominant groups or parties. This is commonly done by segregating different types of activities and institutions which depend on different standards of performance, and that cannot be compared to, or put in direct competition with, other fields of activity.[32] Being a good teacher is different from being a good basketball player, or a good nurse. Everyone understands that being good in one field has no bearing on the person's capacity in a different one. Moreover, performance in any field can ultimately only be judged by the people that engage in, or specialize, in it. Every segregated field provides its members or practitioners a set of challenges, a sense of social belonging, standards of performance, and opportunities for accomplishment. The divisions between the male and female worlds in more traditional societies have this characteristic. In the domestic sphere, women ruled and controlled its standards, while the men did the same outside it, and neither could normally interfere with the other, while society acknowledged the value and necessity of both.

---

[31] As Foucault reminds us, "A society without power relations can only be an abstraction" (2000, 343).
[32] Béteille 1994, 1018.

This does not mean, however, and as we all know, that all fields are equally valued.[33] In many societies with stark divisions between male and female domains, the male activities were frequently considered more prestigious. In our societies, where money rules, the tendency is to overvalue those activities that make more money, since money confers power and status. All societies have, indeed, and independently of their level of complexity, an overall system of evaluation that ranks its activities and occupations. Bourdieu's types of capital can actually be interpreted as attributes of social fields, similarly separate and ranked.

One way in which powerful groups extend their power is precisely by trying to make all fields of activity comparable by establishing some common metric of evaluation. In capitalist societies, this metric is obviously money. In order to avoid losing power, and in order to preserve the social benefits of the different fields, groups normally resist this expansionistic power grab. After all, when everything is reduced to money, those with more of it end up with the advantage. We thus resist the idea that art museums, symphony orchestras, or universities be rated solely in terms of how much money they make. We defend the value of professions or activities regardless of their "monetary" worth, and ask instead for a fair compensation based on society's understanding of their importance. We reject the idea that school teachers, university professors, or firefighters have a "market value," and we oppose any mechanism that would allow moneyed persons to "buy their way" into positions that should be defined by expertise and skill.

These dynamics are pervasive, and apply equally to the rarefied fields of high earners. Most of us would find senseless to ask who was a better sportsman between Michael Jordan and Diego Armando Maradona, since they played completely different sports. To compare earnings among them would also seem to be irrelevant, since they played to different markets and, in any case, their performance can only be measured in regards to the particular standards of their own fields, not the money they made. This is a classic case of trying to compare apples with oranges and, indeed, this is the right metaphor for all such cases. The defense of cultural life and the autonomy of its fields is all about resisting comparisons between apples and oranges, or rather, the defense of apples as apples, and of oranges as oranges.

[33] Ibid., 1019.

Finally, and critically, people's sense of power is intimately tied to the stability of their relationships and their emotional attachments, not only to their capacity to influence the actions of total strangers. A job, a marriage, a family, a place, and a community can all be components of a person's sense of identity, and critically ground her in the world. The loss of any of these relationships or attachments can have a more negative emotional impact for a person than the simple loss of income or material resources.[34] Here the key issue is less about the right to resources, and more about the right to have a life, in the terms the society defines it. I will come back to this key point in Chapter 7.

This all implies that, however important power differentials are, they are ultimately just one aspect of social life, which, in the best of cases, should offer a diverse set of fields for success, accomplishment, and belonging. Life cannot consist solely of what happens after power differentials have been "resolved." Life is what happens through the use of power, however limited; and in the bleakest of cases, in spite of its lack.

[34] Marris, op. cit.

6 AN EXCUSE TO PRODUCE

All the toys that infatuate men, and which they play for, – houses, land, money, luxury, power, fame, are the selfsame thing, with a new gauze or two of illusion overlaid.
    Ralph Waldo Emerson, *Fate*

Most of the topics that have been discussed in this book so far, such as religion, culture, or psychology, pertain the world of ideas and emotions. The economy seems to be something much more concrete. Selling and buying goods and services could be seen as practical activities that meet human needs, and that have perhaps less to tell us about morality, the meaning of life, and other dimensions of cultural cosmologies. Sure, what we buy and sell is culturally determined; that is obvious enough. We know that in different regions of the world people tend to eat different things more regularly. But once we understand what the local tastes are, the production and distribution of the corresponding goods follow the same principles of supply and demand, regardless of whether we're talking about rice, bread, or potatoes.

The reader might already suspect that I'm going to challenge this simplistic view. As in the case with religion, it is not that obvious what the "economy" actually refers to. Since the goods we consume have social meanings, it is not clear how acquiring something in the "market" is all that different from other forms of social interaction.

This is an old problem in anthropology. Most of us would consider that an economic transaction has taken place if we see a peasant transferring a horse to another peasant and receiving money in return. But what if the horse is traded for bags of rice (a case of barter)? That still looks "economic." But what about trading the horse for the right to marry his sister (a dowry)? That does not look very "economic" anymore. Anthropologists solve these ambiguities by replacing the concepts of buying and selling with the concept of "exchange." Exchange theory accounts for all kinds of transactions between individuals and groups, regardless of what is being transacted – goods, services, people, or rights over people. The purpose of exchange is always to establish and shape social relations. What is exchanged, and how it is exchanged, defines the nature of the relationship between the trading partners, and also their relationship to the society they live in. In other words, what we call the economic field is just one more form of organizing social relationships, that is, what cultures do by definition. The fact that we treat the economy as something separate and amenable to technical, objective analysis, responds in part to the need we have of concealing to ourselves what we are actually doing. Modern economic discourse is extraordinarily ideological, and a privileged domain of collective self-deception. It does today what official religions did in the past: justify the existing power structure and cover its tracks. This it does by presenting the economy not as a social phenomenon, but as a natural process. This becomes clear when analyzing our own definitions of it.

The definition of economics that most university students around the world receive in introductory courses goes something like this: Economics is the study of how societies distribute goods and services that are scarce.[1] The students then proceed to study how the intersection between people's preferences and scarcity determines prices. Because people want things, and since there's always a limited supply of everything, prices adjust to the willingness of potential buyers, leading to the sale of the whole lot of whatever is on sale at prices that inevitably produce "rational" and "efficient" results. The system is efficient and rational because it gives everyone what they want,

---

[1] See Chang 2014. What I will refer to in the following pages as economic theory is the neoclassical version, which is the dominant one internationally. Chang does a useful job in mapping other schools. The aforementioned standard definition was initially formulated by Lionel Robbins in the 1930s (Mazzucato 2018, 64).

subject to the unavoidable scarcities of the world and the limitations of everyone's pocketbooks. An economy where things sell at prices determined through this process generate markets "in equilibrium," since it automatically matches availability with desirability. It doesn't make much sense to interfere with such a "free market" because we would be second-guessing what people want and how much they're willing to pay for it. Governments should stay out of the business of providing goods, since that would replace the consumers' criteria with that of distant bureaucrats. Besides, who knows what people are thinking? The results of the market reflect transparently people's choices, so there is no need to bother ourselves much with speculations about people's motivations. Every consumer is treated as an independent entity entering the giant supermarket of the economy by themselves, and the thing we should be mainly looking at is what they end up carrying in their shopping carts when they get to the cashier. The main virtue defended here is choice – people are free to buy and sell, and to express their unique preferences through their behavior as consumers.[2]

There are several problems with this model. The first one we already touched upon in Chapter 5: Freedom is dependent on power, in this case, purchasing power or wealth. The above model has no adequate way of dealing with the interdependency between choice and power. It proposes and advocates for a free market, but it is does not acknowledge that the market is going to be more free for those with more money, and less free for those with less. If, for example, the government were to provide affordable healthcare for everyone, this would not restrict the choices of the poor, but rather expand them, since they would have one less thing to worry about, and surplus funds to use on a wider variety of goods. The freedom that the capitalist free market proposes is thus a formal one: *In theory*, you're free to buy anything you want; *in practice*, your level of choice will match the level of your bank account. Equilibrium, rationality, and efficiency are thus simply the attributes of the status quo – the outcomes of the free market are efficient and rational only if you consider that it is okay for the wealthy to obtain what they want, and for the poor to obtain what they can.

The second problem is the assumption of the isolated, independent consumer. By not exploring the social meanings behind

---

[2] See Carrier (1996) for a useful assessment of the "free market" paradigm from an anthropological view.

consumption, standard economic theory cannot realize that what people are doing when they shop is not satisfying some private and mysterious needs, but *communicating with one another*. This has a direct bearing on the notion of scarcity. The reason that some goods are scarce may be due to the fact that they're not meant for everyone, that is, that they're produced in low quantities in order to afford social distinction. As I will argue further below, scarcity in capitalist systems is not a precondition, but a result. The purpose of capitalist systems is to *create* scarcity, not to solve it.

* * *

Let's start by characterizing the type of human relations that are generated by capitalist exchanges. Anthropologists have typified different forms of exchange in relation to the level of *reciprocity* that they involve. If I give someone a gift, I usually expect something in return, even if it's just another gift or a dinner invitation sometime in the future. Among equals, gifts always call for some level of reciprocity. We tend to see gift giving as the quintessential example of disinterested behavior, but as all anthropologists know at least since the publication of Marcel Mauss' classic essay, *The Gift* (1950),[3] there is no such thing as a free gift, and a disinterested gift is an oxymoron. How much reciprocity is expected depends on the type of relation being fashioned. At the most intense level, gifts are offered plentifully without keeping account. This characterizes the relationship between parents and their children, or between spouses or intimate friends. Parents give their time and resources without measure, and without expecting any type of "exact" return. They nonetheless anticipate love and respect from their children, as well as perhaps some economic aid in the future. The relationships forged through these types of "gift exchanges" are open-ended, that is, they are continuous and have no end date. When they are successful and satisfying, the people involved in such long-term relationships get the sense that the "debts" incurred are actually "unpayable."

When gifts are offered in the context of more distant relationships, we tend to be more alert toward exact equivalences. "I gave my very special friend a gold necklace for her birthday, so why did she give me a trinket for mine?!" The more impersonal the relationship, the

[3] Mauss 1990 [1950].

more the exchanged gifts will be compared.[4] But the expectation of reciprocity still holds – to offer a gift and never receive anything in return is considered an offense, or a sign of rejection. All gifts are instruments of engagement. In addition, as commented, reciprocity in gifts always implies a certain level of equality. To offer a gift and then receive one in return implies that we have a somewhat equivalent relationship. By contrast, any gift exchange that dispenses with reciprocity implies a clear power differential. Giving without expecting anything in return is the realm of charity. Receiving without giving back implies that I cannot offer anything worthwhile in return, thus confirming my dependent status. Conversely, it can also mean that I'm too powerful to bother; reciprocating would indeed give the wrong impression that we're equal.

Precapitalist societies relied on "gifts" to fashion social relationships, and their exchange systems have been sometimes called "gift economies." Within households, the first, more personal mode of gift-giving prevailed, much like it still does today, while the second, more competitive mode, shaped relationships with other social groups. The first mode prevailed at the level of the whole group only in the more egalitarian cultures. In these cases, social equality was maintained by having everyone give away whatever material surpluses they had. In return, the giver was entitled to someone else's surplus in their times of need. Many hunter-gatherer societies followed this model. The system guaranteed that no one really suffered from "scarcity" – if there was a shortage of something, everyone suffered equally from it. These societies fulfilled Marx's ideal of "From each according to his ability, to each according to his needs."[5] In our days, this mode has been circumscribed to the family, nuclear or extended. In other words, most families today are "communist" in this sense, but the range of the modality typically ends at the household's doorstep.

---

[4] The more personal form of gift exchange is called in the anthropological literature "generalized reciprocity," while the more impersonal one is called "balanced reciprocity." Barter and market exchange are forms of "negative reciprocity." "Social distance" increases as we move through that sequence. The typology was developed by Sahlins 2017 [1972]. Graeber (2014, Ch. 5) has argued that conventional exchange theory is culturally biased because "exchange," in his view, is a concept brought from Western market economics to explain social processes where reciprocity does not really hold. Beyond the obvious (and inevitable) fact that all theories rely on somewhat exotic terms to describe diverse situations, the critique misrepresents at least some of this corpus, because he assumes that "Exchange is all about equivalence" (p. 103) and that reciprocity necessarily follows the same logic, which is not what Sahlin's exchange theory contends.

[5] Marx and Engels 2001, 20.

In more stratified societies, gift giving beyond the household was rather used to create situations of dependence and submission, in other words, to generate and enhance power differentials. A striking example were the tribes of the Northwest coast of the American continent who organized the famous "potlatch" feasts. Chiefs acquired and augmented their prestige and power by offering gifts to their competitors – gifts that had to be then reciprocated in due time, sometimes with interest. The inability to adequately reciprocate was a source of shame and an admission of defeat. The exchange goods had little to do with physical survival, which was guaranteed by a generous coastal ecosystem that provided an abundance of fish and game. The gifts rather consisted of mats, baskets, canoes, blankets, shells, and etched sheets of copper, most of which were manufactured for purposes of exchange and wealth accumulation, not for daily use. During the potlatches, the hosting chiefs not only offered gifts to their rivals; they also destroyed them. Chiefs presided over a bonfire of their own goods as a demonstration of their surplus wealth, sometimes allowing their own houses to catch fire. The purpose of the ritual was to put pressure on competitors, challenging them to surpass the provocation.[6] In this culture, there was never a doubt that the giving of a gift was the imposition of a debt.

Competitive gift exchanges with established exchange rates take us closer to barter, an even more impersonal mode of exchange. In small-scale, precapitalist societies, barter was typically practiced with foreigners and enemies.[7] It is different from gift exchanges in that the relationship between the parties ends at the moment of exchange. Bartering a bag of maize for a blanket with a foreign trader implied no further commitments. Both parties left the scene with what they sought, and no further contact was required. When barter includes haggling, it is very similar to *market exchange*, the form of exchange that dominates in capitalist systems. Market exchange implies exchanging a good for an established form of currency, and for a price that is negotiated in the transaction. Like barter, market exchange is a *terminal form of exchange*, in that it doesn't establish any kind of permanent or ongoing form of reciprocity. I have a problem with my kitchen sink and an acquaintance comes over and takes care of it. If I pay him, the

[6] I'm following here Ruth Benedict's description of the Kwakiutl of Vancouver Island.
[7] Graeber 2014, 29.

transaction ends right there – neither of us "owes" the other anything. If, on the other hand, the acquaintance refuses to accept money and argues that it be considered a "favor," I will feel obliged to reciprocate sometime in the future, perhaps offering a favor of my own when he has some kind of need. In other words, while most forms of gift giving imply some form of ongoing reciprocity, market exchanges are special in that they don't.[8]

Market exchange is thus the most impersonal form of exchange possible. It can be accompanied by anonymity and indifference toward the trading partners, and lends itself to all kinds of abuse. Since I might never see the trading partner again, I might sell them a defective good (a "lemon") or withhold important information about it. The seller is entitled to use all kinds of stratagems to sell for more, while the buyer can respond in kind to lower the price. That is why these types of exchanges tended to be excluded from the social life of the group in small scale, precapitalist societies. From the perspective of exchange theory, what characterizes modern capitalist societies is the transformation of the entire social scene into a world of strangers, where anyone can be taken advantage of. The free market admits, in theory at least, no notion of a fair price, of continuous relationships, or of a commitment to a common welfare. Every market actor seeks the best deal possible, which means selling high and buying cheap. This is what the "law of supply and demand" in economics refers to. The same principle could be called the "law of extortion," if we were to adopt a more moral language, since what is sought by all actors is to extort a more convenient price by taking advantage of the constraints weighing on sellers or buyers at any particular moment, such as shortages or economic downturns. A capitalist free market can in fact be defined as a socially integrated system of mutual extortion.

Capitalist markets are thus highly regulated institutions. There is no such thing as an "unregulated" or "free" market, and can never be, not only because markets are creatures of culture and law, as everything else, but also because market exchanges are, in general, too risky to be left alone. Our laws establish clear procedures for the conducting

---

[8] It should be noted that the terminal nature of market transactions, which depends on the identification of monetary price with value, is characteristic of capitalist systems, rather than a universal way in which moneyed exchanges operate. Gifts can indeed consist of money, as when we give our children cash for their birthdays – without implying that we just established their "price" (see discussion in Bloch and Parry 1989).

of businesses, including protections against fraud. Consumer Protection Bureaus are set up, and professional codes of ethics are drafted. These are all necessary measures for a system that works under the assumption that everyone is a selfish, self-interested maximizer.

We should never see markets, however, as purely impersonal institutions guided exclusively by legal compliance and enforcement. Most markets depend on established forms of sociality that provide a minimum level of perceived trust. The language of personal relations is frequently brought into market transactions to provide a sense that the exchanges are not purely instrumental. Banks, businesses, and salespeople present themselves as part of the "family" or "community," as concerned partners at the service of the customers' life projects. This might be mostly a marketing strategy, but it also evinces people's need for reassurance that self-interest is not the only operating motive.[9] Most established businesses depend, of course, on the trust that they instill in their customer base in order to guarantee consumer loyalty and expansion. (Perceived trust or, if you prefer, follow-the-leader copycat behavior, is also pervasive in the stock market and other speculative sectors of the economy). In the real world, few market systems could survive without some form of generalized ethics, since the enforcement apparatus would be overwhelmed if most economic actors decided to behave deceitfully. As Durkheim argued, "no contract is sufficient by itself," but is backed by certain shared moral expectations.[10] Thus, the language and outlooks of gift giving and reciprocity have a way of sneaking into the more impersonal modes of exchange. Still, markets are hazardous contraptions, offering both advantages and dangers for societies, as I will expand below. But before delving further into this topic, let's go back to the issue of why we consume goods to begin with.

***

I have already commented that one of the characteristics of standard modern economic theory is its indifference to the motivations behind consumption. Economic analysis focuses mostly on consumer behavior – what people buy, at what prices, and in what quantities.

---

[9] Gudeman 2016, 9.
[10] Durkheim 1984, 162. See also Giddens 1971, 69.

The market for any type of good can be analyzed more minutely in order to understand the different tastes it has to respond to, but the origins of these tastes are less of a concern. This does not mean, however, that we don't handle different theories about the matter. These theories have a presence both in the social sciences and in popular culture, and indeed try to explain why people buy things. According to Douglas and Isherwood, the two main ones are the "hygienic or materialist theory" and the "envy theory."[11]

The materialist theory argues that humans consume goods to keep themselves alive in a biological sense. Humans have "basic needs," such as food and shelter, and the economy is simply the mechanism through which these needs are satisfied. Humans are just one kind of animal, subject to the same survival imperatives as the rest. The theory has important uses throughout the modern ideological spectrum and corresponds to the mechanistic view of the world we described in Chapter 3. If human needs are simple and quantifiable, then public policy and social justice debates are correspondingly simplified. Many Marxists believe that, real human needs being limited, our consumerism cannot be other than a ploy of capitalists to sell us stuff we don't really need. Socialism or communism would thus focus on addressing those fundamental demands and dispense with the rest. Instead of sacrificing the elementary needs of the poor in this sea of false luxuries, economic systems should orient their productive forces to those goods which really matter. The materialist theory likewise informs the policy debates about "basic needs." Political stability would be furthered if we can just provide everyone with food, shelter, and drinking water. It also underlay such influential theories as Abraham Maslow's "hierarchy of needs," which argued that humans had to take care of their physiological and safety needs first, before addressing those "higher" ones related to self-realization.[12]

We have already commented on the limitations of this worldview. Humans not only want to survive; they also want to *belong*. All human consumption is, in consequence, always multivalent. Food is never *just* food, and shelter is never *just* shelter. Any consumption, however basic, is pregnant with social meanings. Any government or corporation that addresses human needs as the needs of a

[11] Douglas and Isherwood 1996, 4.
[12] Maslow 1943.

more intelligent form of livestock (as the term "workforce" suggests) is looking for trouble. All strategies of survival are also strategies of belonging, and any menu of basic needs is also a menu of belonging. The main difference between slum housing and middle-class housing is not just their relative effectiveness in keeping out the rain. Their respective locations, conditions, size, aesthetics, and amenities speak of different social statuses and degrees of power. When the poor fight for better living conditions they're not only trying to improve their physiological status, but also their social one. It's not only about "satisfying," but also about *becoming*. In this sense, we are *always* looking for self-realization.[13]

The envy theory has an advantage over the materialist one in that it at least acknowledges the social nature of consumption. Envy theory sees consumption as a terrain of competition, where consumers are always trying to improve their social status through the goods they purchase and use. In other words, we consume mainly to "keep up with the Joneses." Bourdieu's theory of power, described in Chapter 5, subscribes to this view. When we consume, we are sending signals about our position in society, and our position can in turn be improved by acquiring more prestigious goods. The possession of wealth is not enough – its existence has to be confirmed by "conspicuous consumption," to use Thorstein Veblen's famous term.[14] In fact, the less wealth we have, the more urgent might be the need to show off, since the possibilities for confusing our status are greater.[15]

Since capitalist societies are indeed competitive ones, the envy theory has a lot to offer, and I will be using it extensively in the following pages. The problem with this outlook is that it cannot explain the consumption patterns of more egalitarian groups or societies, where goods are much more standardized and stable. It also has trouble

---

[13] Here, it might be useful to recall Heilbroner's dictum: "Among animals, self-preservation is a response mobilized by a threat to existence, but in the social world – especially that of economic competition – the threat is not that of death but of social diminution" (1985, 58).

[14] Veblen 1926.

[15] As pointed out in Chapter 5, conspicuous consumption tends to be more common in the *nouveaux riches*, that is, the social classes that are new to wealth. The established wealthy (that is, the *anciens riches*) may in fact engage in a rejection of consumption as a demonstration of a wealth everyone knows they have, a sort of "conspicuous non-consumption" (Girard 2013a, 21 ff.) reflected in a certain informal style, rumpled look, and austere aesthetic that signal that they are "above" the tasteless ostentation of the *arriviste* classes.

explaining the enormous amount of goods that our societies produce that don't seem to have any clear social status connotations, and that don't satisfy any clear physiological need, either. If consumption is always about outplaying others, how do you explain cultures or sub-cultures where everyone always wears the same (weird) clothes? Or where a bewildering variety of goods are regularly used and consumed without changing anyone's social position?

* * *

In order to account for different forms of consumption, we need to see goods as *the material props of a society's cosmology*.[16] If a society or group sees itself as egalitarian, the objects everyone will use will be the same, expressing the idea that, indeed, there are no differences between us. If a society or group is competitive, goods will be used as weapons to outdo others in status and prestige. Any group that enforces equal-ity will enforce uniformity – in the case of clothes, frequently an actual uniform. Sports teams, military troops, schoolchildren, and monks, all use uniforms to express the fact that no one has special privileges. In special occasions, such as school proms, these same organizations can give free reign to individual competition or expression, at which time consumption explodes in variety.

When a society offers diverse and shifting power positions, it is inevitable that consumption give expression to the corresponding struggles. The same will happen if there are a variety of social roles. In Chapter 3, we stated that cultures function through the distribution of roles, the enactment of rituals, and the division of space and time, all mediated through the use of symbols. We could have equally said "mediated through the use of goods." The more complex the soci-ety, the more complex its material paraphernalia.[17] Capitalist societies don't produce lots of goods because people's fancies are intrinsically infinite. Rather, the diversity of goods is a reflection of the stratification and complexity of their social organization, and the encouragement they give to individual agendas.

---

[16] For Douglas and Isherwood (1996), goods are "mediating materials" (p. viii) and the visible part of culture (p. 44), used for "making visible and stable the categories of culture" (p. 38).

[17] I mean here structural complexity. Many "simple" societies are highly complex regarding their belief systems and other parameters.

It is important to highlight the tradeoffs involved in these different modes of social organization, as well as their ideological biases. Any egalitarian society necessarily represses individual advancement, which means it will also repress individual expression through consumption. That is why in egalitarian nomadic bands, everyone more or less has the same objects and dresses the same way. Anthropologists have documented numerous mechanisms used in egalitarian cultures to clamp down on any individual's potential rise above the rest. Among the Ju/'hoansi hunter-gatherers of the Kalahari, the hunter lucky or talented enough to bring priced meat to the camp was mercilessly mocked for his efforts, regardless of the amount of meat he brought, so that he would not put on airs and consider himself better than the other hunters. Sometimes the owner of the meat, and thus the designated distributer of it, was not considered to be the actual hunter, but the owner of the arrow the hunter used, which could be a much less able, competent, or hardworking individual.[18] Through these kinds of mechanisms, everyone thus always benefited from the talents of the few. At the same time, who was successful or when was less important, since the benefits would inevitably percolate to the group. The suppression of individual advancement is compensated here with protection from any adversity confronting the group. The group is responsible for everyone's welfare, which is only possible because everyone sacrifices for the group.

Capitalist ideologies reject this notion of mutual responsibility and instead propose that every individual pursue their own success independently from the group. The corollary can only be that the group is indifferent to the fate of the individual. But we need to be careful here, since this position can lead us fully into the realm of pure ideology. The idea of an absolutely indifferent society is as much a mirage as the idea of an absolutely free market. For the more radical defenders of unregulated capitalism, society has indeed no responsibility toward anyone's welfare beyond the enforcement of fair rules for competition. This was perhaps best expressed by British Prime Minister Margaret Thatcher's striking phrase: "There's no such thing as society. There are individual men and women and there are families."[19] But the rules of the capitalist market have to be enforced by a "society," and all societies imply, by definition, some sense of mutual

---

[18] Suzman 2021, 163–164.
[19] Thatcher 1987, 30.

responsibility and solidarity. Every time we draw the line around a human group and establish common rules of coexistence, we are in the presence of a "society." We have seen that all human societies are inevitably moral organizations that establish ethical standards for its members. We have also argued that modern nations have replaced the smaller communities of the past as the bearers of social allegiance. We root for our country, we defend its borders, and look out for its common interests. None of this would make any sense if the nation were only a large agglomeration of individual competitors. As explained in Chapter 3, humans have to belong to a group, and they cannot belong to a group that acknowledges no belonging. Thatcher's extremely ideological phrase is striking for a head of state, since if there is no society, there's nothing to be Prime Minister of.

This ideological current is not only typical of economic libertarians, but in fact informs standard economic theory. The terms and models used in neoclassical economics assume indeed that society does not exist, or rather, that what is happening in the market is not a negotiation of people's statuses or power positions within an integrated group, but rather the transaction of goods between anonymous traders in a sort of borderland. In Bourdieu's words, this ideological field engages in a "denial of the social,"[20] which is to say a denial of the moral, since it sees market transactions as morally neutral operations that satisfy people's individual, rather than social, needs. In consequence, free market advocates push an impossible contradiction: They want to defend the rights of individuals to prosper above the rest unimpeded, which leads to dramatic social inequalities; at the same time, they need society to authorize and tolerate such results, which it then frequently resists doing. The ideological solution is to argue that the problem doesn't really exist; that what the market is doing is not transforming the structure of society, but only distributing useful goods and services to people. That one thing is the economy, and another is society – if it really exists at all.

* * *

In sum, capitalism trades social solidarity for individual initiative, which creates an expanded field of consumption that then sustains the

[20] Bourdieu 1984, 11.

capitalist productive sector. In order to do this, it transforms most social exchanges into competitive market transactions and reduces the realm of gift-giving to the domestic sphere. While the system itself is capable of offering adequate employment and resources to a percentage of the population, the inevitable gaps and social exclusions end up, as we all know, in the hands of the modern State, which then has to procure that the whole system doesn't fall apart under its own contradictions. I will have more to say about the relationship between the public and private sectors below, but now I want to deepen our examination of capitalist consumption and the sources of capitalist dynamism.

Capitalist societies dazzle with the variety of the products they produce, and the wealth they can create (for some, at least). The historical productivity of capitalism is undisputable. No other social system in human history has created more material wealth.[21] This it owes to several factors, including potent sources of energy, modern machinery and technology, and an industrial organization of work. These factors are not necessarily intrinsic to capitalism, however, and you can use them in alternative forms of social organization. After all, the Soviet Union became an industrial power without being truly capitalist. What particularly characterizes capitalism is the tendency to commodify and objectify everything. The time of events becomes objective "clock time"; sites become objective "space," measured in distance and surface area; the material world is reduced to "things" that can be traded. The most crucial aspect, however, is its *social technology*, which consists in the commodification of work, or rather, the commodification of people in the form of paid workers. People became mere "labor," "workforce." They became the means to something else, namely, the generation of profit. Left to its own devices, the capitalist market would establish the value of all human work (i.e., wages) like it determines the price of any other merchandise. It is important to understand how historically revolutionary this was.

While human beings had been treated as merchandise before, notably through the institution of slavery, the capitalist worker was now actually "free." He was in possession of a resource (his "labor") that could be sold freely to any employer he wished, or to none at all. In precapitalist societies, most people produced directly many of the goods they consumed, like in the case of subsistence farmers, or

---

[21] Clark 2007; DeLong 2022.

were part of social systems of mutual help, and generally lived under some combination of the two systems. Everyone was "someone," that is, part of some acknowledged social category that entailed some minimum rights. In medieval European cities, even beggars were frequently organized, just as the craftsmen's guilds, and had their own norms and standards for clothing, appearance, and manners, while their social support was considered a duty under the prevailing notions of Christian charity. Social domination was *personal*; everyone knew who they were being oppressed by: the local chief, the feudal lord, or the emperor through his tax collectors. Capitalism did away with these dependencies and preestablished identities, and generated a new type of person: free from traditional social restraints, but also mostly on his own as far as survival was concerned. Even though still a member of society, he was treated as his society would have treated the foreigner in the past. He was now free to fashion his own identity and place in society, but this freedom came at the price of a high degree of social indifference and a new form of dependency: He now depended on the "market" to offer him a job. Social domination in capitalism is thus *impersonal*.[22] A jobless person has no one in particular to blame. He is told that the "economy" is in a slump, that there is no "demand" for his services, or that there is a "recession" going on.

In capitalist societies, the person has a split identity. In the world of work, he is a replaceable cog in a machine, a means to someone else's ends. In the private sphere, he is a unique personality with a rich interior life, dedicated to "finding himself" and discovering his own particular tastes. These are two sides of the same coin.[23] The personhood that is negated in the marketplace is recovered in the domestic or private sphere. There, life explodes in a profusion of eccentric hobbies, tailored consumptions, and snobbish interests. One world serves the other. The person sells himself in the marketplace as workforce, as less than a person. In exchange, he receives money (a salary) that can be used in the same marketplace to cultivate his wholesome individuality and his own ends. The enormous "leisure" industry has a prominent part on the ludic side of the equation. Leisure is whatever work is not; it is the remainder of life after work is subtracted. The world of theme parks, tourism, and recreational consumption in

---

[22] Postone 1996.
[23] Campbell 1987; Graeber 2001.

general, is constituted as a realm of enjoyment, liberty, fantasy, and personal growth – in other words, what is barred in work. The fight for vacation time is, together with the fight for better wages, one of the great social causes in capitalism.

In consequence, the capitalist productive apparatus lives mainly off two types of demand. On the one hand, many goods are purchased and used in the context of status competition. We consume certain goods to improve our standing and climb the social ladder, or just to stay in fashion and not lose ground. On the other hand, there's the mass of goods we buy to support our private activities and lifestyles. Oftentimes, the two types of consumption are difficult to distinguish, since many goods work on both fronts, and also because our identity is difficult to disentangle from our social status.

The competitive nature of capitalist consumption generates a restless economy, and wreaks havoc on any distinction between "necessities" and "luxuries."[24] Because the struggle for power and individual identity is ongoing and knows no limits, goods are being constantly updated, replaced, or invented. The worst thing that can happen to a capitalist system is to end up constantly producing the same set of goods, since that would imply no new businesses and sources of profit. Satiation is antithetical to capitalism. Capitalist societies thus engage in a cult of the new, frequently couched in the language of "innovation." Businesspeople, scientists, artists, and academics are always looking for the new product, the new paradigm, or the new style. When we get tired of the new, we look back nostalgically toward the old, which then acquires the patina of "authenticity" and "humanness" that our current products are supposedly lacking. Since everyone's consumption patterns are considered part of their current identity, but are also constantly changing, any discussion about "superfluous" goods becomes confusing. The necessities of the wealthy become the luxuries of the poor, which will in turn become their own necessities in the future when the whole social ladder moves up. As Douglas notes, "Only relatively stable communities can make and keep a distinction between luxuries and necessities."[25]

But being the mill of emulative consumption is not the only source of dynamism of a capitalist economy. Existing industries are constantly generating new products in the form of spin-offs, or what

---

[24] Douglas and Isherwood 1996.
[25] Douglas 1996b, 123.

Jane Jacobs called "adding new work to old work."[26] Brassieres were originally created by a seamstress as an accessory to dresses, and then became a new product in its own right. The challenges of creating sandpaper by a sand company led to the development of new kinds of adhesives, which then led to the development of the first modern tapes and a host of new similar products.[27] The demand for these products is multidimensional: They make life more comfortable, solve a problem for another industry, save time, or generate a new aesthetic. Crucially, each new product generates a new industrial process, with new suppliers, workers, and intermediate industries and products. A successful capitalist economy is an ever-expanding, interdependent web of supply chains, where the manufacture of any product, and the creation of new ones, generate "chain reactions" of sorts throughout the economy. A craze for a new type of scooter generates a new demand for metal, plastics, paint, and other products, but also workers with new skills, or just more workers, and also, of course, more housing, food, and energy, all of which generate their own demands on other industries.[28]

A key prerequisite for this dynamic is the footloose condition of the labor force. The only way goods and services can multiply and change quickly is through the hiring of workers who can move easily from one job to another. Of course, job insecurity is the dark side of this labor and consumption flexibility. A dynamic, "creative," and "innovative" economy also generates an unstable labor market. As new industries emerge, others are wiped out. Skills quickly turn obsolete; job hierarchies are constantly upended. The precariousness of employment, and of social belonging generally, is the price we pay for living in this exciting, ever-changing world.

It follows that capitalism is incompatible with any social system that includes rigid, preestablished occupations and social statuses. Capitalist powers have, of course, historically sought to undermine these kinds of cultures, since a society that has established roles for everyone, correspondingly accompanied by established objects for everyone, has no need for novel commodities or jobs. The global expansion of capitalism, as Marx correctly pointed out, has meant

[26] Jacobs 1970.
[27] Ibid., Chapter 2.
[28] In this sense, Wassily Leontief's input-output models are one of the most "ethnographic" economic models around, since they describe the actual interdependency and mutual influences of all the industries of a capitalist economy.

the destruction of traditional and indigenous cultures based on self-sufficiency and reciprocity. In these societies, the individual has no status independent from the group, and thus no need for individualized consumption, and no "labor" to sell either. Consequently, in the words of Karl Polanyi, capitalist expansion has meant "the smashing up of social structures in order to extract the element of labor from them."[29] Historically, this process is not related only to European imperialism. The social transformations that European economic and political elites wrought on faraway territories were the same ones that they imposed on the rural communities of their own countryside. In every case, what was destroyed was not only the main "forms of subsistence," but the whole system of social belonging and esteem. The degradation of indigenous and peasant societies around the world was not just a case of economic imperialism, but of cultural obliteration, by which the standards of social belonging were dramatically changed, customary sources of social respect were lost, and "settled folk" were transformed into "shiftless migrants."[30]

We are here very far from any realm of "basic necessities" or "basic goods." Capitalist economies thrive by expanding the production of an increasing variety of goods and services, and it matters little what they actually consist of, as long as they keep the machine moving. The early history of capitalism displays a peculiar list of key commodities whose production transformed the social and cultural landscape of whole regions of the planet.[31] The cultures and civilizations of pre-Columbian South America were smashed to reorient their members toward the production of silver for Spain. Those of North America were transformed by the beaver fur trade with several European nations, fur that was used for the production of fashionable hats. Millions of Africans were forcefully brought to the Americas to produce sugar in the Caribbean and cotton in the mainland British colonies. Europe struggled to find a commodity to sell to China in exchange for its tea, finally discovering, and then promoting, opium addiction. Witnessing the California Gold Rush, Henry David Thoreau amusedly commented, with his characteristic wit and sarcasm, that he "did not know that mankind was suffering

[29] Polanyi 2001 [1944], 172.
[30] Ibid., 164.
[31] Wolf 2010.

for want of gold."[32] We might as well follow Thoreau in wondering if mankind was suffering from want of silver, fur hats, cotton clothing, sugar, tea, or opium.

The consumption of these commodities involved not only adding new objects to daily life but also the reshuffling of social identities and statuses. The industrial revolution started in England with the mass production of textiles and clothing. This was not a coincidence. Up to that point, clothing had been a socially sensitive and highly regulated affair. As befits a society with an explicit hierarchical ideology, what different classes could wear was established through what is known as sumptuary laws, whose purpose was to avoid the confusion of social categories of people in public spaces. For example, bright-colored or smooth fabrics like silk, buttons, or buckles were limited to the gentry.[33] In addition, elites donned highly elaborate styles that were too expensive for the poor to emulate. Lowering the price of clothes and facilitating the imitation of elite fashions was one of the most effective and obvious ways of subverting the hierarchies of traditional society. The modern, capitalist industries not only made this possible, but their success also depended on the buying public seizing these opportunities.[34] The new affordable clothes that capitalist industries were massively producing played a key role in the production of a more mobile society based on economic performance rather than hereditary positions. Thus, from the very beginning, what capitalism was producing was not new goods that would satisfy simple biological or, alternatively, mysterious and inscrutable needs, but as all societies before it, the goods that satisfied the needs its own cosmology created.

Finally, this competitive character of capitalist consumption also renders problematic any claims about the natural scarcity of goods. As commented before, scarcity is treated in standard economic theory as a fact of life that has a logical impact on the dynamics of prices. But instead of understanding prices as a reflection of abundance or scarcity, we must see them rather as a direct expression of social status.[35] As always, it is in the realm of social meanings that the real crux of the matter resides. Certain goods are cheap not because they are abundant.

[32] Thoreau 1964, 639. The phrase comes from his famous essay, "Life without Principle" (1863).
[33] Hunt 1996.
[34] Suzman 2021, 320–322.
[35] Hirsch 1976.

Rather, their abundance and cheapness are both expressions of their low status and their general availability. Low-status goods are, by definition, cheap and available, while high-status goods are, by definition, expensive and scarce.[36] Their status is what determines how much of them will be produced, as well as how much will be charged for them, their price necessarily being an expression of their status. The key variable is social exclusivity, not abundance or scarcity. Once a decision has been made to make a good socially exclusive, its scarcity will logically follow. Like the positions in a royal family, high-status goods are meant to be few and restricted, since if they became common, they would lose their social value. It follows that all products in the market are socially targeted. To the degree that they are meant to be massively used, they will be cheap and abundant; to the degree that they are meant to be exclusive, they will be expensive and "scarce."

Let's take an example of a very cheap and common good, such as paper clips. The low price of paper clips is determined by (1) the low cost of manufacturing them; (2) the fact that they're meant to be massively used; and (3) their prosaic, utilitarian nature, that is, their low status as goods. In a world awash in paper, a devise for holding pages together necessarily has a mundane character. The fact that it is cheap to manufacture clips is just one factor determining their price, and might not even be the most important. Of course, no one is going to sell clips below their production and distribution costs, but the relationship between costs and final price is necessarily a loose one, since the latter is critically defined by their social meanings. You can have very cheap goods selling at very high prices due to their social connotations. A paper clip that was the favorite of Albert Einstein might fetch a very high price in the market. Some goods are sold expensively because of who designed them. Two objects that cost the same to produce can sell at very different prices because of the differing competence, or fame, of their respective designers, which could in itself have an impact on production costs (through higher compensations to the more qualified designers), but not necessarily. Clips designed by a well-known artist can indeed sell at a higher price. Temporal connotations can have similar impacts on price. Second-hand goods generally sell for much less than their original production costs, just because we believe that they have lost value by not being new. We consider that a car has lost value

---

[36] Douglas and Isherwood 1996, 83.

just hours after it has left the store, only because it's not "new" anymore. Of course, some second-hand goods become "antiques," which then increases their price above the original one. In the first case, time works against value; in the second, to its benefit. These variations all occur in response to cultural beliefs, not to any intersections of "supply" and "demand."[37] Goods are not expensive because many people want them and there are too few of them. Rather, the price of goods is an expression of who they're targeted for.

This all means that the status symbolism of a good and its monetary value go up and down together. They mirror each other.[38] This can be clearly discerned, for example, in the processes of urban gentrification. A slum is "turned around" and transformed into a desirable neighborhood; the property values go up, the place becomes more active and attractive, and generates more tax revenue. These results are typically considered a success of urban policy and entrepreneurship. But these processes tend to be also accompanied with complaints about the unfortunate displacements of poorer families and the increase in house prices that now exclude the previous residents. But there is nothing unfortunate about the process, since it is completely predictable.[39] Here, a change in prices is simply a reflection of a change in customers. The neighborhood is pricier because the newly interested residents are wealthier, which automatically makes it unsuitable for the previous low-income group. Property "values" have gone up because there has been a change in the social "values" of the place. The neighborhood has changed its social status, which means its prices will change as well. To miss this point is to believe that "value" has no social dimension, as if we were talking about value in the eyes of God. In this case, the increase in the price of land and buildings has nothing to do with scarcity. The place was cheap before simply because it had not become fashionable among the wealthy. Under capitalism, as in all competitive societies, all points of value are points of social distinction, and thus of created scarcity.[40]

The reader might object, "wait a minute, many goods are really scarce, such as those extracted from nature. There is a finite amount of oil and minerals in the ground, and we use all of that. Surely the market

[37] Thompson 2017.
[38] Sahlins 1976.
[39] I study the relationship between urban social segregation and social status in modern societies in my first book (Espino 2015).
[40] Bourdieu 1984; Dumouchel 2014.

economy deals with goods that are really scarce, not only artificially so!" Two important points can be made in this regard. First, for a good to be truly scarce, it not only needs to be available in limited quantities; it also needs to be desired or needed. Nature offers plenty of resources that are not, in this sense, "scarce," mainly because no one wants them.[41] When I was a kid, I picked up mangoes from the ground in my neighborhood whenever I fancied. I'm sure the supply was limited, but no one considered them to be "scarce." Second, the truly scarce goods, in other words, those that are both in limited supply and highly needed, tend to be those that are absolutely essential for *all* of society, because they support the whole culture and lifestyles of all groups.[42] In modern societies, the main food staples and sources of energy are obvious examples. Without energy, our regular lives would grind to a halt. We couldn't work, cook, heat or cool our buildings, call each other, or get anywhere. Everyone would be affected, rich and poor. So, whatever the sources of our energy are, their scarcity will be of utmost concern. Consequently, and paradoxically, the price of these goods is rarely left to the vagaries of supply and demand, that is, to the law of extortion. They are just too important for that. Japan subsidizes the production of rice, as many other countries do with their basic staples, and most subsidize fuel and electricity, so that prices stay within affordable ranges for the population. In general, the more broadly important a commodity is, the less the rules of the "free market" will apply to it, for few governments are foolish enough to risk a revolution.

The ultimate irony in the relationship of capitalism with scarcity is provided by the phenomenon of inflation. If one would conclude (not unreasonably) that the real scarcity in the system is the availability of money, and proceeded to distribute money to everyone, price inflation, resulting from the exercise of extortion across the market, would quickly raise the cost of everything, effectively annulling the advantages of the increased individual income.[43]

---

[41] I should clarify that, of course, we do live in a planet with limited resources. I'm just emphasizing that, in the context of human societies, scarcities are always culturally mediated.

[42] Douglas and Isherwood 1996, 80.

[43] This means that the control of inflation depends on the premise or belief that money is also scarce. Although countries with monetary sovereignty can create and print money at will, when governments give out money (e.g., through subsidies, bailouts, or transfer payments), the outlays are registered as a "debt" that the government owes itself, and that must be repaid through taxes or other forms of income. The system only works under the

In a capitalist society, the reason some people cannot get what they want is not due to scarcity. They either don't have the money to purchase it, or the market has not found a way to provide it to them with acceptable levels of profit. Since supply is always targeted to a particular social demand, shortages are usually less of an issue. If anything, the problems are normally generated by an *excess* of supply. When a new business opportunity emerges, entrepreneurs make a run for it, producing more goods than the market can actually absorb, and creating the well-known bubbles. Shortages tend to be limited to particular goods, and to respond to particular disruptions. The 2020 global pandemic created all kinds of shortages, but they had nothing to do with natural scarcities, since they didn't exist a year before. In a system built around the principle of the "ability to pay," most people can find what they are looking for – if they have the right amount of money.

* * *

The nature of capitalist production and consumption generates a series of thorny issues for any alternative model. As noted above, communist regimes tried to address the issue of inequality by focusing the productive apparatus on the "basic needs" of the population and guaranteeing universal access to them. But since the definition of basic needs is in itself arbitrary, they ended up producing goods that were questioned for their quality, especially since the populations living under these regimes were conscious of the overwhelming superiority and variety of the goods produced by their capitalist competitors. Just as in capitalism, workers under communism were forced to work for others, in this case the State and its bureaucrats, but without enjoying the flamboyant, compensatory world of recreational consumption of their capitalist counterparts. The goods produced under communism quickly acquired an anachronistic quality, since they didn't evolve through independent social dynamics, but slowly and by bureaucratic decree. For individuals or groups, seeking new products was of no use, since there were no independent suppliers able to create or provide them.

assumption that money is not free (but must be "worked for" or returned) and that all debts must be honored (on this latter point, see Graeber 2014, 367). Even the proponents of Modern Monetary Theory (Kelton 2021), who advocate indifference to government budget deficits, must have their own method for imposing money scarcity and reigning in inflation (in their case, through taxation).

Communist regimes are mostly attractive for populations that are still living under materially modest conditions, such as peasant societies, and that are at the threshold of industrialization.[44] The generations witnessing the changes brought by the socialist revolution can be very supportive, since they are benefiting from what, under any standard of evaluation, are dramatic changes in their quality of life, and in the context of a highly inclusive system and discourse. Their children, however, having grown up with the new amenities in place, are bound to become demoralized and disillusioned with a system that now seems rigid and stuck in time. Since the whole productive infrastructure is centrally run, power is inevitably concentrated, leading consistently to dictatorial regimes. Communist countries liked to frame themselves in opposition to the world of capitalist corporations, but they actually functioned, in many ways, as one big corporation themselves.

Still, political repression aside, one should never underestimate the potential attractiveness of a well-run communist regime in spite of the economic tradeoffs, which Peter Marcuse summarized, for the case of East Germany, as involving "on the good side, kindergartens, health centers, coffee breaks, job security, lack of tension; on the bad side, inefficiency, make-work, waste, lack of innovation."[45] Actress Sandra Hüller's childhood memories of the same regime are also a useful reminder of these compromises, and of the relative value of what capitalism offers:

> She was 11 when the wall came down. Life in the former GDR felt "safe." "People told me I would definitely have a job later: 'Nobody needs to starve here or live in the streets.' There were no drug issues. Maybe it wasn't the truth, but as a child there was not so much fear."
>
> She liked the lack of choice. "We had one sort of milk, one sort of butter, one kind of bread, and you went to the shop to buy the things you really needed. There was no such thing as shopping; walking around and trying to find something you like. It was not so stressful. There was so much more space for leisure, for boredom, for making things out of nothing."[46]

---

[44] Derluguian 2013.
[45] Marcuse 1991, 279.
[46] Shoard 2017.

The cultural pressures of a globalized capitalist system are also a challenge for "developing" countries. Since the key variable in economics is what things mean, who defines the meaning of things establishes the terms of international economic relations. We have already argued that one of the prerogatives of power is to define what is valuable. The history of Western imperialism is not only a history of economic exploitation, but also of cultural domination. Economic dependency is always cultural dependency. The colonies were assigned the task of providing the cheap labor and raw materials for the goods that the imperial, wealthy societies invented and developed. But because these poorer regions were now part of the same cultural system, they ended up consuming and craving for goods that they helped manufacture, but whose meanings and evolution they had limited control over. As new independent countries, these former colonies ended up living under the "allure of the foreign,"[47] since the highly coveted symbols of modernity and progress came almost exclusively from the centers of power abroad. The dynamic still holds today. Having the factories may entail economic benefits, but deciding what the factories make is where the real power and money is. Any factory can churn out shirts, but not necessarily shirts that will sell. In order to sell shirts, you need to know what style is popular now, what kinds of shirts teenagers are buying, and so on. In a globalized economy, this means you need to be integrated to the global taste-making and innovation centers, which tend to be large multinational corporations, and professional and celebrity networks concentrated in key cities of the global north. "World cities" such as New York, Los Angeles, or London, or world centers of technological innovation, such as Silicon Valley, have the power to set the consumer agenda for much of the global market, after which different countries and regions will be assigned their respective roles in the production process. As with the imperial capitals of the past, which concentrated the "surplus, the power, and the glory,"[48] world capitals of today become the places "where the action is;" "the center of things" where the key technologies and cultural products are developed or given their final acceptance and blessing, and to which ambitious global actors make their pilgrimage, as with the religious meccas of the past.[49]

---

[47] Orlove 1997.
[48] Kearns and Philo 1993, 7.
[49] Hannerz 1993.

True "development" in these circumstances entails being able to "nationalize" some of this leadership role. The younger countries that have been able to join the select group of "developed nations" are the ones that have become innovators and inventors themselves, and that have found a way to offer goods that other societies, and their own citizens, crave. This capacity will determine if a society's cities and material culture will look "different" or simply "out of date."[50] As commented before, this process entails a measure of self-confidence that shows up as a certain degree of autonomy in the arts, the sciences, and the intellectual realms. Without this spiritual sovereignty, countries are condemned to a dependent, insecure culture, and reduced to being a bit player in someone else's designs. As with individuals, the power of a society vis-à-vis others begins with self-assertion.

* * *

Let's now focus on the contradictions inherent to capitalism in two different dimensions: the integration of the individual to society and the system's capacity to provide social stability. Every society has its own parameters for establishing the "value" of its members and their relative degree of power. The "currency" of such power can vary considerably. For the Yurok tribes of Northern California, social prestige depended on the accumulation of particular shells, feathers, pelts, and obsidian blades. For the Lele men of Central Africa, it depended on the number of women they controlled, both as wives, and as daughters they could offer in marriage to other men.[51] As Douglas comments, the double nature of women as people and currency gave them a particular form of power in the whole "economy" that the men inevitably resented.

As we all know, in capitalism, power is defined mainly by the person's monetary wealth. Although a person's social influence has different dimensions, as we saw with Bourdieu's scheme of forms of capital, the most important source of power in our society is the possession of money, or of goods that can be transformed into money. This means that the most important attribute a person can offer in the social scene is his capacity to produce money. Consequently, we

---

[50] "The tropics are less exotic than out of date," wrote Lévi-Strauss in his famous travelogue *Tristes Tropiques* (1992 [1955], 87).

[51] Douglas 2002, 184 ff.

pay relatively more to the people that contribute more critically to the "bottom line" of a corporation. These individuals have special knowledge, skills, or leadership talents, that is, they are less "replaceable" and must be snatched from competitors by means of higher compensation. Similarly, the activities that generate more wealth are also privileged, since they offer their owners and beneficiaries more social power. The source of profitability may be the activity's capacity to access larger markets, its monopolistic nature, a preferential treatment by governments, and any number of circumstantial factors.

This overall logic leaves at a disadvantage any activity or occupation whose capacity to directly generate wealth is limited or negligeable, regardless of its social importance. The most obvious example is the world of domestic tasks and the care of people, such as children and other family members. In peasant or tribal societies, men, women, and different age groups divided the crucial tasks of family life among them, so that all tasks were understood as different types of "work." Farming and cooking, herding and weaving, or fishing and nursing, were all seen as necessary tasks that had a certain equivalence as different subsistence activities. Under capitalism, "work" is limited to those activities that are exchanged for money; consequently, domestic chores and family obligations are conducted by people who "do not work." By making the pursuit of money the principal means of achieving social respect, a whole set of regular life activities end up socially devalued.

The situation extends to a large number of occupations, activities, and goods that society needs, but that the market has no way of properly providing or compensating. Parks, general education, or public transportation cannot be "sold" at "market price" because then only those with enough money would be able to access them. If society requires that everyone learn to read and write, it has to offer the corresponding training to every child regardless of his family's means. These services and goods that the market fails to guarantee to everyone are then called, in the language of economics, "market failures." The term itself is telling. It assumes that the market generally provides what we need, except in those particular cases when it can't (there are no "market victories").

"Market failures" end up, of course, in the hands of the modern State, and their list can be quite extensive. Capitalism seeks to free the individual from social obligations, only to have them reappear through the back door in the form of public policy. Public services present a number of economic conundrums, because their prices cannot be determined "rationally," that is, through the law of extortion. What is the "price," after all, of a public-school teacher? Inevitably, the solution comes with its own form of imposition. If the price of a good or service in the free market is the result of the application of force (the might of the wealthiest), the price of a public good is the result of another (the enforcement of a policy, such as a minimum salary). I will return to this key issue.

It is important to understand the purported rationales behind capitalist social valuations. We tend to assume that it makes sense to pay more to people that have more knowledge or skills, but this assumption only holds under an individualist ideology. Individual talents are seen as just another form of "competitive advantage," like owning the piece of land where a valuable mineral is found. The individual owns a "scarce" resource (his exceptional talents) that can be deployed competitively in the market to extort the best price possible. In a society with an egalitarian ideology, the situation is quite different. The individual's talents are, as everything else, a property of the group, and must be put at its service. Whatever "surplus" an individual generates is the group's gain, since it will be distributed equitably anyway. Special compensations or privileges for exceptional individuals can be offered, but only as a recognition for their contributions to the group. The idea that an individual can accumulate power unlimitedly just because he is better in some respect is rejected.

Even in highly stratified societies, individually accumulated wealth can be seen as a resource of the group. In many societies of the ancient world, the rich were considered the "treasurers of the community," and the distribution or sharing of their wealth was expected and ritualized.[52] In modern societies, especially those with more "collectivist" ideologies, exceptional individuals can also be seen as a common patrimony. The Soviet Union went to great lengths to pamper its outstanding artists, and to protect them from harm during World War II. In his heyday, Brazil passed a law declaring the football star Pelé a "national treasure," in order to bar him from playing professionally abroad.

---

[52] Graeber 2001, 160.

The freedoms afforded to individuals are thus a function of the balance societies strike between individualism and social responsibility. In modern, liberal societies, we tend to understand such freedoms in the classical way John Stuart Mill did, which today sounds completely commonsensical: "Liberty is doing as we like, subject to such consequences as may follow, without impediment from our fellow creatures, as long as what we do does not harm them even though they should think our conduct foolish, perverse or wrong."[53] But anytime a group has a clear common purpose, the tolerance for unconventional behavior necessarily decreases. In a modern army, a soldier who decided to behave foolishly or eccentrically would be summarily court-martialed.

Regarding power, societies or groups with egalitarian ideologies are very straightforward: Concentrations of power are bad, so they have to be controlled. Societies with hierarchical ideologies are likewise transparent: Everyone has a fixed place in the hierarchy, so each person must simply assume theirs. Capitalist societies have, in contrast, a conflicted view of the issue, so it is denied or covered up. On the one hand, the system asserts the radical equality of everyone, both in the political realm ("one person, one vote") and in the economic one ("freedom of choice"). On the other hand, the system's commitment to unrestricted individual action generates dramatic power differentials that it then has to contend with and justify, and that belies its egalitarian principles *in practice*. In the process, it tries to ignore what all other competitive societies know very well: that power begets power and that wealth begets wealth. We all know that it is far easier to make money if you already have money; that making money can be the result of luck, connections, and unearned advantages as much as of effort and talent; that money buys political power, which then leads to more preferential treatment; and that the logic of the system leads not toward competition but toward monopoly, that the big prize awaits those who can get rid of their competitors. In spite of this, we insist that the system is meritocratic; that the main reason some people have more money is because they have worked harder, which means they deserve the fruits of their efforts and should not be curtailed in their capacity to accumulate it. In other words, we believe wealth is not an expression of a social imbalance, but just one more "thing" that can be hoarded or collected, such as antique cars. In fact, sociologist Michael

[53] Mill 1880, 7.

Young, the initial popularizer of the term "meritocracy," used it sarcastically as a way of describing an ideology that pretended to justify wealth imbalances with the language of merit, so as to hide their true source and excuse the opposition to distributive efforts.[54]

The clash between our ideals of equality and our unequal realities leads to all kinds of contradictory policies and attitudes that generate predictable social conflicts. In order to help disadvantaged groups, we favor them with special measures that go against the principle of "equality under the law." The contentious quota systems based on race or gender are a case in point. They represent an effort to correct an imbalance of the system by betraying the principles of the system. This is a typical, and paradoxical, clash of two "goods." The imbalances obviously exist, and a basic principle is obviously being violated. Both contending parties are thus fully justified in their complaints.

Something similar happens with the policing of humor. Aggressive humor (teasing, taunting) works very much like gifts. If I can tease you, and you can tease me back, we're in a fairly equal relationship. Any repression of reciprocity in teasing evinces a power differential that we feel uncomfortable with. We tend to disapprove of powerful people mocking their inferiors, since we see it as abusive in light of the equality that supposedly exists between everyone, even though, by disapproving, we're implicitly acknowledging the imbalance. By contrast, everyone feels entitled to publicly mock the powerful. Politicians and the rich are constantly ridiculed; at the same time, we expect them to avoid responding in kind. In a truly equal and democratic society, mockery can be freely exercised in any direction. By contrast, mockery in a society with a hierarchical ideology simply follows the power structure – mocking the powerful is clearly subversive, and comes at a cost. But the conflicted and paradoxical relationship between equality and inequality in our societies leads us to want our cake and eat it too. We claim equality in order to ridicule those more powerful than us, but claim inequality and victim status in order to protect ourselves from ridicule. The more scandalous comedians spot the ruse, take our egalitarian ideology at its word, and turn into "equal opportunity offenders."

I should clarify again that the previous comments on meritocracy are not meant to suggest that actual merit has no role in capitalist

---

[54] Young 2017 [1958].

societies. The fact is, capitalism has probably produced some of the most merit-oriented human societies in history. By eliminating all hereditary and preestablished social positions, and opening the social field to competitive struggles, capitalism frequently allows any social actor to excel based on his own talents. But not all talents produce wealth, and not all wealth is the result of talent. By concealing power issues behind a discourse of merit, we try to avoid confronting topics we have no clear answer to. In the process, we open our own cosmology to accusations of deceit and hypocrisy.

In the best formulated version, people in liberal, capitalist societies are entrepreneurial and creative, displaying their unique talents in a system that allows for a seemingly infinite number of individual initiatives and business opportunities. As pertains to the structure of developed economies, this is largely a myth. The great majority of working people in the developed world are not entrepreneurs, but work for a company or institution they don't own.[55] This is exactly the opposite of the situation in the "developing" world, where sometimes a majority are "self-employed," that is, eke out a living in a variety of low-cost and informal activities, such as selling things on the street, all the while hoping for someone to offer them a "real" job.[56] The most common version of the good life in a developed capitalist society is not that of an independent entrepreneur, but rather that of an employee who works permanently in a private or public organization that has figured out a way to survive in the dynamic, and unforgiving, capitalist economy.

In this context, the "humanization" of the capitalist workplace has become a key issue in our times. This has proceeded through a number of different paths. First, there is the traditional one focused on "workers' rights." Salary increases, paid vacations, workplace security regulations, and paid maternity and paternity leaves are the salient topics. Then there are the varied schemes of "employee-ownership" of companies, where workers participate partially or fully of the profits and decision-making processes of an organization. From the side of company owners, the "corporate social responsibility" movement aims at guaranteeing that businesses align their mission and procedures toward principled societal goals, not only regarding their own employees, but also the society at large. Environmentally sustainable business

---

[55] Chang 2011, 157 ff.
[56] What Banerjee and Duflo call "reluctant entrepreneurs" (2011, Ch. 9).

practices have become a key terrain of debate and application of the movement in recent years. The general thrust of all these efforts inevitably leads to a questioning of the profit motive and the ultimate purpose of corporations. For Howard Stevenson, profit should be seen mainly as a *constraint*, rather than as the mission of a business, which should be related to the good or service that it is committed to.[57] Since without financial viability there would no business, profit becomes a condition, but not necessarily a *raison d'être*. For Stevenson, entrepreneurship is fundamentally about transforming the world through "the pursuit of opportunity without regard to resources currently controlled."[58] It is thus only partially related to profitability, and encompasses all efforts to bring about social change.

At the individual level, these business philosophies try to incorporate personal agency and initiative to the workplace, so that all employees are active creators in their positions. In the ideal case, everyone's jobs represent a good match between organizational responsibilities and personal capabilities and preferences. The workplace becomes then an actual site of self-realization, instead of the simple means of survival or status acquisition that "savage" capitalism offers. The job is not just about the money, just as the corporation is not just about the money, either. This implies a rethinking of such classic formulations as Adam Smith's oft-cited phrase: "It is not from the benevolence of the butcher, the brewer, or the baker, that we expect our dinner, but from their regard to their own interest."[59] The self-interest here would not be mainly the pursuit of profit, but rather the commitment to a particular vocation. We benefit not from the baker's greed, but from his desire to excel in his chosen path. Profit becomes a means, rather than the ends, of the service. Of course, as in many human actions, motivations would most likely be mixed in this regard.

The realization of these possibilities will depend, of course, on the type of organization, and it also has an international dimension. In many economic contexts, and also "developing" countries, creativity and individual initiative are still seen as a privilege of the bosses, rather than as a regular workplace feature. The legacy of colonialism presents an important challenge here. Historically, colonialism entailed the rule

[57] Sinoway 2012, 53, 211.
[58] Stevenson 1983, 3.
[59] Smith 1976 [1776], 27.

of a miniscule elite over large masses of workers, whether peasants or slaves, in a rigid system that offered very few positions of high status. Leadership was identified with domination, and entrepreneurship with exploitation and looting. For many people in former colonies, accessing better jobs is mainly about accessing positions of social privilege and prestige that have been historically denied. In these contexts, the quest for status can be desperate, and can override subtler considerations about self-realization. Frequently, this leads people to simply reproduce the colonialist logic in contemporary workplaces, such as government institutions. This was perfectly captured by Naipaul in his description of a military takeover of a government in his fictional African nation:

> They didn't see, these young men, that there was anything to build in their country. As far as they were concerned, it was all there already. They had only to take. They believed that, by being what they were, they had earned the right to take; and the higher the officer, the greater the crookedness – if that word had any meaning.[60]

The key difference is here between "building" and "taking," between creating something new and simply seizing what is already there; between the idea of power as leadership, and the idea of power as a source of perks and privileges. What is "taken" here are the spoils of a social position that one has finally accessed, and that had been denied before. It corresponds to the mentality of someone whose turn to be on top has finally arrived.

Colonialism also colors the relationship with the law. Many colonies lived under laws drafted in the faraway imperial centers of power. They thus acquired the character of an alien imposition designed to protect an unfair power structure. The local way to get ahead was to work around them. This then became a pattern. In subaltern countries, the popular and admired figure of the "trickster" represents a resourceful character that, through ingenuity and cunning, circumvents the established order in order to prevail. Of course, the trickster is inevitably a lawbreaker. One of the most popular comedies in Latin American history is La Tremenda Corte ("The Great Court"), produced as a radio program in Cuba between 1942 and

[60] Naipaul 1989, 91.

1961, and as a TV show in Mexico between 1966 and 1969, and retransmitted through the region to this day. Every episode consists of a different court trial of the main character, *Trespatines* (literally "Three Skates"), a ne'er-do-well who is invariably tried for fraud, and condemned to jail time at the end of each episode. *Trespatines* is recursively accused of deceiving some hapless victim for money, and the comic element consists of the ingenuity of his methods and arguments, which are unmasked by the impatient and grumpy judge, another fixed character. He is able to sell a car that has no engine (it does roll downhill) or a house with only one room (the bed in the corner represents the "bedroom," the pot represents the "kitchen," and so on). Culturally, the show allows for the celebration of the trickster, but since he is always punished at the end, also defends the rule of law. It is thus a typically ambivalent creation that allows for the psychological processing of contradictory pulls, in this case respecting, and also disrespecting, the rules. Such a show is unthinkable in a country like the United States, with its almost religious reverence for the law.

Regarding these issues, debates about the cultural aspects of underdevelopment sometimes point toward the wrong "values" in the developing world that impede the creation of modern, successful societies. Government corruption, disrespect for the law, or lack of entrepreneurship are blamed on a dysfunctional culture adverse to modern progress. But, to a large extent, these cultures *are the result of modern progress*, only the dark side that is destined for the subordinate components of the system. The main challenge now is, in any case, not a change in "values," but a change in the conditions of social belonging. People in these societies would need to experience forms of social advancement that do not depend on patronage, graft, or pillage. Once these alternatives are sufficiently common, the "values" will adjust accordingly. As Aristotle understood well, virtuous behavior is the child of habit; it relates to our habitual responses to the world, rather than to abstract ideals that can be promoted in campaigns on ethical behavior.[61]

Here, we can point to a false dichotomy between "cultural" and "structural" factors in development, that relates to the debate regarding the work of Lawrence Harrison mentioned at the beginning

[61] Aristotle 2009.

of the book. Cultures and institutions are not completely separate variables that have an independent influence on a society's evolution and prospects. In general, certain institutions can only work with certain cultures, but certain cultures are always the result of certain institutions.[62] For a society to function, a minimum match between mentalities (or ideology) and social structures is essential; any stark disconnect is a sure source of instability.[63] Consequently, social transformations can be led by institutional or ideological change, and whichever moves first is bound to force shifts on the other.

In the end, if we want to understand the moral compass of a group, we need to identify its moral imperatives and compulsions, that is, the values and behaviors it imposes on its members. The talk about "values" is frequently one more individualization of forces that should be analyzed at the social scale, in this case, in the realm of social pressures. This reflection applies to all societies, rich and poor. If in a capitalist society, greed takes you far, people will be greedy. If advancement depends on who you know, people will form powerful cabals. If creativity is the key to success, people will deploy their creativity in the workplace. In this sense, societies, groups, and individuals don't have the "wrong" culture or values; they all tend to have the culture and values they can afford.

* * *

Going back to the issue of stability, capitalism clearly doesn't only generate uncertainty to individuals; it also does so, of course, for the whole of society. Both defenders and detractors of capitalism agree that the system is intrinsically unstable and cyclical. Capital is constantly exhausting existing profit opportunities and trying to open new ones. New industries are highly profitable as long as they involve some form of monopoly power due to proprietary technological innovations, good timing, State protections, imperialistic maneuvers, or all

---

[62] In this regard, I'm mostly in agreement with Acemoglu and Robinson's analyses of development challenges (2012; 2019), and the way they handle politics, institutions, and culture under a single, integrated approach. I do take issue, however, with their uncritical view of what "development" means, and consequently, with their assumption that there's a clear psychocultural profile that leads to it.

[63] "The community that puts its categories at risk puts itself at risk. The institution and the categories by which it knows itself are one" (Douglas 1992, 286).

of the above. Once competitors are able to catch up, profits drop, and new frontiers have to be explored.[64]

The system is also indifferent to larger goals of social welfare. The most important thing to know about the social goals of a "free market" capitalist economy is that it doesn't have any. It is useless to expect such a system to offer full employment, preserve the environment, or reduce inequality, since these kinds of objectives are extraneous to its logic, which is centered on the pursuit of profit. If any of these goals are attained, it is usually temporarily and by accident. These kinds of goals have to be regulated in by the State, or brought into play by enlightened entrepreneurs who, at any rate, need the State's support in order to be competitive against their more cut-throat colleagues.

This means that the State ends up being responsible for providing a common social vision for the economy, because the private market can only offer a jumble of uncoordinated individual initiatives. Since everything in the market is for sale to the highest bidder, the State becomes the representative of the community, the protector of its ideals and symbols, and the provider of its common goods and services. This view is anathema for libertarian thinkers, who would rather see the State as a "neutral" administrator of fair rules for private action, not an agent of the collective will. But, as commented before, all societies imply a notion of a common purpose, and some institution has to channel it. Reducing public officials to the role of referees implies making them an appendix to the private industry, rather than a balancing, directing, or monitoring force. Under this model, it is not surprising that corruption can increase, since if the mission of the government bureaucracy is simply to help the private sector make money, why not share in the spoils? By eliminating the sense of a public mission, which gives public officials a distinct and different role than the private actor, they end up as the unfairly underpaid servants of private corporations. In this sense, the ultimate form of government corruption is not the stealing of public funds, but the stealing of public purpose.[65]

The furtherance of a common vision might include not only complementing the market, but shaping it as well. As argued before, markets are creatures of the State, which means the State can also create new ones, expand existing ones, or lead them in new directions.

---

[64] Wallerstein 2013.
[65] Haller and Shore 2005, 9.

Economic crises or cyclical disruptions can also be managed through State interventions. In the most proactive mode, States can be entrepreneurial themselves, and create business initiatives that the private sector is incapable or unwilling to pursue.[66] There are, of course, more practical and regular duties. The private sector cannot actually function without the goods and services provided by the State. It cannot provide the public roads that carry everyone and everything, the basic education of the workforce, or the general utilities. The government is thus the "silent partner" of every private business, and legitimately claims its share of the profits through taxation. In addition, it handles the private market's "externalities," or the environmental and social impacts of private operations, such as pollution or plant closings. Economists usually consider that, ideally, businesses should be able to "internalize" these impacts, that is, the price of goods and services should incorporate the cost of dealing with these spill-over effects. But since we live in highly interdependent social and environmental systems, "externalities" can be difficult to measure fully, and their actual cost could make many businesses unviable. Governments thus force as much internalization as they can short of bankrupting the industry, and simply deal (or not) with the rest.[67]

The balance between taxation and the costs of externalities is one of the most difficult and politically fraught problems in capitalist societies, and can even threaten the viability of the whole system. Normally, governments do not estimate the spill-over costs of private operations and verify if the collected taxes can actually cover them. This requires a level of technical expertise and planning that is either generally lacking or discouraged. In the realm of urban development, for example, it would require governments to estimate the maintenance costs of whatever public infrastructure private developers build, and check if the taxes collected from the new residents can actually finance them in the long term.[68] (Otherwise, someone else will have to, which is, in itself, a topic worthy of discussion). In the realm of environmental impacts, we have been dumping externalities into the biosphere for centuries now, with the result that their unpostponable handling has become almost unpayable.

[66] This is the concept of the "entrepreneurial State" theorized and advocated by Mazzucato (2015; 2018; 2021).
[67] Calhoun 2013.
[68] Marohn 2020.

Deferring the management of externalities tends to be, in consequence, the norm. The common philosophy is to stimulate private development in any way possible, since economic growth is what generates employment and public revenue. What is produced, where, and how becomes secondary, while the balance sheet of development is ignored. Invariably, this leads to environmental destruction and social mayhem, as private industries move from one business opportunity to another, leaving the governments to pick up the pieces behind them – if they can or are willing to. One more polluted water body, deteriorating infrastructure, or jobless community is then added to the long list of pending problems that demand "urgent" government action. The gap between impacts and remedial costs is usually covered through public borrowing, which sooner or later leads to a spiral of indebtedness that generates accusations of government waste and inefficiency, which is actually a fair accusation given the lack of government planning behind the mess. Unfortunately, the business leaders usually making the condemnation would normally reject the restrictions that could help avoid the whole situation. The externality throw-and-catch game between the State and the private sector, in which the most frequent occurrence is that both players drop the ball, can easily become a source of public financial overextension, one of the most common causes of the collapse of complex societies throughout human history.[69]

---

[69] Tainter 1988. I'm not advocating here for balanced government budgets, a traditional hobbyhorse of conservatives, but rather for efficient and strategic use of public resources. As authors such as Keen (2022) have argued, government deficits are probably an essential component of healthy capitalist economies.

7 KEEPING THE KING'S HEAD IN PLACE

Nothing is more difficult than admitting the final nullity of human conflict.

> René Girard, *Things Hidden Since the Foundation of the World*

Chapter 6's characterization of capitalism allows us to return with fresh eyes to those fundamental components of the modern worldview we singled out in Chapter 3: our individualistic outlook, the mechanistic view of the world, and our linear perception of time. Our societies' tendency to see everything through the lens of the individual is clearly related to capitalism's particular form of organizing power in society. Because the individual is given free rein to concentrate power at the expense of the group, we tend to see social life as originating in the inner world of the person and to keep out of sight the cultural contexts that frame the individual's life. Since human agency and initiative are located in the individual, we assume that general ideas about the world have that same origin point. The world is the way it is because *individuals* willingly shape it, not because we behave in the context of a culture that always precedes us. To see the individual as part of a larger system would entail paying attention to the social consequences of private actions, which is exactly what we don't want to do. The mechanistic view of the world is likewise clearly related to capitalism's objectification of the world, where everything is converted to objective "things" that lend themselves to measurements and market transactions. Modern science obviously shares the same outlook. Both the economy and science tend to treat the world as a realm of inanimate objects whose behavior can be deduced through mechanistic reasoning. If, in the case of science, this has allowed the discovery of laws of nature that have a clear autonomous logic, in the case of the economy, the assumption allows us to ignore the social nature of exchange – a convenient move if we want no restrictions on individual initiative. Finally, temporal linearity is the necessary result of the objectification of time itself. Precapitalist societies saw life as defined by "events" that followed each other or regularly returned. Although we preserve much of this, we now handle also a concept of time as something separate from social life, as an objective reality that can be counted, accumulated, and projected. Time flows independently of its "users" and always moves forward indefinitely. Time and space are not dimensions of life itself, intrinsic components of what is happening, but "things" in themselves.

It is important to emphasize the self-serving usefulness of this worldview. The competitive and open-ended nature of capitalist economies puts a strain on social relations, because it proposes what amounts to a "law of the jungle" in the world of social exchange. Since admitting this straightforwardly, and operating explicitly under this premise, would be highly conflictive, we have transposed any language of relationships between people into a language of relationships between things. Modern technical jargon in economics, and social policy fields generally, speak about people without speaking about people. In economics, we talk about supply, demand, rationality, and efficiency; in urban and social planning, about land uses, activities, and indicators. Societies with hierarchical ideologies had no need for this. Since the social order was preestablished and justified ideologically, there was nothing to hide in terms of the nature of social relations. If people of a certain class were considered "inferior," they were simply labeled and treated as such. There, the "deceit," if you will, resided in the arbitrariness of the whole cosmology and religious ideology that justified the established social pyramid. In our case, there is no agreed-upon social pyramid to defend, so technical language functions rather as a generalized form of psychological diversion, as a sort of defense mechanism that lessens the anxiety and conflict that the system inevitably entails.

The open-ended nature of individual power and identity in capitalist societies accounts for their runaway philosophy, no doubt buttressed by their extraordinary accomplishments in wealth creation and technological progress. Capitalist societies are unique in that they do not foresee or posit any type of final satisfaction. We toil not to arrive anywhere, but to keep on toiling. There can always be more progress, more wealth. We see the attitude in the peculiar and popular notion that every generation should be able to attain a higher living standard than that of their parents. One struggles to find a clear logic behind this, which turns preposterous when applied to high earners. Should the children of millionaires aim to become billionaires, lest they forfeit their good name? And should those of billionaires become trillionaires?

The thrust to pursue wealth for its own sake has always baffled analysts of the modern condition, famously including Max Weber, who wrote his well-known essay *The Protestant Ethic and the Spirit of Modern Capitalism* (1905) as a potential explanation. As Weber pointed out, most societies in the past had based their economic goals on particular ways of living. To be successful economically meant having enough resources to live a specific type of life, which varied according to social class. One of the problems capitalists initially had, was that agricultural workers prioritized their established lifestyle over the possibilities of increased income; in other words, they refused to work more once they had met their accustomed economic goals. If their piece rates were increased, they simply worked less hours. As Weber saw it, "A man does not 'by nature' wish to cam more and more money, but simply to live as he is accustomed to live and to earn as much as is necessary for that purpose."[1] The shift away from this "economic traditionalism," as he called it, was what demanded explanation, and he speculated that its origins were in the Calvinist doctrine of predestination, according to which our salvation was predetermined, and one could only look for clues as to one's particular verdict. Protestant businessmen saw economic success as such proof, which unleashed an unrestrained desire for wealth accumulation. In other words, Weber saw the transition as triggered by religion, that is, by a change in cosmology.

In the mainstream Western philosophical and religious traditions, not to mention other traditions, the unending pursuit of material

---

[1] Weber 1930, 37.

wealth comes across as morally problematic, while at the individual level, such radical insatiability can only be considered pathological in most psychotherapy offices.[2] The environmental consequences require little elaboration. A gigantic productive sector churns out merchandise that is quickly phased out and circulates ever more briefly before arriving at the trash dump. Since many goods function as little more than symbols, their value is as fickle as our social fads. For all our complaints about our "materialist" society, we are strikingly indifferent to our material possessions, which do not hold enough interest for us to hang around for very long. Of course, questioning the productive apparatus and its continued growth becomes problematic, since it's the source of jobs and our ambivalently valued modern goods.

Capitalism's boundless perspective is mirrored inevitably by some of its main opponents. As normally happens, a cultural system sets the terms for its critique. Capitalism's permanent dissatisfaction is shared by its most utopian critics, who also look forward to an unending accretion of benefits, in this case of equality and social justice. Since things can always be better, the present is always found wanting. If capitalists can never have enough money, some of their critics can never have enough equality. In consequence, they both reject settling for any constrained social vision that would block an unimpeded view toward an infinitely open future. Utopian excess is baked into the system.

If we go back to our view of wealth as just our particular currency for social power, the obsessive capitalist quest for accumulation loses much of its mystery. We want more money because we want more power, and power can indeed grow indefinitely, especially if we're competing with determined others. In other words, the system produces its own unstoppable incentives. Once the possibilities for individual power have been unleashed, any curtailment gets complicated. Even those groups who commit to a communitarian life will have to come to terms with their corresponding weakness in the general social context. In a world that places few restrictions to private accumulation, those who opt for frugality, egalitarianism, and community end up necessarily disadvantaged, and thus require a particularly high level of self-confidence and psychological (personal) power, which makes the option even more unlikely. It is one thing to be an ascetic monk in a society that values and supports your option, and quite another in

---

[2] Skidelsky and Skidelsky 2013; Fromm 1976.

one that sees you as just one more eccentric.[3] Countries that refuse to play the capitalist game also end up handicapped. They can compete or feign opposition, proposing an autarkic alternative based on alternative values. The communist experiment can be seen as a gigantic move of "reaction formation," the aforementioned psychological defense mechanism typical of those who want something but cannot get it, and thus react by hating it and opposing it. We all know how that ended.

The dynamic, unstable, and competitive nature of capitalist systems presents particular challenges to social stability, which is the topic I want to explore in this chapter. Environmental collapse looms over humanity's experiment, but social collapse, in the form of intractable conflicts and war, is never far behind, threatening to block any possibility of joint ecological action at any level. Regarding social stability, the main problem with capitalist societies is their uneven distribution of power coupled with their promise of exactly the opposite. The system promises freedom and wealth for everyone while increasingly making them exclusive, at least when growth sputters. The solution cannot come by simply attending to the "basic needs" of the population, since, due to the dynamism of the system, these cannot be objectively defined. At the end of the day, capitalist poverty is a product of the system itself. There are poor people because they do not meet the standards that the system itself defines for success – standards that are being continuously redefined upwards. The discourse about basic needs is, in this sense, another defensive, psychological evasion. As Douglas and Isherwood argue, "the problem of getting people out of poverty is not to get them enough to eat and drink; this is the condition for sustaining people in poverty."[4] The solution to poverty cannot consist solely of the satisfaction of physiological needs, since this just keeps people alive, while doing little to integrate them to society. By focusing our attention on an arbitrary list of needs, we avoid the much trickier issue of social belonging, which involves questioning the power structure of our society – and the protection of our own place in it.

The issue of stability pertains not only "social justice," but crucially, ideology. Since all systems have power differentials, the key to stability is legitimacy, in other words, how effectively a society justifies its social order. People will not take to the streets if they feel that the

---

[3] Skidelsky and Skidelsky, op. cit., 93.
[4] Douglas and Isherwood 1996, 114.

deal they live under is relatively fair. Societies with hierarchical ideologies relied typically on the official religion – the order of society was sanctioned by the gods. Modern societies have forfeited this option. What are, then, the current alternatives?

Capitalist societies tend to handle, as commented, a discourse of meritocracy and equality of opportunities. Formally, the system offers everyone equal opportunities to succeed; in consequence, the resulting social structure is the direct result of merit. Those who put in more effort end up with more. We have already pointed out the limitations of this ideological track. Equality of opportunities is largely a mirage, not only because we are all born to families with different degrees of power, but also because the system is self-reinforcing: The more power you have or acquire, the more additional power you can get, at which point merit recedes as a relevant variable. It's not that merit is not a critical factor in competitive, capitalist dynamics. It's just that it is only part of the story – and people know it. Any modern society that ignores stark power differentials and tries to compensate exclusively with an ideology of merit and equality of opportunities is truly playing with fire.

Something similar happens with political liberalism. Just as libertarians sacralize the free market, liberals sacralize the political process. Free elections, political equality, ample participation, and government transparency are seen as the key to a just society, one that offers everyone the possibility to come together and decide a collective future. In both cases, an institution (the market, the liberal political system) is seen as the basis of everything else, a conduct for implementing society's highest aspirations. The problem, as already emphasized, is that free participation depends on the possession of freedom, which in turn depends on the possession of power. Unless participation is highly regulated in order to balance everyone's degree of access, those with more power will exert a disproportionate influence on the public debate, including the selection of topics, the way they are framed, and the solutions that are envisioned, all of which will set the alternatives that show up at the voting booth. Libertarians and liberals share the same enthusiastic trust on rules and procedures: They see the market and the political system as neutral mechanisms of popular expression. Through the market and the liberal political system, people supposedly express what they want, which then offers a cover of legitimacy to the political and economic results. However, these institutions do not work in a vacuum, but in the context of real social imbalances that condition the results – and results are what people are obstinately concerned about. We have to come to terms with the fact that a reasonable level of social equality may not be result of democracy, but rather, its prerequisite.[5] For most people, staving off threats of social death will always override commitments to democracy. Societies will give formal economic or political rules a chance, but they will ultimately abandon them if the distance between their intentions and their results is too wide to bear. We have seen this situation play out all over the world.

It is important to emphasize the role of coercion in these dynamics. All societies constrain the behavior of their members, not only because they all involve power differentials, but in a more basic sense, because, as we posited in Chapter 3, they are all based on cultural selectivity. Modern societies, obsessed as they are with equality and freedom, tend to hide this elemental fact, and to deal inefficiently with the corresponding contradictions, which take different forms depending on the model in question. Simplifying considerably, in communist societies, you are coerced to be everyone's brother; in exchange, you transfer political power to the select group of equality enforcers, who then enjoy the benefits of being on top, that is, of not being everyone's brother. You enjoy the benefits of a limited solidarity, and pay with a fundamental inequality. In capitalist societies, coercion comes as a result of individual weakness, that is, of not being considered anyone's brother. Power can be more diffuse, but so can exclusion. Communist systems reinstate the traditional, personalized mode of domination: We all know who's on top and who's to blame. By contrast, capitalist societies are fans of the automatisms that scientists see in the natural world, and want to hide power relations behind impersonal market mechanisms that distribute power without acknowledging it. Both systems tend to make promises they can't keep, and to betray their own principles. In consequence, they will both try to paper over their contradictions with ideology and their particular Orwellian languages: Citizens will have to endure ardent discourses about the virtues of the "free market," the "revolution," and so on. In this sense, any discussion of reform needs to acknowledge that all complex societies

[5] Let's remember that the incompatibility of democracy with stark social inequalities has been argued by authors going all the way back to Jean-Jacques Rousseau and Alexis de Tocqueville.

distribute power one way or another, but never equitably. In addition, it has to come to terms with the capabilities of the ideologies they engage in, and in particular their stabilizing potentials and limitations.

In the following pages, I will discuss the parameters of a plausible and modified alternative, in terms of consumption organization and ideology, to the liberal capitalist project, so it is important that I define clearly my position on some key issues. I believe markets and classical liberal freedoms are here to stay. Their benefits are important, and their absence entails real tradeoffs that have to be seriously considered. Their virtues are frequently exaggerated, but not more than those of more egalitarian alternatives. The dearth of social solidarity in capitalist societies has its bright side in the possibilities for individual expression and even liberating anonymity, not to speak of wealth creation, while the committed solidarity of more egalitarian systems has its dark side in the intrusive and suffocating style of the group. The key reflections involve evaluating different combinations of modes of social belonging and relating. Market exchange has been a regular feature of human societies throughout history, albeit at the margins. The question is, what dimensions of social life should be left to its devices? And what dimensions should be channeled through other modes of social relating and exchange? The discussion has to be carried out at this, more abstract, level of analysis. The conventional terminologies of capitalism versus socialism, or progressivism versus conservatism, will have to be dropped, because once you approach the nuts and bolts of cultural systems, these labels tend to obscure more than enlighten.

But before proceeding with this exercise, I need to make a strategic stop at the important and highly relevant work of René Girard.

* * *

The intellectual journey of Girard, who started his career as a US-based professor of French, took him from literature, to anthropology, to religion, in the way formulating a very insightful framework for understanding cultural dynamics. His first book, *Deceit, Desire and the Novel*, published originally in French in 1961, compared authors from different countries and eras, finding striking similarities in the way they wrote about desire and the vicissitudes of their characters around it.[6]

---

[6] Girard 1966.

In Cervantes's *The Curious-Impertinent*, a novella within *Don Quixote*, the main character obsessively asks his best friend to seduce his wife in order to test her love, leading to an actual affair, with tragic consequences. In Dostoevsky's *The Eternal Husband*, a man is constantly involving a friend in his amorous plans, thus always exposing himself to cuckoldry.[7] In several prominent literary works, Girard found that there was always a third party involved in the characters' desires. They didn't just desire something or someone, but they also sought validation through other people. This wasn't just a trait of romantic *ménages à trois* of sorts, but of all kinds of desires. Girard tracks parallel processes in the work of Stendhal, Flaubert, and Proust related to class relations, art, and religion. For Don Quixote, the imitation of legendary errant knights, such as Amadis of Gaul, and their imaginary world, guides all his desires and pursuits. When he sees a barber wearing a basin on his head as protection from the rain, he confuses the basin for the magic helmet of Mambrino, a mythic Moorish king, and chases the barber, who, terrorized, runs away, and leaves his basin and mule behind. For Don Quixote, what everyone else sees as a common basin is transformed into an enchanted helmet through the detour of the fictional world of knights that fuels his fantasies. Girard concludes that human desires are always *triangular*, working through the interaction of three vertices. There is the desiring subject, the desired object (which can be a person, a thing, a human attribute, and so on), and the mediator or model. We always desire the object through the model, that is, the reason we desire something is because the possession of that something would transform us into the admired model. The origin of desire, then, is always located in the drive to imitate, or turn into, our models. We desire what our models desire; this way, we step into their shoes. It follows that desire for the object wanes when the mediation is weak. The husbands in the aforementioned stories needed another man to desire their wives in order to make them more desirable for themselves. Their friends were their models, which meant they must love their wives, too. It also means that Don Quixote's insane behavior is metaphoric of regular behavior – we are always turning basins into magic helmets. The object has no true hold on us; it is the mediator that does the trick.

---

[7] Girard 2017, 19.

To typify the phenomenon, Girard calls human desire *mimetic desire*. The idea that all human desires are imitative is congruent with what we already argued in Chapter 3: Humans don't have an instinctual agenda, but must derive meaning from the society they live in. Humans must figure out what it is to be human from their culture, and this they can only do by learning, which is based on imitation.[8] We structure our lives through the models we choose, some of which originate in our childhoods and personal histories, and all of which are ultimately provided by the society at large. We can argue that the cultures we live in are the mediators of last resort, since they circumscribe the universe of models and desirable things. If there is any freedom for humans, it resides in their choice of models; and when we choose our models (consciously or not), we are also choosing our desires. Human freedom consists basically in our ability to choose who we want to copy.

Psychoanalytic theory provides its own version of the claim. As Person argues in the case of romantic love, we tend to fall in love with an infantile, idealized version of our parents, or conversely, with people that offer what they failed to deliver.[9] In both cases, the parent offers the model to follow or reject. Romantic love depends crucially on a mutual idealization of the other, where both lovers seek in the relationship an experience of wholeness and unconditional love, pursued as a refinding of a lost state or the construction of a longed-for one.[10] For this to occur, the beloved must fit a certain profile, for we are looking for a specific actor for a very specific play. Person, following H. G. Wells, calls this ideal the "Lover-Shadow."[11] In other words, people looking for love are trying to match a real person with their Lover-Shadow. Thus, a model of lover and relationship presides over all romantic desires. In a more general sense, Girard's mediator can be related to the psychoanalytic "ego ideal," the inner image of oneself

---

[8] Girard 1987, 7. "Humankind is that creature who lost part of its animal instinct in order to gain access to 'desire', as it is called" (Girard 2001, 15).

[9] Person 1988. Girard was not very fond of psychanalytic theory and never incorporated the theory of defense mechanisms into his work. Although he engaged deeply with Freud, he mostly ignored post-Freudian authors who, I believe, would have been very useful for his purposes (see Garrels and Bustrum 2019 for a critique of Girard's position in this regard).

[10] I should clarify that romantic love, as we understand it today, is another clear modern phenomenon, as Person argues, since it is the result of converging in a single person the functions of affection, sexual desire, and practical partnership that previous societies tended to distribute among different people.

[11] Person 1988, 34.

that one wants to become. For Person, the ego ideal is a "generative fantasy," a type of fantasy that works as lodestar in our lives, organizing and providing coherence to our life plans, and supplying our sense of identity and self.[12] Inevitably, these fantasies are largely borrowed from our culture. While personal histories play a role in determining what we end up borrowing, our generative fantasies are always shared with other people, and consist of "variations on familiar themes."[13] In fact, what we have been calling cultural cosmologies are presented by Person as a type of "shared fantasy" around which whole cultures cohere. For Person, shared fantasies "form part of the very ground of human relationships."[14] We are always shadowed by our culture.

But the most interesting part of Girard's theory relates to his use of the concept of mimetic desire to explain social conflict. For Girard, mimetic desire is the main source of conflict in *any* society, and the intensity of the conflict depends on the particular relationship between the subject and the model. If the model is far removed, in space, time, or status, from the subject, the level of conflict is potentially low, because the subject's attraction is to a model with whom the subject cannot enter into direct competition. Girard calls this modality "external mediation." This is what happens when we take as our model a Hollywood film star or a historical figure. It is, of course, the nature of Don Quixote's delusional mimetic desires. But when the model is a person, or group of people, that are more accessible and potentially comparable to us (i.e., peers), we step into "internal mediation," which then quickly leads to "mimetic rivalry." Taking as our mediator the neighbor, the political opponent, or the colleague next door sets us into a path of real confrontation. It should be noted that all forms of mimetic desire have an element of rivalry or competition, in that we not only seek to equal our models, but potentially to *surpass them*.[15] Mimetic desire thus accounts for learning and cultural transmission, but also for cultural evolution, since it is the source of our ambition to move beyond the status quo. (Think, e.g., of sport stars who surpass their idols. This also means that "innovation" is always squarely dependent on imitation.)[16]

---

[12] Person 1995.
[13] Ibid., 122.
[14] Ibid., 123.
[15] Girard 2010, 42.
[16] Girard 2008.

Crucially, mimetic rivalries have a way of escalating into "mimetic crises," which, if unresolved or controlled, lead to social violence. Mimetic rivalries are always based on envy. We want what our models have, but more specifically, we envy what our models *are*. In many ideal scenarios, we would replace our models.

Since mimetic rivalries are the source of most social conflict, it follows that most social conflicts are mimetic in origin. For Girard, we fight not because we are different, *but because we are the same.*[17] In this, he coincides with the psychoanalysts that see the opposite of love not in hate, but in indifference.[18] We have no reason to hate someone if we don't really care for them. Hate or antagonism necessarily involve something both parties covet. All fights presuppose a common desire, and the desired object both unites and separates the rivals. Girard is adamant in critiquing the popular arguments that see social or cultural conflicts as stemming from differences, lack of tolerance, or disrespect for diversity. It is what both parties want, *and agree on,* that generates the conflict. They are two hands reaching for the same object.[19]

One party moves against another out of envy, of mimetic desire. The other one reacts defensively, a resistance that then increases the desire of the first, which then reinforces the desire of the second, because it has been confirmed and buttressed by the desire of the first, and so on in a self-reinforcing cycle. The process escalates because both desires confirm and enhance the desirability of what is desired, which lacks an autonomous capacity to be desirable. It is important to highlight that while one party might seem to be reacting defensively, its position is equally acquisitive (aggressive), because envy undergirds the whole system. Libertarians are fond of critiquing Marxists because they purportedly foment class warfare, envy, and resentment, but capitalism is mostly based on class warfare, envy, and resentment. It could not operate without these passions. Whoever defends himself in such a system is already committed to a game of envy, which was the driving force behind the original, privileged position. Capitalists and Marxists agree wholly on the desirable goods; they just disagree on the methods to acquire them.

---

[17] Haven 2018, 2.
[18] The role of envy in romantic love is analyzed by Person (1988, Ch. 9).
[19] Girard 1978, 201.

Mimetic crises are contagious and tend to engulf whole social groups or societies. They also follow a typical pattern. At their end point, a curious thing happens: The object of desire fades away. The rivals forget what they were fighting for, and the objective becomes simply the defeat or destruction of the opponent. At this point, the rivals become, in Girard's terminology, "doubles," that is, twins, or, more precisely, a mirror image of each other. Doubling leads to all kinds of nihilistic violence, including of the self-destructive variety. The frustration is felt as a threat to the self, to the possibility of being. All terrorisms, including suicide terrorisms, work from a position of pure antagonism, where the "cause" has been swept away by the obsession with the rival. We are here in the territory of Freud's "death instinct," which Girard considers no instinct at all, but the predictable end point of all human mimetic crises.[20]

In one of his illustrations, he analyzes the famous Biblical story of King Solomon and the two prostitutes who dispute the maternity of a baby.[21] Since no agreement seems to be possible, Solomon orders the baby to be cut in half with a sword and distributed among the women. While one woman accepts the proposed solution, the other one pleads for the baby to be saved and turned over to her rival, since she would rather relinquish the baby than see him die. Solomon then orders the baby to be given to this woman, who has proven to be the real mother. The first prostitute was behaving here as a typical double – she was more focused on beating her rival than on the baby's welfare. ("Neither I nor you shall have him. Cut him in two!" she says.) It is a common position in mimetic crises: If I can't have it, no one will. The other woman, in contrast, reacted out of love and substituted the baby's sacrifice for her own. For Girard, love is what always has the power to short-circuit mimetic escalations. I will return to this key argument.

The fact that doubles behave alike does not mean, of course, that they resemble each other. In fact, they couldn't be more different – their rivalry is reflected in opposing styles, positions, and principles. But the contrast is fueled by the antagonism itself, in a perfect example of psychological "reaction formation." *They will make a point of being different to their rivals*. Being different from my rival is what

---

[20] Freud 2010, 106 ff.; Girard 1987, 412–413.
[21] 1 Kings 3:16–28; Girard 2014a, 42 ff.

makes me superior to him, what distances me from his lot; at the same time, my obsession with the distinction evinces the outsize role my rival plays in the dynamic.

Given the pervasiveness of mimetic rivalry, Girard considers human societies to be intrinsically unstable and conflict-prone, in fact, potentially unviable.[22] Human desires are not only naturally undefined, but also unbound, which means that human conflicts have a tendency to escalate to self-destructive extremes. No other animal kills out of frustrated desire, with no "practical" objective in mind, such as nourishment or defense. No other animal kills limitlessly either. How human societies managed to survive under these circumstances became Girard's preoccupation after *Deceit, Desire and the Novel*, and the explanation coalesced in his second mayor book, *Violence and the Sacred* (1972),[23] which set the path for all his subsequent work.

In Girard's telling, early human societies must have been haunted by the self-destructiveness brought about by the loss of an instinctual behavioral basis. After examining the classical anthropological literature, Girard concluded that a plausibly universal solution to mimetic crises had been found in the form of *ritualized sacrifice*. In a surprising number of small-scale and complex societies, both human and animal sacrifice appeared as a distinguishing feature, linked to religious practices and mythology. In his analysis, the key to the dissolution of the inevitable mimetic crises had been the selection and sacrifice of a *scapegoat*. Faced with intractable and escalating social conflicts, resulting from contagious mimetic rivalries, human societies had proceeded through the path of psychological "displacement," concentrating the group's aggression on a single person who would be blamed for the disturbance and correspondingly killed, in the way restoring a modicum of peace, albeit transitory. Through the process, unruly social divisions were turned temporarily into social consensus, as everyone agreed on who to blame. The sacrifice would be ritualized, that is, turned into a regular event, and in many cultures, eventually transformed into animal sacrifice. The scapegoat would typically be a marginal or outside member of society too weak to fight back or to represent a threat to the established order, such as foreigners, prisoners, or children. Since the sacrifice brought peace, the scapegoat, and

[22] Girard 1978, 201.
[23] Girard 2013b.

the whole ritual, would have a sacred character, and correspondingly offered to sacrifice-demanding gods. The pattern could be found not only in recorded customs from different parts of the world but also in many origin myths, which frequently included a "founding murder," and which Girard interpreted not symbolically, but quite literally.

For Girard, human cultures in general had their origin in this phenomenon of sacrificial killing, in the sense that scapegoating allowed for the survival of the group and the control of the mimetic crises that made social life impossible. Sacrifices were complemented with prohibitions, likewise religiously sanctioned, whose purpose was also to control the spread of mimetic rivalries, keeping them within strict boundaries. The (almost) universal prohibitions against incest impeded mimetic crises within the household, blocking the competition for sexual partners between parents, their progeny, and the siblings, while kinship rules did the same on a wider scale. The need to have animals available for sacrifice led to their domestication, which then opened the door to more mundane uses, such as nourishment or transportation. The first monuments were actually tombs, commemorations of the scapegoat that solved the riddle of social strife.[24] Since no social life could proceed without the control of violence, sacrifices and prohibitions were the first order of business of all societies, after which cultural development could then proceed on this foundation. To assume that cultural evolution had its thrust in practical matters of biological survival ignored the treacherous predicament of human societies, with their tragic, doubled-edge dependency on mimesis, which hurls them forward, but also against themselves. "[I]n human relations there is a conflict principle that can't be resolved by rational means," says Girard.[25] After food and water, the most important "practical" human problem is to keep everyone from each other's throats.

The argument also implied that religious systems, developed through rituals, beliefs, myths, and prohibitions, were foundational to human cultures. The purpose of religions was to control violence, even if they ended up producing other types. As discussed in Chapter 2, the sacred encompassed the immovable principles and rituals that existed apart from the group, and that in this version kept the peace and protected people from their own violence. Girard turned on its head the

[24] Girard 1987, Ch. 2.
[25] Girard 2014b, 15.

modern view that sees religions as a source of violence, and argued that they developed for exactly the opposite purpose. The management and prevention of (more) violence was "the heart and secret soul of the sacred."[26] We are, quite literally, "the children of religion."[27]

At this point the reader may be wondering what is the relevance of all this for modern societies, which have dispensed not only of sacrificial rituals of any type but also, in many cases, of religion as well. If indeed sacrificial rituals are mostly absent from the scene these days, scapegoating is not – you only have to put on the news. As in the past, psychological displacement is a privileged way to shift problems to third parties, and to unite the previously disunited people around a common enemy. It also usually works in tandem with its psychological cousins: splitting and reaction formation. The scapegoat, in the form of the immigrant, the foreigner, the poor, the rich, the ideological opponent, or whoever, is still the father of ingroup unity, harmony, and identification. The quickest way to establish your identity and your group affiliation is by "choosing the same scapegoat as everybody else."[28]

For Girard, what distinguishes modern societies is their particular method for stopping the escalation of mimetic rivalries. In "primitive" societies, ritual sacrifice was the typical mechanism for arresting the unending cycles of vengeance and counter-vengeance that mimetic crises inevitably unleashed. Modern societies, in contrast, have outsourced vengeance to an external agent: the judicial system of the modern State, which is set up as the ultimate, and sole, agent of retribution.[29] The modern judicial system is not only established as the exclusive body that can exact revenge; its punishments are also final, in the sense that aggrieved parties cannot proceed with further punitive measures. The law functions as a "lesser form of violence," just as sacrifice had previously replaced all-out war in a historic process of progressive de-escalation.[30]

Mimetic rivalries have also been attenuated by capitalism's extensive division of labor and its diversity of professional activities. By generating multiple fields for human accomplishment and

[26] Girard 2013b, 34.
[27] Girard 2010, ix.
[28] Girard 2017, 60.
[29] Girard 2013b, 16 ff.
[30] Girard 2010, 108.

competition through the development of its supply chains, capitalism diversifies the opportunities for mimetic rivalry, thus diluting the dangers that more constrained systems entail.[31] It should be noted that this diversification is, however, always being undermined by capitalism's own thrust to reduce all endeavors to their monetary worth, that is, and as argued in Chapter 5, to impose the predominance of economic capital over the other forms, and to drown all human passions "in the icy water of egotistical calculation," in the famous words of Marx and Engels.[32] Economic diversification and the generation of separate and regulated fields of professional work replace the religious prohibitions of the past, by establishing different social roles and keeping them within segregated spheres of competition. The laws that establish professional accreditations, technical competencies, and minimum salaries replace the grid of religious taboos that previously kept everyone from wanting the same things. At the same time, the whole system is always being threatened by its own tendency to assert a sole, definitive measure of social value (money), which given the inequality that characterizes its distribution, always spells doom for social stability.

Finally, and crucially, the modern transition has been, according to Girard, also spurred by the spread of the Christian faith. The crucifixion of Christ, a paradigmatic execution of a scapegoat, fell clearly within the traditions of the previous sacrificial religions. ("You do not realize that it is better for you that one man die for the people than that the whole nation perish," says the high priest.)[33] But then something unusual happened: The scapegoat was declared innocent and identified as the messiah and savior. This uncovered the scapegoating mechanism and revealed its true nature: the murder of a blameless victim by a murderous mob. Scapegoating, like all defense mechanisms, depends on self-deception and misrecognition. In order for it to work, we need to believe that the scapegoat is actually guilty; otherwise, *we* are the guilty party. "Having a scapegoat means not knowing that we have one."[34] For his followers, Christ's life and message closed the door of easy displacement. Scapegoating

---

[31] Girard 2017, 172

[32] Marx 2018, 12.

[33] John 11:50.

[34] Girard 2010, xiv.

and psychological splitting were severely undermined by his injunctions to love our enemies and refuse to judge; to check on the beam in our eye before the mote in our neighbor's; to hand down our cloak as well when our tunic is taken; and in general, to radically renounce to vengeance and approach the other as our brother and equal. In spite of the Christian churches becoming inevitably as violent and persecutory as many other religious apparatuses, Girard believed that, through the centuries, the core Christian message ended up having a critical impact in the evolution of Western culture.[35] The steady concern about the poor and the marginalized, and the notion of universal human rights and of the radical equality of all humans, all have their origin, according to Girard, in the Christian message and its focus on the innocence of the victim.[36] "Christianity eliminates sacrifice wherever it gains a foothold," writes Girard, and deprives us of our enemies.[37] ("If all men loved their enemies, there would be no more enemies".[38]) Christian love sidesteps not only the cycles of retaliation but also all exact (and exacting) reciprocities. It undermines our eternal arguments of self-defense, and holds up a mirror to our indictments.[39] Christian love is always authentic in that it does not rely on human mediations and rivalries. Its coin is the rare, true gift – radically generous and nonacquisitive.

Paradoxically, the diffusion of the Christian ethos, both in its explicitly religious form and in its more common "secular" version, came however, at a price. Girard became increasingly concerned about the type of violent escalations that Christianity *itself* was inevitably bound to unleash. By eliminating or weakening the traditional

---

[35] Girard 2001, 161 ff. By recognizing the execution of Christ as originating in a very human mob, rather than in God's will, early Christians desacralized sacrifice, and engaged with the idea that *we* are responsible for our violence. This desacralization, which led to the undermining of the idea of an interventionist divinity, paved the way, according to Girard, to the development of modern science, which depends on the idea of an autonomous realm of nature, and also to Western cultural secularization in general (Vattimo and Girard 2010). The history of Christianity illustrates the tension between two currents: one that sees Christ's crucifixion as preordained by a sacrifice-demanding God, and that has led to a sadomasochistic faith, and one that sees it as the revelation of our ultimate responsibility to others (Girard 1986, 159, 204–205). In this, his view is similar to that of theologians such as the aforementioned Torres Queiruga (2000; 2008; 2011).

[36] Girard 2001, xix.

[37] Girard 2010, 214, 199.

[38] Girard 1987, 211.

[39] Ibid., 198.

guardrails of sacrifice, the Christian path demanded higher ethical standards from societies, which they were not necessarily ready to guarantee. Toward the end of his life, his vision of the future darkened as he witnessed the novel twenty-first–century forms of terrorism and the wars they spawned, the increasing social tensions, and the continuing threat of nuclear Armageddon.[40] Legal systems were losing legitimacy, and social movements purportedly devoted to social justice and peace were creating their own forms of polarization. Adamson's "masochistic nationalism" is clearly delineated in Girard's writings as Christianity gone mad – a movement in favor of victims and scapegoats that creates its own victims and scapegoats in its path.[41] As a historical process, Christianity disables our worst fixes, but in exchange demands a level of compassion (or, in an alternate formulation, of psychological maturity) that we may be unprepared to offer. Our crutches have been removed, but we cannot walk.

The apparent failure of Christianity did not take Girard by surprise, however, since it had been foreseen in the Christian texts themselves. A devout Catholic, he saw in the Book of Revelation a clear-eyed projection of how it was all going to end, given the radical nature of the Christian message and its inevitably bungled reception by an unprepared humanity. The development and proliferation of nuclear arms made the end of world a true possibility, rather than just a fanciful, nightmarish vision on the part of St. John. "Christianity is the only religion that has foreseen its own failure," says Girard; "This prescience is known as the apocalypse."[42] The only exit he envisioned was conversion. The time had come to become true Christians; otherwise, we would fall in the same trap

---

[40] Haven 2018, 253, 261.

[41] Girard 2014b, 37 ff. This is how Pierpaolo Antonello summarizes Girard's position on this topic: "What the identitarian logic of politically correct postmodern discourse promotes as an 'incommensurability' among the visions of the world, among the discourses and conceptual schemas proper to the various cultures of the globalized world, turns out to be permeated with sacrificial residue. Precisely in the exercise of this 'incommensurability' a principle of 'exclusion' is activated: it is permissible to persecute and exclude the other in order to affirm one's own identity. From this perspective, the terrain of shared dialogue for Girard can only be a victimology that does not produce more victims, given that the conflict between religions, or between ethnic groups, is often grounded in the ostentatious assumption of victim status in order to put the rival group at a disadvantage – in the claim to be more of a victim than the other side and so justify one's own retaliatory violence" (see the introduction to Vattimo and Girard 2010, 21).

[42] Girard 2010, x.

as all other past societies, that is, in the illusion that we can conquer violence through violence, but this time armed to the teeth with world-ending weapons. We have not been able to meet the Christian challenge, for "We are not Christian enough."[43]

* * *

Girard's framework allows for a revisiting of the topics discussed in the previous chapters from a slightly different angle. Social differences have now an ambiguous character. They can be the result of cultural classifications that organize society in a way that lessens competition and rivalries between individuals and groups. But, on the other hand, they can also result from rivalries themselves, as reactions to frustrated desires. In these latter cases, differences are all about pursuing distinctions, which belie the identification with the opponent, that is, a commonality of desires. Conflicts are the result of *sameness*; it is when social differences collapse that antagonism appears. Social polarization is the result of all parties being captive of the same desires, of the same models.

The erasure of all traditional social classifications under capitalism and liberalism is a recipe for social conflict. By radically establishing that we are all equal, both economically and politically, the gates are opened for widespread conflicts – between social classes, genders, age groups, and all other categories that previously lived under culturally and religiously sanctioned separations. At the same time, capitalism's decentralized and dynamic economy generates its own forms of social divisions, which in many cases can again provide stability through differences and the development of separate fields of social action and accomplishment. Of course, the system undermines such differentiations too, since it also tends to homogenize the social

---

[43] Ibid. In spite of his copious use of anthropological literature, Girard has been mostly ignored by professional anthropologists (probably, in part, due to his evolutionary approach to culture), and his plunge into Christian theology further alienated him in the mostly irreligious US academy, although he has been well debated by professional theologians (Haven 2018; although see Scubla 2002, and Graeber and Sahlins 2017, 71 ff.). In other words, he was rejected by one group of cosmologists and embraced by another. On the other hand, his theories on the importance of ritualized sacrifice for human cultural evolution have never been seriously examined in light of the available evidence, and since clear and definitive proof would be hard to come by, he himself was sceptic of the prospects of such efforts. I'm using his framework because I obviously believe he's on to something.

landscape by reducing everything to its monetary worth. Thus, as is typical, the capitalist system is both a generator of conflict, and a potential solution to it.

From a more psychological perspective, love appears in Girard as the antidote to the mimetic rivalries that generate social divisions. By adopting the alternate model of Christ, whose relation to the world is not based on envy or rivalry, we can dispense of mimetic crises and of the destructive mechanisms we typically use to deal with them: scapegoating, splitting, and reaction formation. Girard's concept of love, however, can best be translated as "compassion," since "love" can encompass romantic and family love, which can be possessive and exclusivist, and thus less expansive and applicable to strangers.[44] The distinction is important, since this more specific notion of love, related more closely to emotional attachment, also has important functions in reducing social conflict, but is largely left unexplored in Girard's work.[45] While attachment may not save us from all conflicts, it can also be anti-mimetic. We are emotionally attached to specific people, which means they're irreplaceable, and are not "in competition" with others. As I argued in Chapter 5, people's identities and sense of power can spring from their attachments to people, places, or vocations, rather than simply from their relative position in status games.[46] In fact, and following this line of argument, we can define neurosis as an incapacity to develop attachments, and, consequently, as an emotional entrapment in unending mimetic rivalries. Horney's neurotic personalities seek social validation at the expense of actual love. Their emotional connections are weak and superficial, while most of their energies are spent in the defense or pursuit of social esteem. Childhood trauma, which originates itself in an inadequate emotional attachment between the caregivers and the child, leaves the individual exposed to the unforgiving powers of mimetic rivalry, of "Satan" in Girard's theological interpretation, who is framed as the metaphorical

---

[44] See Vaillant (2008, 151 ff) for an analysis of this difference.

[45] See Frost (2019) for an exploration of the potential relationship between the concept of attachment and the work of Girard.

[46] Adding to that chapter's discussion, we could now productively bring in the work of philosopher Harry Frankfurt (2004). For Frankfurt, freedom does not spring from an absence of constraints or a wealth of choices, but from certainty regarding the things we love or care about. Such certainty focuses our energies and bolsters our sense of power. In his framework, the person who does not know what he loves is a prisoner of indecision and conflicting desires.

instigator of unending antagonisms.[47] Devoid of adequate defenses, the person falls under the spell of envy, which knows no limit and no satisfaction. A world without attachment, without love, is indeed Hell, or eternal unhappiness, which comes by the hand of the inability to love, to commit, and to attach.

***

Let's now turn to the issue of present-day conflicts and our options for de-escalation. In Girard's view, the demise of ritual sacrifices or scape-goating, brought about by the spread of the Christian ethos, has lim-ited the options for dealing with mimetic crises. While this transition is undoubtedly positive, it demands a level of compassion that societies lack, which then leads to militantly selective forms of empathy which create new scapegoats and leaves many key conflicts unchanged. The fragmented mediations of capitalism can diffuse the tensions, but not permanently, since the system also works to undermine them. Girard thus advocates for religious conversion to avert disaster.

The problem with this proposal it that it has always been available, so far showing disappointing results.[48] Many religions pos-tulate precisely a path toward conversion or spiritual growth, but as a result of a prolonged personal effort, and whose fruits, if achieved, can come at the later stages of life. To expect salvation from social conflict through mass and immediate conversions is unrealistic – real politics is all about working with real, imperfect people, whose psychologi-cal or spiritual evolution cannot be expected, foreseen, or relied upon. Girard's eschatological stance leads him to a pessimistic dead end, to a specifically Christian type of "limit scenario." Girard's problem is that he gives up too soon. We need to recover his own basic insight: that cultural institutions are historical artifacts devised to manage social conflicts, and that social stability depends on finding the right tools for the right place and time.[49] If there is currently an urgent innova-tion required in the realm of public policy, it is precisely this: to think through contemporary institutional arrangements that can guarantee reasonable stability through their particular anti-mimetic tools. From a

[47] Girard 1987, 162.
[48] Kolakowski 1982.
[49] Girard 1978, 204.

strictly Girardian point of view, the job of any stable social system, of any viable culture, is to successfully dampen mimetic rivalry.

What options, then, do we currently have? In Chapter 3, I mentioned the "classic utopian" mindset that helps capitalist countries in their initial stages of development. The economy is visibly expanding, the growth rate is high, and so is the tolerance for inequality. However wanting my social position is, I live on the hope that it will improve, since I see forward movement all around me. When growth falters, in contrast, frustration sets in, since such immobility suggests that my low position can become permanent. As commented, more developed economies tend to have slower growth rates, since many of the standard consumer goods that we associate with "progress" are already massively available, leaving more reduced space for transformational industries that everyone is impacted by, and that can increase economic output. When slow growth is combined with high inequality, mimetic tensions are bound to worsen, taking the form of masochistic or aggressive mentalities that thrive on scapegoating, and that spiral into unresolvable polarizations.[50]

This is where we can revisit the discourses on "basic needs" and their associated Welfare State policies. As discussed before, there are no basic needs that can be objectively defined, since they participate of the same realm of mimetic desires as everything else. Biology cannot take us very far, and certainly not far enough to save us from civil strife. What discourses on basic needs do, however, is to build an *imaginary* set of common, minimum standards that define a baseline of belonging and social dignity, that is, a baseline of legitimate, shared desires that must be satisfied for everyone as of right. This then limits mimetic rivalry to a smaller set of goods – those that are framed as "luxuries," and thus of discretional desire, and which purportedly depend on individual effort and performance. Welfare State programs and services work best if indeed they cover everyone, or almost everyone, for only then can they justify themselves as "basic," that is, as socially essential.

---

[50] Haidt (2022), among others, has recently highlighted the role of social media in the worsening of ideological polarization in our times. While I agree that digital platforms contribute to the problem, I don't see them as its *cause*, which I rather locate in the current crises of forms of social belonging. On the other hand, it is clear that social media have ushered in a new type of virtual public square that has lent itself to "digital lynchings," or a novel form of the kind of mob justice and scapegoating that figure prominently in Girard's theories (see Haven 2018, 73, and Wrethed 2022).

When public programs are limited only to the "poor," they lose their efficacy as tools against mimetic rivalry, for they send the message that the goods distributed are exceptional, in that they are destined only for those who don't deserve, or cannot aspire to, anything better. In this way, they confirm, rather than ameliorate, the low status of the recipients. Welfare State programs that target only the poor are invariably stigmatizing, and compound the exclusions generated by the private market, even if they do address some urgent need.

Comprehensive Welfare State policies thus define a realm of "equality," that is, of shared "needs" that we all agree to satisfy for each other. The higher the quality of these services, the higher the image the society projects to itself as an integrated community of shared interests, shared desires, and shared standards. Conversely, when Welfare State programs are small or selective, the field is open for mimetic rivalries in all walks of life. If the society has no effective way for dealing with them, as tends to happen in modern, slow-growth economies, scapegoating, conflict, and polarization are inevitable.

It must be emphasized that discourses on basic needs are as ideological as their alternatives. Hierarchical ideologies argue that everyone has a God-given status; libertarians that inequality is a result of merit; and "basic needs" advocates that these can be objectively determined. If the first one relied on religion for legitimation, the more recent ones draw upon scientific rhetoric. In modern societies, science, and its abstract models, tends to be the ultimate source of authority for the corresponding ideological legitimations. With the demise of formal religions, we tend to rely on justifications and representations that remind us of biology or physics, such as the "law" of supply and demand, or the physiological needs of humans. But in all cases, what we are doing, as ever, is organizing social relations through institutions and cosmologies, and as Girard argued, trying to keep the peace.

The fact that political discourses are "constructed," that is, self-built turtles, should not lead us to the conclusion that they are "false" or promoted just to deceive. Like the "mature" psychological defenses described in Chapter 4, we can be partially conscious of their fragility and arbitrariness, but still "believe" in them. One can argue that all mature cultural mythologies require a good dose of Coleridge's "suspension of disbelief." Like the lover who idealizes his beloved, but also knows better, we can defend beliefs as true in virtue of their necessity and effectiveness, rather than in a narrower sense of "unassailable."

All mythologies are fantasies ("shared fantasies" in Person's terminology), and the cultural landscape is basically composed of two types: those fantasies that rule the world, and those that don't. It follows that people that take ideologies too seriously can be described as fundamentalists. They are de Beauvoir's "serious people," that is, people who seriously believe the stories they tell themselves.[51]

This raises a key point pertaining to social stability and conflict. It is debatable if all societies and groups inevitably constitute themselves through antagonistic opposition to others; in other words, if psychological splitting is an inevitable part of social structures.[52] But we can definitively envision social groups which, although obviously defined through distinctions, have also a sufficient degree of contentment and self-consciousness to allow for a healthy tolerance of others. We are here in the presence of another paradox: societies and groups need closely held beliefs that, when necessary, they can also forge a minimal distance from. We are searching here for that space between the extremes of assertion and empathy, and attachment and competition. But this intermediate state only seems possible if the more critical mimetic rivalries of the culture are kept at bay.

Going then back to the "basic needs" issue, Welfare State policies, such as economic regulations in general, are thus another modern equivalent of the religious "prohibitions" of precapitalist societies, in that they limit competition and circumscribe it to more reduced realms of social exchange. They're institutional tools through which modern societies confirm themselves as a solidary people sharing a common destiny. They're not "solutions" to "market failures," as economists are fond of arguing. The market does not fail in providing "necessary" goods or services, but fails rather in providing a sense of community without which society degenerates into an unwinnable war of all against all. When libertarians complain that economic regulations or the Welfare State impede the efficient functioning of markets, they are mixing up results and intentions. The

---

[51] de Beauvoir 2018, Ch. 2. Philosopher Slavoj Žižek has also emphasized this ambiguous nature of ideologies, which always involve elements of belief and disbelief (2008, 96 ff.; 2006, 353 ff.).

[52] See Douglas 1992, 6–7. Mikulincer and Shaver (2011) argue that "outgroup derogation" is more common from "insecurely attached persons," who can be easily related to Horney's neurotic types. On the other hand, "neurosis," as Horney defines it, can in turn be linked, as argued in Chapter 4, with encompassing political and economic conditions, especially through her concept of "situation neurosis."

market's inefficiency is not an unfortunate, unintended consequence of these government actions, *but their actual purpose*. These government policies try to guarantee the availability of things that society does not want to leave in the hands of the "law of extortion," and thus try to provide them outright, even if inefficiently. In fact, given what we said before about how markets naturally create scarcity, the provision of "basic goods" always has to contend with one true "law" of modern economics: If you want everyone to have access to something, *you need to remove it from the market*.

This power struggle between individual interests and group assertion, or between the desire for personal ascendancy and the demands of social stability, and played out as the conflict between the State and the market, is at the base of what we call "mixed economies." Mixed economies are as unstable as they are, at this point, inescapable. Their contradictions have no "solution," since any attempt to address them through some form of purification is bound to worsen the outcomes: too much statism can be as deadly as too much market. Since the balance between the opposing forces is, by definition, precarious, dynamic, and set by the rules, mixed economies depend critically on competent action and monitoring by the rule-setters, that is, by the government. But as anti-government critics like to point out, such results are far from guaranteed, since government actors are as likely to exploit public office for personal gain as for such key public service. Corruption, incompetence, and ignorance can be the main attributes of those put in charge of steering the ship. Unfortunately, there is just no substitute for good governance, since the "no government" dream of some libertarians and anarchists is another unviable "limit scenario." All societies need a sense of self-control, that is, of self-government. You cannot enjoy the fruits of a large-scale, interdependent, and complex society and pretend that it doesn't exist as a governed entity, that it is just an agglomeration of people doing their own thing. Wherever there is a society, there is going to be a "government," and someone has to be put in charge of it. A viable mixed system is thus an imperfect and permanently contingent arrangement bound to disappoint radicals of all persuasions.

* * *

The problem, however, should not be framed solely in terms of a State-Market polarity, because that would actually sidestep the issue of individual and community power and autonomy, which is not necessarily well served by either institution. To explore this point, we need to introduce the work of Ivan Illich, our last key thinker. Illich, a Catholic priest turned social critic, questioned industrial society not in terms of its relative distributive capacities, but rather focused on how it dispossessed people of the possibility to autonomously lead their lives. For Illich, modern "development" consists fundamentally in the destruction of social forms of subsistence, and their replacement with the consumption of merchandise, produced by either the market or the State. Individuals, families, and communities who erstwhile produced the goods they consumed regularly were stripped of this capacity, and turned into salaried workers who now depended on institutions they did not control to satisfy their needs.[53] This process is the same one described by Marx, of course, but while Marx saw the transition as a liberation from the drudgery of rural life, Illich saw it as a slide into a new form of dependency. He reminds his readers that before the modern era, permanently salaried people had a low social status, since their condition proved that they lacked the means and resources to provide for themselves, in contrast to the small landowner peasants or the urban artisans.

Illich did not advocate for a return to a romantic, idealized life of subsistence farmers. Modern technology clearly allowed productivity to increase, leading to more efficiency and free time. But instead of putting technology at the service of individual aims and initiatives, technology had been appropriated by large institutions that now controlled what was produced and how it was distributed. The gains in efficiency were barred to the individual, whose only option now was to sell his labor in the market or to the State. The result was that goods and services became scarce for many people, since their availability depended on their fortunes in the labor market, and on the unpredictable conditions of the labor market itself. We don't control the satisfaction of our needs anymore; external, large institutions supposedly do that for us, all the while refusing to guarantee us the necessary job or salary.

Central to Illich's philosophy is the concept of "conviviality," which is fundamentally a property of *tools*. Convivial tools are always under the control of the user, and enhance his powers in the world.

[53] Illich 1973; 1981.

Convivial tools can be machines or institutions. A good example of the first one is the bicycle. Bicycles can multiply the speed of a walking person by an extraordinary factor of seven, which makes it an incredibly powerful technology. At the same time, no external sources of energy are needed. In addition, it is relatively economical, and the user can easily repair it when needed (or find readily available help). By contrast, a sophisticated motor vehicle can only be repaired by a costly specialist; the machine itself is costly as well, and it runs on sources of energy that must be brought from elsewhere, and paid for too. Any of these variables can fail. The source of energy can dry up, the specialist can go missing, or I can run out of money for provision, repair, or operation. If I lose my job, I lose my mobility too if I depend on a car, because my mobility, just as my job, is dependent on a complex economic system that I have very little control over. If I live in a city (another tool of sorts) where cycling or walking is impossible, my mobility is vulnerable to all kinds of systemic shocks.

Convivial tools and systems keep solutions close to home, and are a modern version of the subsistence forms of the past. To the degree that the provision of energy (say, through solar panels), food, or mobility can be brought back under the control of the individual, household, or local community, the challenges of market-created scarcities disappear to a certain extent, and with them many of the conflicts that pit the big players of the larger economic scene against one another. Illich rejects any discourse that identifies a human need with an industrial-scale provider, public or private.[54] Education should not critically depend on schools, health should not critically depend on expensive hospitals, machines, or specialists, and mobility should not critically depend on cars and highways. The State should bring convivial resources and means to the purported beneficiaries, so that people can stay healthy, educate and house themselves, and move around without depending exclusively on service providers that they may not be able to afford and that can put them at a disadvantage. Community health workers that help people stay healthy are better and cheaper

---

[54] In Illich's terminology, a "radical monopoly" has taken root when needs can only be satisfied through a formalized, large-scale industry: "I speak about radical monopoly when one industrial production process exercises an exclusive control over the satisfaction of a pressing need, and excludes nonindustrial activities from competition" (Illich 1973, 55). This is different from the conventional concept of monopoly in economics, which relates to a restriction of choice between industrial brands and buying options.

than expensive hospitals; good public libraries are better and cheaper than a world of fully staffed schools who might or might not educate children on subjects they need or are interested in. Illich advocates for involving people with the direct solution of their own problems, and with the forging of their own destinies.[55] Specific kinds of machines, tools, knowledge, and expertise can help people recover a certain level of autonomy in an alienating system that alternates between indifference and charity.

For Illich, tools have *thresholds* of complexity or sophistication, after which they cease to be convivial and become dominating and counterproductive. The key to the development of convivial tools is *to know when to stop*. Bicycle mobility is very convivial, a car-based one less so; one with computerized vehicles, even less. We have seen how healthcare can become more sophisticated even as we become less healthy. We end up more ignorant even as we have more schooling.[56] "Progress" is frequently justified on the basis of some isolated variable whose performance is improved at the expense of the key objectives. We replaced bicycles with cars because the latter were faster, but the resulting traffic congestion slowed all drivers back to the speed of the bicycle, with real gains only in wasted time, pollution, and frustration.[57]

Convivial societies do not dispense with markets or governments, but keeps them at bay, limited to those services that are inevitably large scale. In theory, conviviality can also counteract some of the perverse effects of a conventional capitalist order. In a society where the private sector becomes the only available satisfier of "needs," the health of the market is paramount for both the population (which needs the employment) and the State (which needs the taxes). Anxiety about "investment climate" becomes pervasive, the profit motive becomes difficult to question, and private businesses, framed as the essential "job creators," are supported regardless of their externalities.

---

[55] At the level of social organization, Illich's philosophy can be productively coupled with Elinor Ostrom's advocacy of communal systems of resource management, which also sidestep markets and State institutions (Ostrom 1990).

[56] Illich made famous critiques of the modern educational and health systems in his books *Deschooling Society* (1971) and *Medical Nemesis* (1976), respectively.

[57] It's clear that Illich's "convivial" tools are closer to Frey's (2019) "enabling technologies," and opposed to his "replacing technologies," that is, those that end up replacing human labor, such as automation and artificial intelligence, and that currently not only threaten to increase unemployment but also to proliferate feelings of worthlessness, dependency, and superfluousness among an expanding segment of the world's population.

After all, a longer list of problems can always represent increased business opportunities. More pollution can always be addressed with new pollution-combating industries, and new illnesses with new cutting-edge treatments. Growth proceeds unabated, even though we're worse off, and we pat ourselves on the back on how innovative we are at solving problems we have created ourselves. Governments are denounced as the perennial beggars of the private sector, always trying to exact the funds to meet the increasing demands of a public that has been left wanting by the same private sector. Some degree of modernized subsistence, framed within a shared vision of "basic needs," can do much to sever this toxic dependency on a dynamic that has lost the focus on the purpose of it all.

It should be emphasized that a modern, convivial society can only be born from balance, not from autarky. The idea is not necessarily to dispense with large-scale markets or the State, but to seek a better arrangement that bolsters autonomy, furthers equality, and reduces waste. It tries to undermine the society of scarcity that we have decided to live in, in which the private sector continuously entices us with things we can't afford, and the public sector with promises it can't afford either. If free-market advocates like to promote the fantasy that we can have whatever we want if we work hard enough, some pro-government ideologues advance the equally fantastical notion that better and larger public services can always be paid for, if we just look for the money in the right places. A convivial society can also only be the result of a purposeful vision that is implemented through public policy. It will not happen by itself, or by leaving for the woods. The autonomy it proposes can only be a gift from society.

* * *

With the above discussion, we are now ready to conclude with a modest and schematic proposal of a development model for our times. The picture that emerges is that of a system that is supported by three distinct, but interdependent institutional components, in the manner of a three-legged stool. First, there's the private sector, which clearly needs to be properly regulated in order to control the impacts of negative externalities, but also to further the overall vision that society proposes through its political process. The private sector is not a single thing, of course. Businesses come in all forms and sizes, and it is in the best interest of society that all types thrive. Many of the destructive conflicts pertaining the private sector are not between businesses and the government, but between different types of private businesses. Large corporations gobble up small ones, or purposely run them out of business. Cities are built in such a way that small-scale establishments cannot develop, because real estate is monopolized and too expensive, sometimes on purpose to impose a certain level of social status in an area.[58] Keeping a private market open, accessible, and competitive is hard work, because its own tendency is toward monopoly and exclusion. Many needed enterprises are not even profit-driven, as we all know, and consist of NGOs and all kinds of civic initiatives.

Many libertarian-inclined people question the idea that the government has the right to impose a certain vision for the market, or for society generally, since they see such vision as resulting precisely from private action, not from a preestablished agenda. But all functioning societies *already have a pre-established agenda*, even if it's one as simple as "let those with more resources dominate over those with less." The purpose of the political process should be to make explicit what we want; otherwise, we end up in the hands of implicit decisions that go unexamined. Ideologies protect power structures precisely by naturalizing or sacralizing certain things, that is, by sending them to the realm of the given, of the undebatable. A market is simply what you get when you prioritize commodity-based exchanges between people. Markets are not intrinsically competitive, or open, or fair, or anything, really. Like all institutional forms, they are tools we can use to accomplish certain social goals. But first we need to know what we're after.

The second institutional component is, then, the State. I have already highlighted certain key responsibilities for governments: to implement a social vision, to regulate externalities, to provide certain services that the private market won't. The control of externalities is, as suggested before, a highly imperfect art. If we tried to control all the externalities of all private initiatives, nothing would ever be allowed, since everything is connected to everything else. Some externalities are, however, more ignorable than others. The impacts of businesses on the natural environment seem to be unnegotiable at this point. Clearly, the goals of a "circular" or "green" economy that does not pollute or

---

[58] Espino 2015.

destroy nature can only be attained by appropriate regulatory frame-works for private businesses (and also government corporations).

The control of externalities consists of a balancing act that needs to preserve both the financial viability of businesses and the capacity of governments to carry their social and environmental costs. We want to keep the private market as open and dynamic as possible, but also be able to pick up the tab of its operations. In reality, markets and governments cross-subsidize each other, often in invisible ways. Sometimes it might be necessary for governments to actually carry the externalities of an industry, even by obtaining funds from another one, in order to keep it functioning. It is healthy to forgo the idea, popu-lar among some Marxists, that private initiatives are only that – *pri-vate*, and that they should thus always pay their way. Corporations are forms of social organizations, not just money-making machines for some powerful people. They can provide their members as varied social benefits as a sense of purpose, community, or identity, not to mention the goods and services they provide for the society at large.

As argued above, governments can also have a key role in fash-ioning a realm of "basic needs" that reduces mimetic rivalries, and that is constituted by the goods and services they specifically provide. I contend that these goods and services must be provided for everyone, not just for the unfortunate "poor," since otherwise they just reinforce social divisions, instead of ameliorating them. It is not very difficult to assess if a service is really universal in its orientation. If a public transit system carries a janitor, is it also appropriate for the CEO of his company? Would a public school be a good choice for any child, even for one whose parents can pay for a private one?[59] Ideally, we should cease immediately to do things "for the poor." There is no better way of reinforcing our higher social status than by distinguishing ourselves from a group in need, and then offering our "disinterested" help. In a system charitably oriented toward the massively excluded, charity becomes inevitably the other side of exclusion.

This approach seems to me essential for attaining the kind of "steady state economy" that has been proposed for some time as a more sustainable alternative to the conventional growth-at-all-costs

---

[59] Universal provision does not necessarily imply a single provider or a uniform approach. One can establish universal standards that get implemented through a variety of local strat-egies; see, for example, the discussion on "targeted universalism" by powell et al. (2019).

whirlwind model. Steady state economies aim for quality of life instead of just growth. They seek an adequate standard of living for the population, and put less purchase on growth boosts that continuously strain natural resources and ecosystems, and that frequently generate more costs than benefits. They present a good alternative to the common narrative that identifies "progress" with "more," and for which the solution to social demands and poverty is just around the corner if we just keep moving. The emphasis is on the size of the economic pie and its distribution, rather than on its dynamics. As economist Herman Daly has argued, continued growth (in the form of increasing resource use) in the developed countries is unsustainable; at the same time, it is also unsustainable to try to raise the standards of living of the developing world to meet those of the developed countries.[60] In other words, it is unviable to point to an environmentally onerous "developed" model, and use it as the standard for the whole world. The planet's natural systems simply cannot support that. *Both* rich and poor countries need to engage in a discussion of "what is enough."[61] The challenges of sustainability entail both too much poverty and too much wealth. What is missing is a sufficiently stable vision we can all agree on, that stays within the biosphere's carrying capacity.

This entails defining an acceptable baseline of "development," a new form of Weberian "economic traditionalism" of sorts, which can only result from a general consensus on the "good life." In order for everyone to have "everything you need," you have to define "everything," and while such definition may have considerable individual and cultural leeway, it cannot be completely elastic. Needs are social constructs, like everything else, and as such, are fruits of the imagination. No amount of hygienics and physiology will get us there. If we want to guarantee "decent housing" for everyone, for example, we need to establish what "decent" means. Much of this may consist of utilitarian, safety building standards, but there always will be a more specifically cultural, including an aesthetic, component. Ideally, such common housing should be suitable for *anyone* to occupy, given the need. There might be considerable variations in size, amenities, and luxuries, but it should all be recognized as *good* housing. The absolute worst thing we can do is to build housing "for the poor" that everyone can identify as

[60] Daly 1996.
[61] Skidelsky and Skidelsky, op. cit.

such, and that everyone is terrified of ending up in. The establishment of a realm of "basic needs" has to be an exercise in cultural expression, rather than applied science. It has more to do with a discussion about the "art of living" than with any "science of needs."

Finally, the third institutional component consists of, for lack of a better term, a "convivial infrastructure." Following Illich, we don't want to limit ourselves to a dichotomy of market and State. We should push for a convivial society that also gets things done through autonomous action, without having to recur always to markets or government programs. Illich was right in critiquing a modern transition that replaced a world of precarious subsistence with a world of precarious dependency. By not channeling correctly the possibilities of modern technology, we missed a third option – that of secure and generative subsistence. A future world composed solely of large corporations and large governments looks indeed oppressive, and potentially bankrupt.

Furthering a convivial society means favoring technologies and institutional arrangements that keep the satisfaction of the above "basic needs" as close to individuals and households as possible, and that do not make solutions dependent on the availability of money, the size of the market, or the adequate collection of taxes. Being able to walk or cycle everywhere is better than needing a car. Getting your electricity from your rooftop is better than getting it from a large, far-away plant. Having access to a varied and high-quality set of educational resources is better than depending exclusively on a gigantic, expensive, and mediocre school system. Conviviality is about refusing to believe that good things are always scarce and expensive, and that modern life consists mostly of buying things or asking for them.

As indicated before, conviviality must be the result of a targeted policy. It will not spring automatically from the functioning of markets or conventional politics. In fact, conviviality is not necessarily in the best interests of markets or governments, since it reduces the commodification or institutionalization of services that private business and governments push in order to grow.

In sum, the proposal is to pursue an adequate combination of markets, government policy, and convivial infrastructures. These components already exist, of course, and we already use them. The problem is normally one of imbalance, and of lopsided obsessions. We rail against "big government," and then end up with too little of it, or against the exploitative nature of corporations, and then end up with too little of that, too. We're always throwing the baby out with the bathwater. We try to *solve* polarities, instead of managing them effectively.[62] We think there's a solution to the conflicts, which usually consists, in our minds, of a task of reduction, of making one approach rule over the rest. We repress a key dimension, only to have it come back later to haunt us.

This ideological rigidity is not the result of a cognitive failure, of not knowing better, or alternatively, of living in a society with too many different opinions, or even values. Cultural contradictions spring from the selective nature of culture itself. By always doing things in one specific way, all cultures produce conflicts and exclusions, that is, mimetic rivalries. The culture's cosmology then needs to have a mechanism for diffusing these tensions. The solution, to the degree that there is one, is thus cosmological and collective. We are ideologically polarized not because we are too different, but because our societies are unable to deal with the conflicts they create themselves.

Our unresolved conflicts are thus the source of our polarizations, that is, of our psychological splitting. But once some provisional solution is found, it has to be continuously and properly managed. Monitoring and maintenance are key, because we're dealing with unstable equilibriums, with systems that, due to their intrinsic arbitrariness, have no real resting points or positions. Our fantasies of finding a definitive solution are attractive because they relieve us mentally from the idea of constant work. But this constant work is what modernity is perhaps all about. We vied for more consciousness, for more knowledge about our condition. This consciousness is now our blessing – and our curse.

[62] Johnson 2014.

CONCLUSION

Above all though, to be honest, he simply had too many books in that house. He would have needed a fortune to protect them from damp, silverfish, moths, dust, spiders. His ambition had somehow grown out of control. I complain about having so little time to read, but just imagine a man who has all day and, if he feels like it, the night too. And money to buy every book he wants. There are no limits. He is at the very mercy of his passion. And what is it that passion most wants? If you'll allow me an observation ... it wants to discover its limit.

> Carlos María Domínguez, *The House of Paper*

This book has presented cultures as contradictory concoctions that must nonetheless incorporate their own mechanisms for social stability. It stays away from the idea that social polarizations respond to differences that must be somehow bridged through more dialogue, through more sharing. The individualist ideology that dominates our modern world blinds us to the level of social integration we actually live under. We approach others as if we are just meeting them, when we've been living together all along.

Ideological polarizations cannot be solved, only sidestepped, because the problem is elsewhere. Doubling down on our positions is fruitless, of course, because we would be defending not our values, but the antagonism itself. Social division is the giveaway of all false activisms for a better world.

But as much as we should deplore extremisms, we should also take them seriously. All extreme behavior, like all neurosis, encloses a virtue, like gluttony encloses eating. All extremisms have a virtue buried in them. Our opponents are always right about us, in some respect. Inevitably, our position is always partial, as is theirs. But our lack is not something that we're missing or ignorant about; more frequently, it is something we know about all too well, but rather not deal with.

In these times, our zeal feeds partly from the idea that social progress is a cumulative process. One conquest is supposedly added to another one, like bricks that build a dreamed, final palace of social justice. We're always on the lookout for one more marginalized group that needs incorporation, for one more social or cultural "barrier" to be broken. But the right metaphor is rather that of an unsolvable Rubik's Cube. If you change gender relations, the economy is transformed in the process. The workplace becomes more competitive; household politics are strained. Conversely, economic transformations have implications on gender relations too, as well as in the realm of racial or ethnic conflicts. Try to solve the yellow side, and the blue one gets scrambled. This is not an excuse to do nothing, of course, but rather a warning against our naiveness. As in the world of energy, social conflicts cannot be destroyed, only transformed. Taboos are never eliminated, only transferred.

Our cumulative fantasy is part and parcel of our utopianism, of which we have described two types. If the social justice version holds that an ideal world is possible if we just keep adding social victories, the personalist version argues that the same can be attained if we all become better people. In the first case, paradise never arrives; in the second, it arrives too late. In the meantime, the world spirals out of control, sometimes fueled by our active efforts at betterment.

We are very insistent in our battles because we are very sure of what the final result will be, even though it has only been tried in our heads. The efforts come with various degrees of harmfulness, reaching their extremes in the violent movements of the era, which as their equivalents of centuries past, live off the astonishing belief that a society's problems can be solved by eliminating one of its types of people.

Utopian visions are not the only recourse we have against dealing with the feasible here and now. The procedural fantasies of liberal politics are another option. We believe that the future is actually open, that we only need to sit everyone at the table and discuss. We live in an undetermined world, we tell ourselves, but as all human worlds, ours is already *overdetermined*. The future is not as open as we think, because those who are able to control it will always determine its level of uncertainty. On another plane, we're all standing on the same invisible turtles.

For decades, we have analyzed our modern challenges and characterized them as highly complex. Not only are problems interdependent, as I explained earlier; we sometimes can't even agree on what the problem is, or rather, the formulation of a solution is a prerequisite for the formulation of the problem.[1] The definition of the problem changes depending on what we pretend to do about it. This circular and systemic quality has been taken as proof that we live indeed in a very complicated world, shot through with competing values, positions, and interests, which makes planning and consensus-building a herculean task, if not an impossible one. But maybe the world looks complex because we like it like that. The image relieves us from committing to those always elusive solutions that would reduce the complexity we like to complain about. Maybe we don't understand because we don't want to commit. Repercussions take us by surprise only because we refuse to see what's at stake. We prefer to ignore the truisms about power, the already existing links between groups, and the relational nature of our beliefs and ideas. Perhaps we don't want to understand, but mainly we don't want to choose. We rather entertain the comforting belief that our problems are caused by our diversity, so when things go wrong, we can always blame it on ignorance, lack of information, access to the wrong advisors, or lack of public participation. Committing always has an authoritarian feel to it, because the chosen path tends to originate in our *convictions*, which are not very open to democratic debate.[2] It is better to offer a view of a completely flexible horizon subject to unencumbered public input.

The modern world is devoted to change, but at this point, the main issue is not what can be changed, but what must be chosen. In a postmodern world where we acknowledge that everything is "constructed," the wanton dismantling of conventional social norms

---

[1] These are sometimes described as "wicked problems" (see Rittel and Weber 1973 and Roberts 2014).
[2] See, for example, philosopher Peter Hallward's "politics of prescription" (2005).

looks less like revolution and more like plain vandalism. It is not very clear what we might want to "liberate" ourselves from anymore, for to borrow from Emerson, "every heaven is also a prison."[3] Hence, the real urgency now is less about unmasking "constructs" than about constructing good ones. Our eternal scientific debates about what is genetic and what is environmental (the nature/nurture conundrum) seems to be, in the end, an obsession about knowing what we cannot change, so that we can then proceed to change the rest. But our main social challenge is not the ability to change, but the ability to choose, which is also about the ability to renounce. Choosing always has two sides, as we know: opting for something and renouncing to others. Behind every success there is the shadow of renouncement. A person or society that knows what it wants is willing to forgo those things that stand in the way of its ambitions. But our main obstacle is usually our own ambivalence. This is beautifully expressed by Horney for the case of the conflicted individual:

> Even if we recognize a conflict as such, we must be willing and able to renounce one of the two contradictory issues. But the capacity for clear and conscious renunciation is rare, because our feelings and beliefs are muddled, and perhaps because in the last analysis most people are not secure and happy enough to renounce anything.[4]

The societies that most need transformation are, of course, the ones that are falling apart, but then, not *any* transformation. If it really wants to move forward, a truly creative society must take care of its mimetic rivalries in the process, and this usually entails engaging a system of restrictions. For too long, we have been uncritically selling change as a universal panacea. But we also know how to put limitations to good use. We limit ourselves to one romantic partner in order to explore the possibilities of intimacy. We control the shape of buildings in order to preserve the beauty of a city. We tax certain imports to protect a valuable national industry. Utopianism's true challenger is the confident culture that likes its way of life enough to block its own impulses for blind change. In such context, renouncement is not sacrifice. It is simply part of saying yes to life, a *particular* life, which

---

[3] Emerson 2018, 203.
[4] Horney 1945, 26.

is the only thing humans can dream of. A confident society is willing to limit itself, which is the only way to get more, rather than less. Only by embracing self-imposed limitations can a society discover what it is really capable of.

The limits of our actions are intimately tied to our set of sacred things. The sacred is where all indeterminacy stops, where all doubts go to die. It is the realm of *faith*, but not in the sense of irrational, blind beliefs, but in the sense of those certainties without which human life is impossible. All societies have a realm of the sacred; or rather, *must* have a realm of the sacred, regardless of whether there is a God to back it up. The sacred shows up in the unsayable of our culture, or in the implicit, and in its more conscious version, in the unnegotiable. The sacred is our turtles.

These certainties are present in the way we frame problems, in the way we classify things, in the way we find solutions. Our social sciences tend to discover what we already know, give us what we already have, and confirm us in our scapegoats. "Every day, every act betrays the ill-concealed deity," says, again, Emerson.[5] In this sense, everything in the social world is religion, everything is ideology, or what anthropologists call cosmology, or what psychanalysts call fantasy. Societies stake their future in their cosmology, in the ways they explain and justify their decisions and their institutions. Cosmology is where we have to go for our elusive social harmony, because the only way to undermine a hegemonic fantasy is to replace it with another. "Humans have always found peace in the shadow of their idols," says Girard.[6] And as Person bluntly concludes,

> Fantasy is to cultural evolution as mutation is to biological evolution, and cultural mutations, like biological mutations, may benefit us, but they may also kill us.[7]

Finally, the sacred sets the ground for our emotional investments, and also for our transcendence. Meaning can only come in the form of a particular culture, in the form of those idiosyncratic and quasi-sacred jumbles of routines, rituals, rhythms, and quotidian arts without which a society cannot imagine itself. You cannot simply replace this with

[5] Emerson 2018, 181.
[6] Girard 1978, 255.
[7] Person 1995, 217.

"development," because it is not composed of "things," but rather, of patterned, meaningful actions. Its key mode is not "production," but care and cultivation.[8] The path of meaning that cosmologies send us into is also the path of our devotions, of our passions. And if there is truth, transcendence, and freedom to be found, they can only come by the hand of those attachments.

[8] Harrison 2008.

REFERENCES

Acemoglu, Daron and James A. Robinson. 2012. *Why Nations Fail: The Origins of Power, Prosperity, and Power.* New York: Currency.

2019. *The Narrow Corridor: States, Societies, and the Fate of Liberty.* New York: Penguin Books.

Adamson, Göran. 2021. *Masochistic Nationalism: Multicultural Self-Hatred and the Infatuation with the Exotic.* London: Routledge.

Anderson, Benedict. 1991. *Imagined Communities: Reflections on the Origin and Spread of Nationalism,* Revised Edition. London: Verso.

Arendt, Hannah. 1998. *The Human Condition,* 2nd ed., with an introduction by Margaret Canovan. Chicago: The University of Chicago Press.

Aristotle. 2009. *The Nicomachean Ethics,* translated by David Ross. Oxford: Oxford University Press.

Asad, Talal. 1993. *Genealogies of Religion: Discipline and Reasons of Power in Christianity and Islam.* Baltimore: Johns Hopkins University Press.

Assusa, Gonzalo and Gabriel Kessler. 2021. ¿Percibimos la desigualdad "realmente existente" en América Latina? *Nueva Sociedad* 293 (May–June).

Augé, Marc. 2001. *Ficciones de fin de siglo.* Barcelona: Editorial Gedisa.

Bandura, Albert. 1986. *Social Foundations of Thought and Action: A Social Cognitive Theory.* Upper Saddle River: Prentice Hall.

Banerjee, Abhijit V. and Esther Duflo. 2011. *Poor Economics: A Radical Rethinking of the Way to Fight Global Poverty.* New York: Public Affairs.

Bartra, Roger. 2014. *Anthropology of the Brain: Consciousness, Culture, and Free Will.* Cambridge: Cambridge University Press.

Benedict, Ruth. 1959. *Patterns of Culture,* with a preface by Margaret Mead. Boston: Houghton Mifflin Company.

Berger, Peter L. and Thomas Luckman. 1967. *The Social Construction of Reality: A Treatise in the Sociology of Knowledge.* New York: Anchor Books.

Berman, Marshall. 1988. *All That Is Solid Melts into Air: The Experience of Modernity.* New York: Penguin Books.

Béteille, André. 1994. Inequality and Equality. In *Companion Encyclopedia of Anthropology,* edited by Tim Ingold. London: Routledge.

Bloch, Maurice and Jonathan Parry. 1989. Introduction: Money and the Morality of Exchange. In *Money and the Morality of Exchange,* edited by Maurice Bloch and Jonathan Perry. Cambridge: Cambridge University Press.

Blumenberg, Hans. 1983. *The Legitimacy of the Modern Age,* translated by Robert M. Wallace. Cambridge: MIT Press.

Bock, Philip K. and Stephen C. Leavitt. 2019. *Rethinking Psychological Anthropology: A Critical History,* 3rd ed. Long Grove: Waveland Press, Inc.

Borum, Randy. 2004. *Psychology of Terrorism.* Tampa: University of South Florida.

Bourdieu, Pierre. 1984. *Distinction: A Social Critique of the Judgment of Taste,* translated by Richard Nice. Cambridge: Harvard University Press.

    1990. *The Logic of Practice,* translated by Richard Nice. Stanford: Stanford University Press.

    1998. *Acts of Resistance: Against the Tyranny of the Market,* translated by Richard Nice. New York: The New Press.

Bowles, Samuel, Steven N. Durlauf, and Karla Hoff, eds. 2006. *Poverty Traps.* New York and Princeton: Russel Sage Foundation and Princeton University Press.

Brightman, Robert. 1995. Forget Culture: Replacement, Transcendence, Relexification. *Cultural Anthropology* 10 (4): 509–546.

Brittan, Arthur. 1977. *The Privatised World.* London: Routledge & Kegan Paul.

Burgo, Joseph. 2012. *Why Do I Do That? Psychological Defense Mechanisms and the Hidden Ways They Shape Our Lives.* Chapel Hill: New Rise Press.

Calderón de la Barca, Pedro. 1873. *Calderon's Dramas: The Wonder-Working Magician, Life Is a Dream, The Purgatory of Saint Patrick,* translated fully from the Spanish in the metre of the original by Denis Florence MacCarthy. London: H.S. King.

Calhoun, Craig. 2013. What Threatens Capitalism Now? In *Does Capitalism Have a Future?,* edited by Immanuel Wallerstein et al. Oxford: Oxford University Press.

Campbell, Collin. 1987. *The Romantic Ethic and the Spirit of Modern Consumerism.* Oxford: Basil Blackwell.

Candea, Matei. 2018. Introduction: Echoes of a Conversation. In *Schools and Styles of Anthropological Theory,* edited by Matei Candea. London: Routledge.

    2019. *Comparison in Anthropology: The Impossible Method.* Cambridge: Cambridge University Press.

Carrier, James G., ed. 1996. *Meanings of the Market: The Free Market in Western Culture*. Oxford: Berg.

Chang, Ha-Joon. 2011. *23 Things They Don't Tell You about Capitalism*, with a new postscript by the author. New York: Bloomsbury Publishing.

2014. *Economics: The User's Guide*. New York: Bloomsbury Publishing.

Charpentier, Jarl. 1924. A Treatise on Hindu Cosmography from the Seventeenth Century. *Bulletin of the School of Oriental and African Studies* 3 (2): 317–342.

Clark, Gregory. 2007. *A Farewell to Alms: A Brief Economic History of the World*. Princeton: Princeton University Press.

Daly, Herman E. 1996. *Beyond Growth: The Economics of Sustainable Development*. Boston: Beacon Press.

de Beauvoir, Simone. 2018. *The Ethics of Ambiguity*. New York: Open Road.

DeLong, J. Bradford. 2022. *Slouching towards Utopia: An Economic History of the Twentieth Century*. New York: Basic Books.

Derluguian, Georgi. 2013. What Communism Was. In *Does Capitalism Have a Future?* edited by Immanuel Wallerstein et al. Oxford: Oxford University Press.

Dodson, Lisa and Randy Albelda. 2012. *How Youth Are Put at Risk by Parents' Low-Wage Jobs*. Boston: Center for Social Policy, University of Massachusetts Boston.

Domínguez, Carlos María. 2005. *The House of Paper*, translated by Nick Caistor. Orlando: Harcourt, Inc.

Dumont, Louis. 1980. *Homo Hierarchicus: The Caste System and Its Implications*, translated by Mark Sainsbury, Louis Dumont, and Baisa Gulati. Chicago: The University of Chicago Press.

Douglas, Mary. 1975. Jokes. In *Implicit Meanings: Essays in Anthropology*. London: Routledge & Kegan Paul.

1992. *Risk and Blame: Essays in Cultural Theory*. London: Routledge.

1996a. *Natural Symbols: Explorations in Cosmology*, with a new introduction. London: Routledge.

1996b. The Consumer's Revolt. In *Thought Styles: Critical Essays on Good Taste*. London: Sage Publications.

2002. *Purity and Danger: An Analysis of Concepts of Pollution and Taboo*, with a new preface by the author. London: Routledge.

2004. Traditional Culture – Let's Hear No More about It. In *Culture and Public Action*, edited by Vijayendra Rao and Michael Walton. Stanford: Stanford University Press.

Douglas, Mary and Baron Isherwood. 1996. *The World of Goods: Towards an Anthropology of Consumption*, with a new introduction. London: Routledge.

Dumouchel, Paul. 2014. *The Ambivalence of Scarcity and Other Essays*. East Lansing: Michigan State University Press.

Durkheim, Emile. 1915. *The Elementary Forms of the Religious Life*. London: George Allen & Unwin Ltd.

1972. Chapter 3. In *Selected Writings*, edited with an introduction by Anthony Giddens. Cambridge: Cambridge University Press.

1984. *The Division of Labor in Society*, translated by W. D. Halls, with an introduction by Lewis A. Coser. New York: The Free Press.

Ehrenreich, Barbara. 2006. *Dancing in the Streets: A History of Collective Joy*. New York: Holt.

Emerson, Ralph Waldo. 2018. *Selected Writings of Ralph Waldo Emerson*, edited by Robert D. Habich. Peterborough: Broadview Press.

Espino, Nilson Ariel. 2015. *Building the Inclusive City: Theory and Practice for Confronting Urban Segregation*. London: Routledge.

Fanon, Frantz. 1967. *Black Skin, White Masks*. New York: Grove Press.

Faubion, James D. 2011. *An Anthropology of Ethics*. Cambridge: Cambridge University Press.

Fawcett, Edmund. 2018. *Liberalism: The Life of an Idea*, 2nd ed. Princeton: Princeton University Press.

Flanagan, James G. 1989. Hierarchy in Simple "Egalitarian" Societies. *Annual Review of Anthropology* 18: 245–266.

Foucault, Michel. 2000. The Subject and Power. In *Power*, edited by James D. Faubion and translated by Robert Hurley and others. New York: The New Press.

France, Anatole. 1924. The Red Lily, translated by Winifred Stephens. In *The Works of Anatole France*, Vol. V. New York: G. Wells.

Frankfurt, Harry G. 2004. *The Reasons of Love*. Princeton: Princeton University Press.

Frankl, Victor E. 1985. *Man's Search for Meaning*, Revised and Updated. New York: Pocket Books.

2020. *Yes to Life: In Spite of Everything*. Boston: Beacon Press.

Freud, Sigmund. 1961a. *The Future of an Illusion*, translated by James Strachey. New York: W.W. Norton & Company Inc.

1961b. Dostoevsky and Parricide. In The Standard Edition of the Complete Psychological Works of Sigmund Freud, Vol. XXI, translated by James Strachey, in collaboration with Anna Freud and assisted by Alix Strachey and Alan Tyson. London: The Hogarth Press and the Institute of Psycho-Analysis.

2010. *Civilization and Its Discontents*, translated by James Strachey. New York: W.W. Norton & Company Inc.

Frey, Carl Benedikt. 2019. *The Technology Trap: Capital, Labor, and Power in the Age of Automation*. Princeton: Princeton University Press.

Fromm, Erich. 1969. *Escape from Freedom*. New York: Henry Holt & Company.

1976. *To Have or to Be*. New York: Harper & Row.

Frost, Kathryn M. 2019. Exploring Girard's Concerns about Human Proximity: Attachment and Mimetic Theory in Conversation. *Contagion: Journal of Violence, Mimesis, and Culture* 26: 47–63.

Gans, Herbert. 1995. *The War against the Poor: The Underclass and Antipoverty Policy*. New York: Basic Books.

Garrels, Scott R. and Joy M. Bustrum. 2019. From Mimetic Rivalry to Mutual Recognition: Girardian Theory and Contemporary Psychoanalysis. *Contagion: Journal of Violence, Mimesis, and Culture* 26: 9–46.

Geertz, Clifford. 1973. *The Interpretation of Cultures*. New York: Basic Books.

Giddens, Anthony. 1971. *Capitalism and Modern Social Theory: An Analysis of the Writings of Marx, Durkheim, and Max Weber*. Cambridge: Cambridge University Press.

1984. *The Constitution of Society: Outline of a Theory of Structuration*. Berkeley: University of California Press.

1991. *Modernity and Self-Identity: Self and Society in the Late Modern Age*. Stanford: Stanford University Press.

Gilligan, James. 2001. *Preventing Violence*. New York: Thames & Hudson.

Girard, René. 1966. *Deceit, Desire, and the Novel: Self and Other in Literary Structure*, translated by Yvonne Freccero. Baltimore: The Johns Hopkins University Press.

1978. *To Double Business Bound: Essays on Literature, Mimesis, and Anthropology*. Baltimore: The Johns Hopkins University Press.

1986. *The Scapegoat*, translated by Yvonne Freccero. Baltimore: The Johns Hopkins University Press.

1987. *Things Hidden since the Foundation of the World: Research Undertaken in Collaboration with Jean-Michel Oughourlian and Guy Lefort*, translated by Stephen Bann and Michael Metteer. Stanford: Stanford University Press.

2001. *I See Satan Falling Like Lightning*, translated and with a foreword by James G. Williams. Maryknoll: Orbis Books.

2008. Innovation & Repetition. In *Mimesis and Theory: Essays on Literature and Criticism, 1953–2005*, edited and with an introduction by Robert Doran. Stanford: Stanford University Press.

2010. *Battling to the End: Conversations with Benoît Chantre*, translated by Mary Baker. East Lansing: Michigan State University Press.

2013a. *Anorexia and Mimetic Desire*, translated by Mark R. Anspach. East Lansing: Michigan State University Press.

2013b. *Violence and the Sacred*, translated by Patrick Gregory. London: Bloomsbury.

2014a. *The One by Whom Scandal Comes*, translated by M. B. DeBevoise. East Lansing: Michigan State University Press.

2014b. *When These Things Begin: Conversations with Michel Treguer*, translated by Trevor Cribben Merrill. East Lansing: Michigan State University Press.

2017. *Evolution and Conversion: Dialogues on the Origins of Culture*, with Pierpaolo Antonello and João Cezar de Castro Rocha. London: Bloomsbury.

Goffman, Erving. 1959. *The Presentation of Self in Everyday Life*. New York: Anchor Books.

Gordon, Robert J. 2017. *The Rise and Fall of American Growth: The U.S. Standard of Living since the Civil War*, with a new afterword by the author. Princeton: Princeton University Press.

Graeber, David. 2001. *Toward and Anthropological Theory of Value: The False Coin of Our Own Dreams*. New York: Palgrave.

2014. *Debt: The First 5,000 Years*. Brooklyn: Melville House.

Graeber, David and David Wengrow. 2021. *The Dawn of Everything: A New History of Humanity*. New York: Farrar, Strauss and Giroux.

Graeber, David and Marshall Sahlins. 2017. *On Kings*. Chicago: Hau Books.

Gray, Alasdair. 2021. *Lanark: A Life in Four Books*. Edinburgh: Canongate Books Ltd.

Gray, John. 2018. *Seven Types of Atheism*. New York: Farrar, Straus and Giroux.

Gudeman, Stephen. 2016. *Anthropology and Economy*. Cambridge: Cambridge University Press.

Haidt, Jonathan. 2022. Why the Past 10 Years of American Life Have Been Uniquely Stupid. *The Atlantic* (May Issue).

Haller, Dieter and Cris Shore. 2005. Introduction – Sharp Practice: Anthropology and the Study of Corruption. In *Corruption: Anthropological Perspectives*, edited by Dieter Haller and Cris Shore. London: Pluto Press.

Hallward, Peter. 2005. The Politics of Prescription. *South Atlantic Quarterly* 104 (4): 769–789.

Hannerz, Ulf. 1993. The Cultural Role of World Cities. In *Humanizing the City? Social Contexts of Urban Life at the Turn of the Millenium*, edited by Anthony P. Cohen and Katsuyoshi Fukui. Edinburgh: Edinburgh University Press.

Harrington, Anne. 2019. *Mind Fixers: Psychiatry's Troubled Search for the Biology of Mental Illness*. New York: W. W. Norton & Company.

Harrison, Lawrence E. 1985. *Underdevelopment Is a State of Mind: The Latin American Case*. Lanham: Center for International Affairs, Harvard University, and University Press of America.

Harrison, Robert Pogue. 2008. *Gardens: An Essay on the Human Condition*. Chicago: Chicago University Press.

Haven, Cynthia L. 2018. *Evolution of Desire: A Life of René Girard*. East Lansing: Michigan State University Press.

Heilbroner, Robert. 1985. *The Nature and Logic of Capitalism*. New York: W. W. Norton.

Hinkelammert, Franz J. 1984. *Crítica a la razón utópica*. San José: Departamento ecuménico de investigaciones.

Hirsch, Fred. 1976. *Social Limits to Growth*. Cambridge: Harvard University Press.

Hirschman, Albert O. 1971. *A Bias for Hope: Essays on Development and Latin America*. New Haven: Yale University Press.

1991. *The Rhetoric of Reaction: Perversity, Futility, Jeopardy*. Cambridge: Harvard University Press.

Hirschman, Albert O. and Michael Rothschild. 1973. The Changing Tolerance for Income Inequality in the Course of Economic Development. *The Quarterly Journal of Economics* 87 (4): 544–566.

Horney, Karen. 1937. *The Neurotic Personality of Our Time*. New York: W. W. Norton & Company.

1945. *Our Inner Conflicts: A Constructive Theory of Neurosis*. New York: W. W. Norton & Company.

1991. *Neurosis and Human Growth: The Struggle toward Self-Realization*. New York: W. W. Norton & Company.

Hunt, Alan. 1996. *Governance of the Consuming Passions: A History of Sumptuary Law*. New York: St. Martin's Press.

Illich, Ivan. 1971. *Deschooling Society*. New York: Harper & Row.

1973. *Tools for Conviviality*. New York: Harper & Row.

1976. *Medical Nemesis*. New York: Random House.

1981. *Shadow Work*. Boston: Marion Boyars.

Ingold, Tim. 2018. *Anthropology: Why It Matters*. Cambridge: Polity Press.

Jacobs, Jane. 1970. *The Economy of Cities*. New York: Vintage Books.

Johnson, Barry. 2014. *Polarity Management: Identifying and Managing Unsolvable Problems*. Amherst: HRD Press, Inc.

Kearns, Gerry and Chris Philo. 1993. Culture, History, Capital: A Critical Introduction to the Selling of Places. In *Selling Places: The City as Cultural Capital, Past and Present*, edited by Gerry Kearns and Chris Philo. Oxford: Pergamon Press.

Keen, Steve. 2022. *The New Economics: A Manifesto*. Cambridge: Polity Press.

Kelly, Raymond C. 1994. *Constructing Inequality: The Fabrication of a Hierarchy of Virtue among the Etoro*. Ann Arbor: University of Michigan Press.

Kelton, Stephanie. 2021. *The Deficit Myth: Modern Monetary Theory and the Birth of the People's Economy*. New York: Public Affairs.

Kolakowski, Leszek. 1982. *The Death of Utopia Reconsidered: The Tanner Lectures on Human Values*. Lecture, Australian National University, Canberra, ACT, June 22, 1982.

Kopytoff, Igor. 1988. The Cultural Biography of Things: Commoditization as Process. In *The Social Life of Things: Commodities in Cultural Perspective*, edited by Arjun Appadurai. Cambridge: Cambridge University Press.

Koselleck, Reinhart. 2004. *Futures Past: On the Semantics of Historical Time*. New York: Columbia University Press.

Lancy, David F. 2022. *The Anthropology of Childhood: Cherubs, Chattel, Changelings*, 3rd ed. Cambridge: Cambridge University Press.

Leach, Edmund. 1976. *Culture and Communication: The Logic by Which Symbols Are Connected*. Cambridge: Cambridge University Press.

Lechner, Norbert. 1986. *La conflictiva y nunca acabada construcción del orden deseado*. Madrid: Centro de investigaciones sociológicas & Siglo Veintiuno Editores.

Lee, Benjamin. 1997. *Talking Heads: Language, Metalanguage, and the Semiotics of Subjectivity*. Durham: Duke University Press.

Lévi-Strauss, Claude. 1992. *Tristes Tropiques*, translated by John and Doren Weightman. New York: Penguin Books.

1995. *Myth and Meaning: Cracking the Code of Culture*, with a new foreword by Wendy Doniger. New York: Schoken Books.

Lieff, Jon. 2020. *The Secret Language of Cells: What Biological Conversations Tell Us about the Brain-Body Connection, the Future of Medicine, and Life Itself*. Dallas: BenBella Books, Inc.

Lin, Derek, translator and annotator. 2006. *Tao Te Ching*. Nashville: SkyLight Paths Publishing.

Luhmann, Niklas. 1990. *Essays on Self-Reference*. New York: Columbia University Press.

1995. *Social Systems*. Stanford: Stanford University Press.

Lukianoff, Greg, and Jonathan Haidt. 2019. *The Coddling of the American Mind: How Good Intentions and Bad Ideas Are Setting Up a Generation for Failure*. New York: Penguin Books.

Mannheim, Karl. 2000. *Ideology and Utopia*. Collected Works Vol. I, preface by Louis Wirth, with a new introduction by Bryan S. Turner. London: Routledge.

Marohn, Jr., Charles L. 2020. *Strong Towns: A Bottom-Up Revolution to Rebuild American Prosperity*. Hoboken: Wiley.

Marchese, David. 2021. Why Jane Goodall Still Has Hopes for Us Humans. *The New York Times* (July 12).

Marcus, George E. and Michael M. Fischer. 1986. *Anthropology as Cultural Critique: An Experimental Moment in the Human Sciences*. Chicago: University of Chicago Press.

Marcuse, Peter. 1991. *Missing Marx: A Personal and Political Journal of a Year in East Germany, 1989–1990*. New York: Monthly Review Press.

2005. Enclaves Yes, Ghettos No: Segregation and the State. In *Desegregating the City: Ghettos, Enclaves, and Inequality*, edited by David P. Varady. Albany: State University of New York Press.

Marras, Sergio. 1992. *América Latina. Marca Registrada*. Buenos Aires: Grupo Editorial Zeta S. A.

Marris, Peter. 1996. *The Politics of Uncertainty: Attachment in Private and Public Life*. London: Routledge.

Marx, Karl. 2002. *Marx on Religion*, edited by John Raines. Philadelphia: Temple University Press.

2018. *The Communist Manifesto*, edited by Friedrich Engels. Minneapolis: First Avenue Editions.

Marx, Karl and Friedrich Engels. 2001. *Critique of the Gotha Programme*. London: Electric Book Co.

Maslow, Abraham. 1943. A Theory of Human Motivation. *Psychological Review* 50: 370–396.

Maté, Gabor. 2011. *When the Body Says No: Exploring the Stress-Disease Connection*. Hoboken: John Wiley & Sons, Inc.

2022. *The Myth of Normal: Trauma, Illness & Healing in a Toxic Culture*. London: Vermilion.

Mazzucato, Mariana. 2015. *The Entrepreneurial State: Debunking Public vs. Private Sector Myths*. New York: Public Affairs.

2018. *The Value of Everything: Making and Taking in the Global Economy*. New York: Public Affairs.

2021. *Mission Economy: A Moonshot Guide to Changing Capitalism*. New York: Harper Business.

Mauss, Marcel. 1990. *The Gift: The Form and Reason for Exchange in Archaic Societies*, translated by W. D. Halls, foreword by Mary Douglas. New York: W. W. Norton.

Mikulincer, Mario and Phillip R. Shaver. 2011. An Attachment Perspective on Interpersonal and Intergroup Conflict. In *The Psychology of Social Conflict and Aggression*, edited by Joseph P. Forgas, Arie W. Kruglanski, and Kipling D. Williams. New York: Psychology Press.

Mill, John Stuart. 1880. *On Liberty*. London: Longmans, Green, Reader, and Dyer.

Miller, Jay. 1974. Why the World Is on the Back of a Turtle. *Man* 9 (2): 306–308.

Morgenthau, Hans and Ethel Person. 1978. The Roots of Narcissism. *Partisan Review* 45 (3): 337–347.

Naipaul, V. S. 1989. *A Bend in the River*. New York: Vintage International.

Nuckolls, Charles W. 1997. *The Cultural Dialectics of Knowledge and Desire*. Madison: The University of Wisconsin Press.

1998. *Culture: A Problem That Cannot Be Solved*. Madison: The University of Wisconsin Press.

Olmsted, Frederick Law and Laura Wood Roper. 1952. The Yosemite Valley and the Mariposa Big Trees: A Preliminary Report (1865). *Landscape Architecture* 43 (1): 12–25.

Orlove, Benjamin, ed. 1993. *The Allure of the Foreign: Imported Goods in Postcolonial Latin America*. Ann Arbor: The University of Michigan Press.

Ostrom, Elinor. 1990. *Governing the Commons: The Evolution of Institutions for Collective Action*. Cambridge: Cambridge University Press.

Person, Ethel. 1988. *Dreams of Love and Fateful Encounters: The Power of Romantic Passion*. New York: Penguin Books.

   1995. *By Force of Fantasy: How We Make Our Lives*. New York: Penguin Books.

   2002. *Feeling Strong: The Achievement of Authentic Power*. New York: William Morrow.

Piketty, Thomas. 2014. *Capital in the Twenty-First Century*, translated by Arthur Goldhammer. Cambridge: The Belknap Press.

Polanyi, Karl. 2001. *The Great Transformation: The Political and Economic Origins of Our Time*, foreword by Joseph E. Stiglitz, with a new introduction by Fred Block. Boston: Beacon Press.

Postone, Moishe. 1996. *Time, Labor, and Social Domination: A Reinterpretation of Marx's Critical Theory*. Cambridge: Cambridge University Press.

powell, john a., Stephen Menendian, and Wendy Ake. 2019. *Targeted Universalism: Policy & Practice*. Berkeley: Othering & Belonging Institute.

Rao, Vijayendra and Michael Walton, eds. 2004. *Culture and Public Action*. Stanford: Stanford University Press.

Rittel, Horst W. and Melvin M. Webber. 1973. Dilemmas in a General Theory of Planning. *Policy Sciences* 4: 155–169

Roberts, Nancy. 2014. Wicked Problems and Network Approaches to Resolution. *International Public Management Review* 1 (1): 1–19.

Rosaldo, Renato. 1993. *Culture & Truth: The Remaking of Social Analysis*, with a new introduction. Boston: Beacon Press.

Ross, John Robert. 1967. *Constraints on Variables in Syntax* (Doctoral dissertation, Massachusetts Institute of Technology).

Sahlins, Marshall. 1976. *Culture and Practical Reason*. Chicago: The University of Chicago Press.

   2013. *What Kinship Is – And Is Not*. Chicago: The University of Chicago Press.

   2017. *Stone Age Economics*, with a new foreword by David Graeber. London: Routledge.

Samuels, Andrew. 2016. *The Political Psyche*. Classic Edition. London: Routledge.

Scubla, Lucien. 2002. Hocart and the Royal Road to Anthropological Understanding. *Social Anthropology* 10 (3): 359–76.

Seneca, Lucius Annaeus, John Davie, and Tobias Reinhardt. 2007. *Dialogues and Essays*. Oxford: Oxford University Press.

Shoard, Catherine. 2017. Toni Erdmann's Sandra Hüller: 'Everybody Knows the German Clichés. Maybe They're True.' *The Guardian* (January 26).

Shore, Bradd. 1996. *Culture in Mind: Cognition, Culture, and the Problem of Meaning*. New York: Oxford University Press.

Sinoway, Eric C. (with Merrill Meadow). 2012. *Howard's Gift*. New York: St. Martin's Griffin.

Skidelsky, Robert and Edward Skidelsky. 2013. *How Much Is Enough? Money and the Good Life*, with a new afterword by the authors. New York: Other Press.

Smith, Adam. 1976. *An Inquiry into the Nature and Causes of the Wealth of Nations: The Glasgow Edition of the Works and Correspondence of Adam Smith*, Vol. II, edited by R. H. Campbell and A. S. Skinner. Oxford: Oxford University Press.

Solomon, Andrew. 2012. *Far from the Tree: Parents, Children, and the Search for Identity*. New York: Scribner.

Southall, Aidan. 1998. *The City in Time and Space*. Cambridge: Cambridge University Press.

Stahl, Titus. 2022. *Immanent Critique*, translated by John-Baptiste Oduor. Lanham: Rowman & Littlefield.

Stavrakakis, Yannis, ed. 2020. *Routledge Handbook of Psychoanalytic Political Theory*. New York: Routledge.

Stein, Howard F. 1994. *The Dream of Culture: Essays on Culture's Elusiveness*. New York: Psyche Press.

Stevenson, Howard H. 1983 (October; Revised April 2006). A Perspective on Entrepreneurship. *Harvard Business School Background Note*: 384–131.

Strathern, Marilyn. 2018. Persons and Partible Persons. In *Schools and Styles of Anthropological Theory*, edited by Matei Candea. London: Routledge.

Suzman, James. 2021. *Work: A Deep History, from the Stone Age to the Age of Robots*. New York: Penguin Press.

Tainter, Joseph A. 1988. *The Collapse of Complex Societies*. Cambridge: Cambridge University Press.

Taylor, Charles. 2004. *Modern Social Imaginaries*. Durham: Duke University Press.

2007. *A Secular Age*. Cambridge: The Belknap Press.

Thatcher, Margaret. 1987. Interview by Douglas Keay. *Women's Own Magazine*, September 23, 1–45.

Thompson, Michael. 2017. *Rubbish Theory: The Creation and Destruction of Value*, 2nd ed. London: Pluto Press.

Thoreau, Henry David. 1964. *The Portable Thoreau*. Revised Edition, edited by Carl Bode. New York: The Viking Press.

Torres Queiruga, Andrés. 2000. *Fin del cristianismo premoderno. Retos hacia un nuevo horizonte*. Maliaño: Sal Terrae.

2008. *Repensar la revelación. La revelación divina en la realización humana*. Madrid: Editorial Trotta.

2011. *Repensar el mal. De la ponerología a la teodicea.* Madrid: Editorial Trotta.

Turner, Victor. 1970. *The Forest of Symbols: Aspects of Ndembu Ritual.* Ithaca: Cornell University Press.

2008. *The Ritual Process: Structure and Anti-structure,* with a foreword by Roger D. Abrahams. New Brunswick: Aldine Transaction.

2020. *Schism and Continuity in an African Society: A Study of a Ndembu Village Life.* London: Routledge.

Vaillant, George E. 1993. *The Wisdom of the Ego.* Cambridge: Harvard University Press.

2008. *Spiritual Evolution: How We Are Wired for Faith, Hope, and Love.* New York: Broadway Books.

Van Der Elst, Dirk. 2003. *Culture as Given, Culture as Choice.* 2nd ed. Long Grove: Waveland Press, Inc.

Van Der Kolk, Bessel. 2014. *The Body Keeps the Score: Brain, Mind, and Body in the Healing of Trauma.* New York: Penguin Books.

Van Gennep, Arnold. 1960. *The Rites of Passage.* Chicago: The University of Chicago Press.

Vattimo, Gianni and René Girard. 2010. *Christianity, Truth, and Weakening Faith: A Dialogue,* edited by Pierpaolo Antonello and translated by William McCuaig. New York: Columbia University Press.

Veblen, Thorstein. 1926. *The Theory of the Leisure Class: An Economic Study of Institutions.* New York: Vanguard Press.

Wallerstein, Immanuel. 2013. Structural Crisis, or Why Capitalists May No Longer Find Capitalism Rewarding. In, *Does Capitalism Have A Future?,* edited by Immanuel Wallerstein et al. Oxford: Oxford University Press.

Weber, Max. 1930. *The Protestant Ethic and the Spirit of Modern Capitalism,* translated by Talcott Parsons. Pantianos Classics.

2019. Power, Domination, and Legitimacy. In *Power in Modern Societies,* edited by Marvin Marger and Valencia Fonseca. London: Routledge.

Wilkinson, Richard and Kate Pickett. 2009. *The Spirit Level: Why Greater Equality Makes Societies Stronger.* New York: Bloomsbury Press.

Wilson, Mitchell. 1993. DSM-III and the Transformation of American Psychiatry. *American Journal of Psychiatry* 150 (3): 399–410.

Wolf, Eric R. 1994. Perilous Ideas: Race, Culture, People. *Current Anthropology* 35 (1): 1–12.

2010. *Europe and the People without History,* with a new foreword by Thomas Hylland Eriksen. Berkeley: University of California Press.

Wrethed, Joakim. 2022. Cancel Culture and the Trope of the Scapegoat: A Girardian Defense of the Importance of Contemplative Reading. *Contagion: Journal of Violence, Mimesis, and Culture* 29: 15–37.

Wright, Robert. 2017. *Why Buddhism Is True: The Science and Philosophy of Meditation and Enlightenment*. New York: Simon & Schuster.

Young, Michael. 2017. *The Rise of the Meritocracy*, with a new introduction by the author. London: Routledge.

Žižek, Slavoj. 2006. *The Parallax View*. Cambridge: The MIT Press.

2008. *Violence*. New York: Picador.

INDEX

splitting, psychological defense
    mechanism
  and classic utopianism, 68
  and masochistic nationalism, 70
  and mimetic desire, 145
  and polarization, 164
  masochistic and aggressive
    nationalisms, 71
  overview, 50, 51
statism *vs* market, 155–156
status symbolism of goods, 112
steady state economics, 161–162
Stein, Howard F., 67n43
stereotyping, 59–60
Stevenson, Howard, 123, 123n58
strangers, capitalist world of, 98
strategic use of rules, 28, 42–43
Strathern, Marilyn, 54n20
stratigraphic model of culture, xiin6
stress, mitigation of, 44–45
Structure of Scientific Revolutions, The
    (Kuhn), 11
subaltern groups, 86–87, 124–125
subaltern power, 79
sublimation, psychological defense
    mechanism, 51
subsidies of essential commodities,
    112–113
subsistence and conviviality, 157, 163
sugar production, Caribbean, 109
sumptuary laws, 110
super-ego, 43–44
supernatural, the, 6–7
superstition *vs* science, 9–10
supply and demand, law of, 98
surplus gifting, 96
surplus wealth, 97
surveillance, social, 20–22
sustainability, global, 162
Suzman, James, 103n18, 110n34
symbolic capital, 84, 86
symbols, 26–27

Tao Te Ching, 74
target consumers, 111–112

targeted universalism, 161n59
taste and power, 84–85
taxation, 128, 168
Taylor, Charles, 11n10, 78n7
technology and growth, 68
terminal exchanges, 97–98
terrorism, 70, 142
Thatcher, Margaret, 103–104, 103n19
Thompson, Michael, xin3, 88n29,
    112n37
Thoreau, Henry David, x, 109–110,
    110n32
threshold of convivial tools, 158
time, views of, 26, 105, 107,
    131, 156
Tocqueville, Alexis de, 136n5
toil, infinite, 131–133
tolerance, 3, 16–17, 154
tools, convivial, 156–159
trade and exchange, relationships of,
    92–93
trade-offs of communism, 115
transcendence, 169–170
transformational growth, 68
triangular desire, human, 138
tribal societies, 7, 20
trickster, celebration of, 124–125
tunnel effect, 67
Turner, Victor, xvi, 26, 26n15, 29n22,
    31–32, 31n26
turtle cosmologies, 1

uncertainty and social power,
    47, 87
unchanging social hierarchies, 77–78
unconscious, the, 43–45
Underdevelopment is a State of Mind
    (Harrison), x
universal human problems, xiv–xv
utopianism
  classic utopianism, 67–68
  and excess, in capitalism, 133
  and linear time, 39–40
  and social change, 32–34, 166, 168
  and the tunnel effect, 67

Printed in the USA
CPSIA information can be obtained
at www.ICGtesting.com
CBHW020726060624
9554CB00022B/57